GEOMETRY
A Contemporary Approach

THOMAS G. LATHROP
Massachusetts State College at Salem

LEE A. STEVENS
Foothill College, Los Altos Hills, California

GEOMETRY
A Contemporary Approach

Wadsworth Publishing Company, Inc., Belmont, California

To Ina, Wilma, and Professor E. S. Hammond

11-15-71
L.C. Cat. Card No.: 66–23450
Printed in the United States of America

Preface

This book is dedicated to the idea that present-day students need a contemporary treatment of geometry. To this end such discredited concepts as superposition are not used, and widely recommended analytic methods are an essential part of the material. In fact, the development of the geometry proper begins with a set of axioms that makes swift construction of a coordinate system possible. Then other analytic concepts are introduced rapidly. Thus the student learns them early and uses them often.

Such a treatment has many advantages. For example, the student can make greater progress in grasping second-degree functions and relations in Algebra II. He is better prepared to succeed in the modern type of analytic trigonometry course, in calculus, or in courses in the behavioral sciences where important use is made of graphing and slope. He will capitalize on his knowledge of arithmetic and algebra rather than allow number concepts to rust while studying geometry. These factors should be of special benefit to the hard-pressed student who must complete his mathematics sequence in college, where time is necessarily short.

A good course in elementary algebra through use of the quadratic formula provides the necessary background for the material in this text. However, it is concepts rather than techniques that are stressed. For example, the student is not asked to solve complicated quadratic equations or to do intricate manipulations with radicals. He is expected to see when the nature of the quadratic discriminant guarantees certain points of intersection. He is asked only to square radicals or to remove a common factor.

Practice with the synthetic method is introduced into the material. After a point in Chapter 9 is reached, almost all the traditional synthetic techniques have been established. Heavy use is then made of them in the latter part of the chapter and in Chapter 11.

In general, new concepts are intuitively introduced before axioms or definitions are officially stated. Approximately three hundred illustrations and a wealth of examples are provided. These features should greatly aid students of all ability levels. The exercises are graded and those with asterisks can be considered as optional.

The text has been designed to meet the requirements of a one-semester or one-quarter course in beginning geometry. There is sufficient flexibility so that an adequate continuous development of geometry can be presented in a three-, four-, or five-hour-per-week class schedule.

In any arrangement of class time, the topics contained in Chapter 3 should be considered as review material. Although the set concepts in Chapter 3 are discussed only to the extent needed in the remainder of the book, they are presented in sufficient detail so that one who has no previous training in sets will gain an adequate foundation.

A good deal of time could be spent on Chapter 2. The formal logic has been treated thoroughly because geometry is traditionally the first course in logic. However, an adequate discussion of the use of the converse and contrapositive would suffice for the succeeding chapters.

The constructions have been deliberately gathered together in Chapter 10. The sections can be brought in as desired or done all at once. The proofs of the constructions have been emphasized. In any case, the exercises of Chapter 10 provide an excellent review of material from Chapters 4 through 9.

The Appendix contains proofs of some of the more involved theorems. Discussion on axial projections is also included there.

In Chapter 4 the Cartesian plane is built very carefully from a set of seven axioms. The topics in this chapter can be dealt with rapidly, or more time can be spent in showing how an axiom system creates a desired result.

For a three-hour-per-week course, Sections 3a, 3b, 3d, 4c, 4d, 4e, 5f, all or any part of Chapter 10, Chapter 13, and the Appendix could be omitted without the loss of any continuity in the geometry. Also, less time should be spent on Chapters 2 and 3; reference to these chapters can be made when needed in working proofs and exercises.

For a four-hour course, the material in the Appendix and Chapter 13 could be left out and the topics of Chapter 3 considered review work.

In a five-hour course, all the material in the book can be used. The Appendix can be integrated into the course and Chapter 2 studied carefully.

The theorems are numbered for easy cross reference. Theorem (5f-3) means, for example, that it is the third theorem of Section 5f. Definition (9-d) indicates that it is the fourth definition in Chapter 9.

Any such work as this necessarily reflects attitudes formed and ideas learned from former teachers and others with whom we have studied. We wish it were possible to thank each such person directly. We can and do express sincere appreciation to all those members of the Mathematics Department at Bowdoin College who took the time to discuss points with us and particularly to Professor Emeritus Hammond for giving us initial help and encouragement; to Coordinator William Devitt and others of the staff of the Intensive Training Program at the State College at Salem, where some of the material was used; to instructors Herbert Schmidt, Davis Davies, Raymond Strauss, and Jack Paarlberg for providing helpful suggestions while teaching the preliminary version at Foothill College and Masconomet Regional High School; to Professors Irving Drooyan of Los Angeles Pierce College; John Fujii of Merritt College, Richard Lord of Yakima Valley College, Katherine Raymond of Skagit Valley College, and George Wallace of the College of San Mateo for their suggestions in the manuscript stage; to student Robert Brennan for preparing the answers; and, finally, to our wives for their yeoman service as typists and for their unfailing patience and understanding.

Contents

CHAPTER 5   LOCI   68

CHAPTER 6   PROPERTIES OF STRAIGHT LINES   96

CHAPTER 7   CIRCLES   129

CHAPTER 8   PROPERTIES OF ANGLES   159

Table of Notation

$\therefore$	therefore
$\vee$	inclusive "or"
$\underline{\vee}$	exclusive "or"
$\wedge$	conjective "and"
$\Rightarrow$	if ..., then ..., implication
iff	propositional equivalence
$\Leftrightarrow$	logical equivalence
$\sim(\ldots)$	negation of the proposition $(\ldots)$
$\forall x$	for all x
$\exists x$	for some x
$\in$	belongs to; contained in
$\notin$	not contained in
$\ni$	contains
$\leftrightarrow$	corresponds to
$A \subset B$	A is a subset of B; A is included in B
$A \supset B$	A includes B as a subset
$\{1,2,3\}$	a set with elements 1,2,3
$\{x \mid p(x)\}$	the set of all x such that the open sentence $p(x)$ is true
$\cup$	union
$\cap$	intersection
$\emptyset$	null (empty) set
$A,B,C,\ldots$	points, sets
$\mathscr{L},\mathscr{M}$	loci
$=$	equal
$\neq$	not equal
$a,b,c,\ldots$	numbers, propositions in Chapter 1
$a > b$	a greater than b
$a < b$	a less than b
π	the number 3.14159...
$\mathscr{R}$	the set of real numbers
(x,y)	any ordered pair
(x_i,y_i)	a particular ordered pair for $i = 1,2,3,\ldots$
AB	line segment having A and B as endpoints
(AB)	measure (length) of line segment AB
$\overleftrightarrow{OX}$	x axis
$\overleftrightarrow{OY}$	y axis
$\overrightarrow{AF}$	ray with endpoint A

$\overleftrightarrow{AB}$ straight line containing points A and B

$\overline{ABC}$ B is between points A and C on line AC

$\perp$ perpendicular

$//$ parallel

$\sim$ similar

$\cong$ congruent

$\triangle ABC$ triangle ABC

$\sphericalangle ABC$ angle ABC with vertex B

$\alpha, \beta, \ldots$ angles

$(\alpha), (\sphericalangle ABC)$ measure of angles α and ABC

(A, AB) circle having center A and radius AB

$\overparen{AB}$ arc AB

$(\overparen{AB})$ measure of arc AB

Greek Alphabet

(Pronunciation in italics)

A	α	Alpha	N	ν	Nu
B	β	Beta (*bayta*)	Ξ	ξ	Xi (*ksee*)
Γ	γ	Gamma	O	o	Omicron
Δ	δ	Delta	Π	π	Pi (*py**)
E	ϵ	Epsilon	P	ρ	Rho (*ro*)
Z	ζ	Zeta (*dzayta*)	Σ	σ	Sigma
H	η	Eta (*ayta*)	T	τ	Tau (*tou*, as in "town")
Θ	θ	Theta (*thayta*)	Υ	υ	Upsilon
I	ι	Iota	Φ	ϕ	Phi (*fee*)
K	κ	Kappa	X	χ	Chi (*ky**)
Λ	λ	Lambda	Ψ	ψ	Psi (*psee*)
M	μ	Mu	Ω	ω	Omega (*omayga*)

* Longstanding usage in mathematics sanctions these pronunciations.

Greek Number Prefixes

1	mono-	6	hexa-
2	di-	7	hepta-
3	tri-	8	octa-
4	tetra-	9	nona-
5	penta-	10	deca-

chapter 1

Introduction

1a Introduction to the Student

If we were asked for the solution of the equation

(1) $$2x + 3 = 0,$$

after some simple computation we would be able to answer that the solution is

(2) $$x = -\tfrac{3}{2}.$$

In solving (1) for the variable x, we have essentially used the end results of our work in learning the principles of numbers called algebra. We shall build upon such algebraic skills to develop a subject that combines the algebra of the real numbers with figures of the types we might draw. Here we are referring to triangles, circles, rectangles, and straight lines, to mention a few such figures.

We shall want to make this development a careful one. Thus in Section 1c we shall investigate an example of what we could call a *finite geometry*. This will provide us with some insight into why the subject is presented as it is in the remainder of this book.

One of the most important skills that we need to develop in a geometry course is that of *proof*. We must be able to answer questions like " What is a proof?" " Is this a valid (correct) argument?" " Is this a logical system?" Therefore, as we read and study the material, we want to concentrate particularly on the proofs of the theorems that are illustrated and eventually be able to provide our own proofs. The need of ability to construct a proof cannot be stressed too much. You should keep in mind at all times that this is one of the concepts that you are trying to develop into a usable skill.

In a subject of this type, the student must quickly realize that there will be many concepts which need to be memorized. As was the case in algebra, where formulas and procedures were memorized, so it will be in geometry, where there are axioms, definitions, and theorems that must be memorized. Do not wait until too late to come to the realization that geometry is like building a brick wall. The bricks on the top row depend on those in the rows beneath them for their support. Thus in geometry the theorems in the last chapter need the support of theorems, definitions, and axioms that precede them.

Every theorem, definition, and axiom has an identifying number in this textbook. Each number helps to locate where the principle is found in the book. For example, Theorem (6e-2) is located in Chapter 6, Section e, and it is the second theorem in that section. The definitions are numbered consecutively by letter throughout a chapter. When proofs of theorems are given, the reference numbers of theorems used in that proof are given. This has been done to conserve space. In constructing his own proofs, the reader should rarely use the theorem numbers; rather he should paraphrase the theorem itself. A general rule to go by is to be sure that what you write can be read by someone else without his having to refer to the textbook.

This geometry course will make use of your previous course (or courses) in algebra. There are no topics which will employ any concept that is not traditionally taught in a first course in algebra. One topic, however, may not have been included in your background for this course. This is the language of *sets*. A section in Chapter 3 discusses sets sufficiently for this treatment of geometry.

In Chapter 3 we have also included a short discussion of the real numbers. These should be familiar from your algebra course. Since our geometry is essentially based on the real numbers and their properties, a good understanding of them is important. Whenever reference is made to a real number property in the course of a proof, the phrase *properties of $\mathscr{R}$* will probably appear. This means that some axiom, definition, theorem, or algebraic operation on real numbers has been used. You should familiarize yourself with whichever one is indicated.

Whenever algebraic operations are used in the geometry, examples and sample problems are included for your review. Study the examples carefully, for they can be of valuable help in your work in geometry.

In summary, we urge you to remember three points. (1) Read carefully and study the examples thoroughly. (2) Memorize what is necessary and continually review concepts with which you have difficulty. (3) Ask questions. Good luck!

1b   Historical Retrospect

Geometry is an ancient subject. Its roots go far back to the ages when the first civilizations began to appear along the Tigris, the Euphrates, and the Nile. The peoples who lived by these rivers began to work out some rough geometric methods as they learned to erect buildings and to resurvey fields after the yearly floodings.

By the third millennium B.C., when the great I-em-hotep built the first pyramid, the Egyptians and Sumerians had developed many concepts we would now call *geometric*. As ages passed, a considerable storehouse of mathematical knowledge was assembled for use in architecture, navigation, astronomy, and other fields requiring measurement. It seems, however, that most, if not all, of their methods were developed solely by trial and error or by observation of chance results. Even though this meant that the collected knowledge of these ancient people was not free of error, the foundation they laid was one on which later peoples were able to build.

The Greeks in particular made enormous strides in advancing the subject. Thales of Miletus (640?–546 B.C.), Pythagoras (572?–500 B.C.), Eudoxos (?), Euclid (about 300 B.C.), and Archimedes (287?–212 B.C.) were among the greatest of the contributors to this development. *The Elements* by Euclid is one of the most famous books of all time. In it he summed up all the geometric knowledge of his day. Until quite recently every high school geometry text was in essence a modification of this great work.

These Greeks added new ingredients to the study of mathematics. For one thing, they developed the concept that results based on given information ought to be proved. For another, they learned to regard some mathematical entities as *abstractions*.

An abstraction is simply a concept that has been reduced solely to its essential aspects; that is, all superfluous associations have been removed from the idea. The Sumerians and Egyptians seem never to have regarded geometry as more than a description of properties of the physical world. To them it treated visible *dots*, *edges* of stones or boards, *physical surfaces*, and actual *solid objects*. From the concept of a visible dot the Greeks distilled the *abstract concept* of a point having neither breadth nor thickness. The physical idea of an edge became the *abstract concept* of a line like a ray of light that continues indefinitely and possesses no thickness. Geometry in this abstract sense became an *idealized* representation of the physical world.

Little important progress occurred after the Greek age until about 1600 A.D. By that time knowledge of arithmetic and the algebra of numbers had developed to the point where number properties could successfully be used to simplify and illuminate various aspects of the study of geometry. In 1637 René Descartes (1596–1650) published a book in which he made very successful use of algebraic techniques for solving geometric problems. From that day to the present, the use of number properties in geometric work (called the *analytic* method) has shown steady increase.

Such improvements in the study of geometry and various useful refinements of results did not change the essential nature of the subject. The universally recognized basic principles were still those set down by Euclid in his *Elements*. Hence we call this geometry *Euclidean*.

In the first half of the nineteenth century, three men, N. I. Lobachevsky (1793–1856), J. Bolyai (1802–1860), and K. F. Gauss (1777–1855), all developed a particular kind of non-Euclidean geometry called *hyperbolic* geometry. A little later, Bernhard Riemann (1826–1866) developed a second kind of non-Euclidean geometry and showed that it was possible to develop still others.

As the name non-Euclidean implies, these newer geometries differ from Euclidean geometry in some very fundamental ways. Various relationships among lines and triangles, for example, are far from being the same. This fact may seem strange, but possibly even stranger is the fact that scientists cannot tell at present which of these geometries is the best model of the physical world. In fact, scientists have been able to make use of some non-Euclidean geometry in relativity theory.

The development of non-Euclidean geometries was a great landmark in the history of mathematics. Euclidean geometry is still the most useful, but it is important to realize that we can no longer regard Euclidean geometry as describing the physical world as the ancient people did. All we can ask is that the geometric relationships we study produce a model that fits the real world to within useful accuracy of measurement.

1c Deductive Reasoning

For some unknown reason the Greek mathematicians put their primary efforts into the study of geometry and did little with other branches of mathematics. Since they also developed the idea of proof, geometry and proof have been inseparable concepts for over 2000 years. Until very recently the geometry course was most often the first and only experience a student had with proof outside of college mathematics classes.

What is a proof? Almost anyone would agree that it is a method used to show that a statement is true. The beginner realizes that he is to prove a particular statement by using known true statements in support of an argument leading to the truth of the statement to be proved. As outlined, this may not seem like a formidable task but a thoughtful person might well ask the following questions: (i) How do we know when a statement is true and thus available for use in proving further statements true? (ii) How can we make a proof for the first given statement if all proofs are to be in a single sequence?

In attempting to answer these somewhat thorny questions, let us examine a statement that one might classify as true:

(1)   The tax bill on my house and lot is $40 a month.

Is this statement true or false? Probably there are people who could label it true. However, most persons would find that the given figure is higher or lower than the amount they actually pay. Hence they would label (1) false. The answer obviously depends on the community in which the person lives, on the tax rate in that community, and on the value of the property. Notice that the tax rate is set arbitrarily. If the local authorities change the rate, statement (1) might become true for some persons, whereas it had been false previously, or vice versa.

Statement (1) also presents a further difficulty. What if the person who is to label it does not own a house or lot? For him (1) is actually a meaningless statement.

Thus in answering question (i) we must conclude that the appropriate label for a statement depends on having an arbitrary standard (such as a particular tax rate) available. Furthermore, a statement must be meaningful relative to the standard. We can call such an arbitrary standard a *truth standard*.

Now (ii) can also be answered in part. It is obviously impossible to "prove" that very first statement, but since we need an arbitrary truth standard in any case, the statements that are used to build it are arbitrarily labeled *true*. The arbitrarily true statements of a truth standard are called *axioms*. Other statements are proved or disproved *relative* to the axioms for that structure. The preceding discussion shows that a statement which is true relative to a particular axiom system may be false or meaningless relative to a different axiom system.

In any branch of mathematics we prove facts about terms that have special meaning in that subject. *Point* and *line* are such terms in geometry. We try to define as many such terms as possible and state each new definition using only the specialized terms previously defined or nonspecialized words of English. If we now imagine ourselves going backward through any sequence of mathematical definitions, we realize that it is *impossible* to define all specialized terms—just as it is impossible to prove all statements. How would one make the first, or even the second definition? At that point there would be no previously defined specialized terms to use in making a definition. Hence we must leave some specialized terms undefined. These we call the *primitive terms* of an axiomatic structure.

When we say that a term is left "undefined," we do not imply that we never know its meaning. Since these primitive terms are the first specialized terms we introduce into an axiomatic development, they are available for use in stating the axioms. In fact, the axioms tell us how the primitive concepts are interrelated, thereby providing us with *implicit* definitions for them.

The axioms, then, are the first true *statements* in a mathematical structure such as geometry. The primitive terms are the first specialized terms in the structure. When specialized terms other than the primitives are needed, the meaning of each is given by an *explicit* definition. *Such a definition must never contradict any principle established by the axioms.*

With axioms, primitive terms, and defined terms available, it is possible to enlarge the structure by proving new statements. To prove a statement true, we make an argument based ultimately on the axioms of the system. *That is, each step in the argument is justified relative to an axiom, a definition, or a previously proved statement.* The answer to the question "Why?" in mathematics is always one of these three kinds of statements. When we construct such an argument correctly, we say that we are using *deductive logical reasoning.*

We shall now consider an example of a finite logical system. We must first establish two primary concepts. That is, we list first the primitive terms and then the axioms.

Example 1: Primitive terms: α, β, δ, square.

Axiom 1: All α's are square β's.

Axiom 2: All β's are δ's.

Using these two axioms, the following theorem can be established.

Theorem 1: All α's are square δ's.

We now make a definition.

Definition 1: A farm is a δ.

Theorem 2: All α's are square farms.

Theorem 3: All β's are square farms.

In Example 1 we have performed three basic operations of geometry. We wrote a theorem, made a definition, and then wrote another theorem. Each of these processes seemed to be correct and appears to make good sense. But why? Because we simply *feel* that they do? This is not enough for us to be sure that we would never reach a point with our theorems where one contradicted another. In Example 1, suppose we continued until we wrote a theorem as follows.

Theorem "13": All β's are α's.

Is it true? How can we determine whether it is true or false? This is what logic is all about. It develops the method and procedure of "proof" for us and tells us what constitutes a "logical system."

In a way, Example 1 illustrates what we will be doing in Chapters 4 through 13. Starting with a basic axiom system that has been preceded with some primitive terms, we shall carefully build the body of knowledge we call geometry by stating definitions and proving theorems. It would be of value for the reader to take time out now and then and carefully examine the *structure* that is being built as he proceeds through the remainder of this book.

Exercise Set

In the following exercises, a logical system is implied. For each set of primitive terms and axioms, write as many theorems as seem reasonable.

1. Primitive terms: x, y, z.
   Axiom 1: Every x is a z.
   Axiom 2: Every y is an x.

2. Primitive terms: a, b, c.
   Axiom 1: All a's are b's.
   Axiom 2: Some b's are c's.

3. Primitive terms: wires, beads.
   Axiom 1: Every wire contains exactly two beads.
   Axiom 2: Every bead is on at least two wires.
   Axiom 3: There are exactly three beads.

4. In Exercise 3, replace the word "bead" by the word "point" and the word "wire" by the word "line." Rewrite your theorems using these words and draw a picture of what is happening.

5. Replace Axiom 3 of Exercise 3 with the following: "There are exactly five beads."

6. Redo Exercise 5 except also replace Axiom 2 with the following: "Every bead is on exactly four wires."

chapter 2

Logic

2a Logical Reasoning

In Section 1c we pointed out that each step in establishing a theorem is justified by appealing to a previously proven theorem, a definition, or an axiom. It may not always be clear why a particular statement is a theorem in a given logical system or (see Example 1, Section 1c), if it is, how to prove it.

To develop the ability to write theorems, we need the help of logic. It provides us with the necessary tools to build various logical systems. We start by considering a few simple arguments to see how they should be constructed. Consider the following:

(1)
p_1: Foothill College is in California.
p_2: California is in the U.S.A.
c: Foothill College is in the U.S.A.

Before looking at the argument itself, let us provide some names to make the discussion easier. The final statement c is called the *conclusion*. In a proof this would be the statement whose truth we were trying to establish. The statements p_1 and p_2 are offered in support of the conclusion. They are called the *premises*. In a proof the assertion that each premise is true would be justified by a known true statement (i.e., by an axiom, definition, or previously proved theorem). At this point we shall only assume that taking the facts of geography as a truth standard would be sufficient to ensure the truth of p_1 and p_2.

Now let us consider the argument (1) itself. Does each of the three statements seem true? More important, would you label the conclusion true regardless of how it seems to you so long as p_1 and p_2 are to be considered true? This is the important question to ask about a proof. Consider the following two arguments as further examples.

(2)
p_1: If Polly is a zoy, then Polly is a vlacho.
p_2: Polly is a zoy.
c: Polly is a vlacho.

In this case we certainly do not know anything about zoys or vlachos. We cannot even be certain that Polly is a living being. Ships and other things are given names. Hence we cannot be certain whether p_1 and p_2 are true. Still, we can ask whether the conclusion c seems true if we are willing to accept the premises p_1 and p_2 as true. It should seem true to us on this basis.

(3) $\qquad$ p_1: A grampus is a sea animal.

$\qquad\qquad$ p_2: All fish are animals that live in the sea.

$\qquad\qquad$ c: A grampus is a fish.

Whether or not you ever met a grampus, does the conclusion seem true if the two premises are accepted as true? This time it should not. The argument is not valid.

These examples illustrate two important facts. First, determining whether an argument is valid or invalid *does not depend* on whether the statements used are actually true but only on results obtained when we *consider them true*. Second, there is a difference in the construction of arguments (i.e., the relationships of the premises to each other and to the conclusion), and it is this difference that determines whether an argument is valid.

A valid argument is one that is so constructed that if the premises are true, the conclusion must be regarded as true also. *Deductive* logical reasoning is thus the science of constructing valid arguments. What differences in construction are possible and how these determine validity may not be at all obvious to the beginner at this point.

Exercise Set

Examine each of the following arguments to see whether they seem to be valid. That is, assume that each of the premises is true and see whether the conclusion should be labeled true as a result. Do the best you can at this point in our consideration of logical structures.

1. p_1: Birds are two-legged animals.
   $\quad$ p_2: A zosterops is a bird.
   $\quad$ c: A zosterops has two legs.

2. p_1: If $x = y$, then $2x = 3y$.
   $\quad$ p_2: $x = y$.
   $\quad$ c: $2x = 3y$.

3. p_1: Chicago is in Maine.
   $\quad$ p_2: Maine is in North America.
   $\quad$ c: Chicago is in North America.

4. p_1: John is blond.
   $\quad$ p_2: John is a fisherman.
   $\quad$ c: All fishermen are blond.

5. p_1: All fish swim.
   $\quad$ p_2: I can swim.
   $\quad$ c: I am a fish.

6. p_1:   If you are late, then it must be raining.
   p_2:   It is raining.
   c: You must be late.
7. p_1:   If $4 = 7$, then $8 = 9$.
   p_2: $4 = 7$.
   c: $8 = 9$.
8. p_1:   Lobsters are sea animals.
   p_2:   Lobsters are good to eat.
   c: Lobsters are sea animals that are good to eat.

2b   Propositions

A variety of rules governing the construction of valid deductive arguments can be stated.   The philosopher Aristotle (384–322 B.C.) was the first person to work the rules used in deductive reasoning into a complete system of formal logic.   In its essential features the Aristotelian system is the logic we still use today for the vast majority of our work in mathematics.

Before we can make a precise consideration of why some of the arguments of the preceding section are valid and others invalid, it is necessary to be more precise about the concepts "true" and "false."   Note that we have been applying these labels to statements.   A statement is a declarative sentence; it is a grammatical concept.   Recall that we have had to admit that it is not possible to label all statements true or false.   *In logical argument we can use only statements that can be labeled either true or false.*   We use the term **proposition** for this type of statement.

Here, then, we shall use true, false, and proposition as *primitive* terms. The three principles stated below are among those discussed by Aristotle. They will serve as axioms for our purpose.

L-1:   True and false are the only labels assignable to a proposition.
L-2:   The labels true and false are not assignable to a proposition *simultaneously.*
L-3:   Whenever the possible truth values of one proposition are the same as those of a second, either proposition may replace the other in an argument within that axiomatic structure (Axiom of Substitution).

Recall that the labeling of a proposition may change if the truth standard changes.   As L-3 implies, the use of the term "proposition" is meaningful only relative to a single truth standard (axiom system).   L-1 and L-2 together state that a proposition is labeled either true or false, but not both.   The following theorem is a direct result of this fact.

Theorem (2b-1) (*Principle of Contradiction*):   If the assumption that a proposition has a particular truth value leads to a contradiction, then the proposition must have the other truth value.

The proof of this theorem is postponed until rules of inference have been discussed. (See Section 2d.)

According to L-1, any proposition has the two possible labels. Let p stand for a proposition, T stand for the label "true," and F stand for the label "false." Using these symbols, we can write the possible truth values of p in tabular form as in Fig. 2.1. By L-2 each of the rows represents a *separate* possibility; they are *not* simultaneously possible.

p	
T	Row 1
F	Row 2

Fig. 2.1

Now recall from Section 1c that deductive reasoning is a way of correctly *relating* known true propositions so as to produce valid proofs that other propositions are true. Recall also that any proposition is first of all a sentence. As with other sentences, propositions may be either simple or compound.

We can write negations of English sentences. The following definition provides for negations of propositions.

Definition (2-a): If p is a proposition, then the proposition $\sim p$, called the **negation of p**, is false if p is true and true if p is false.

The tilde ($\sim$) is often read *not*, with the result that $\sim p$ is read *not-p*.

Example 1: Write the negation of "Pappy is happy."

Solution: Either "Pappy is not happy" or "It is false that Pappy is happy" are permissible negation forms unless specifically stated otherwise.

The tabular form of displaying truth values may again be used. (See Fig. 2.2.) The double vertical bar separates the given simple proposition

p	$\sim p$
T	F
F	T

Fig. 2.2

(or propositions) from any derived forms. The truth values for $\sim p$ are filled in according to the requirements of Definition (2-a). Note that $\sim p$ is a proposition according to L-1 and L-2.

Axiom L-3 allows us to substitute one proposition for another in certain circumstances.   Consider the statement p: "A grampus is a fish" in argument (3) of the preceding section.   Consider also, "No grampus is not a fish." Certainly either would be false when the other is false or true when the other is true.   Thus L-3 would allow us to substitute "No grampus is not a fish" for p in the argument.

Example 2:   If q stands for $2x = 3$, is $\sim q$ false?

Solution: Assuming that the truth standard is ordinary arithmetic, $\sim q$ can be either true or false.   If $x = 1$, for example, q is false, and $\sim q$ is true by Definition (2-a).   If $x = \frac{3}{2}$, then q is true and $\sim q$ is false.

Notice that the sentence $2x = 3$ in this example is not directly a proposition.   The name for a specific thing must be substituted for the symbol x before the sentence becomes true or false even relative to a fixed truth standard.   Such a symbol is called a **variable**.   The word *she* in the sentence "She is blond" is another example of a variable.   Until a name is substituted for the variable, we cannot tell whether the sentence is true, false, or meaningless. (See also Section 3b.)

Definition (2-b):   A sentence that contains a variable and becomes a proposition when a meaningful name is substituted for the variable is called a **propositional form** (or *open sentence*).

The symbol $p(x)$ is used here for a propositional form in which the variable is x.

Now let us consider a propositional form $p(x)$ and the meaningful names that can be substituted for x.   Since $p(x)$ must become either true or false by Definition (2-b) when one of the meaningful names is substituted, there are certainly three possibilities.   We may have (i) $p(x)$ true for each meaningful x, (ii) $p(x)$ true for at least one meaningful x, or (iii) $p(x)$ false for all meaningful x.

Definition (2-c):   If a propositional form $p(x)$ is true for each meaningful substitution for x, we write $\forall x, p(x)$.   (Read "For all x, $p(x)$ is true.")   If a propositional form is true for at least one x, we write $\exists x, p(x)$.   (Read "For some (at least one) x, $p(x)$ is true.")   This definition takes care of cases (i) and (ii).   (iii) can be written $\forall x, p(x)$ is false.

The symbol $\forall$ is called the **universal quantifier**.   It is often used for the English words "all," "any," "each," "every."   The symbol $\exists$ is called the **existential quantifier**.   It is often used for the English terms "some," "at least one," "there is," "exists."

Two points are worthy of special note.   The use of the quantifiers *is not exactly equivalent* to English usage in spite of the fact that verbal translations have been given.   Hence it is especially important to learn the provisions of Definition (2-c) with care.   Note also that with a quantifier the symbol $p(x)$ is to be read "$p(x)$ is true" unless otherwise specified.

Example 3: Is the sentence $\forall x,\ 2x + 3 = 1$ a proposition?

Solution: Yes. Substituting 0 for x, certainly $2 \cdot 0 + 3 = 1$ is false. Hence, by Definition (2-c), $\forall x,\ 2x + 3 = 1$ is false. Therefore it is a proposition.

Example 4: Is the sentence $\exists x,\ 2x + 3 = 1$ a proposition?

Solution: Yes. Substituting -1 for x yields the true sentence $2(-1) + 3 = 1$. Then, by Definition (2-c), $\exists x,\ 2x + 3 = 1$ is true. Therefore it is a proposition.

Exercise Set

In Exercises 1 through 12, determine which of the given sentences are propositions. Assume the most obvious truth standard in each case. x and y are variables.

1. Andrew Johnson was president of the United States.

2. $\forall x$, x is a mountain over 4 miles high.

3. Susan is John's sister.

4. x is John's sister.

5. $\exists x$ and $\exists y,\ x \cdot y = y \cdot x$.

6. 7 is a nice number.

7. $5 < 2$.

8. $9 + 4 = 1$.

9. $\forall x,\ x = x + 4$.

10. $\exists x,\ x = x + 4$.

11. Read this book.

12. I wish he were here.

13. How do you think the symbols $\forall$ and $\exists$ were chosen?

14. Explain the statement preceding Example 2 that "$\sim p$ is a proposition according to L-1 and L-2."

15. Consider $\sim(\sim p)$. What are its truth values? What other proposition can be substituted for $\sim(\sim p)$ according to L-3?

*16. Determine the correct form of the negation of $\exists x,\ p(x)$; then, considering Exercise 15, determine the negation of $\forall x,\ p(x)$.

2c Compound Propositions

The axioms of the preceding section do not require a proposition to be a simple sentence. We can make compound sentences provided we adhere to the restriction that the truth values of such a compound sentence must be true or false only, but not both, in each individual case. Any word used to combine two propositions into a compound proposition is called a **connective**.

Definition (2-d): For all propositions p and q, the proposition **p $\vee$ q** (read "p or q") is false whenever both p and q are false; otherwise it is true. The proposition $p \vee q$ is called an **inclusive disjunction**.

Note that the English meaning of the word *or* is ambiguous and that this definition specifies that $\vee$ will stand for the less usual of the two major everyday usages of the word. Whenever *or* is used in this book it will be understood to be a synonym for $\vee$ unless specifically stated otherwise.

If a proposition p happens to be true, a proposition q might be either true or false by L-1. If $\sim p$ is true, q might be either true or false again. Thus the axioms provide four separate cases for arrangement of truth values of any proposition compounded from two single propositions. Using this pattern, Definition (2-d) requires the truth table for disjunction to be as shown in Fig. 2.3.

p	q	$p \vee q$
T	T	T
T	F	T
F	T	T
F	F	F

Fig. 2.3

The most common everyday meaning of *or* is illustrated by the sentence, "If the tide is not either high or low, then it is either going out or coming in." We do not mean that it could be *both* going out and coming in. Thus this exclusive use of disjunction (symbolized $\underline{\vee}$) requires the truth table illustrated in Fig. 2.4. The connective $\underline{\vee}$ is used here occasionally. See, for example, Definition (5-i).

Example 1: Is the proposition "$2 = 3$ or $7 > 1$" true or false?

p	q	$p \underline{\vee} q$
T	T	F
T	F	T
F	T	T
F	F	F

Fig. 2.4

Solution: $2 = 3$ is false, and $7 > 1$ is true. According to Definition (2-d), the compound proposition is true.

Definition (2-e): For all propositions p and q, the proposition **p ∧ q** (read "p and q") is true whenever both p and q are true; otherwise it is false. The proposition $p \wedge q$ is called a **conjunction**.

This definition defines the logical connective $\wedge$ to have about the same meaning as the English *and*. The truth table for conjunction is shown in Fig. 2.5.

p	q	$p \wedge q$
T	T	T
T	F	F
F	T	F
F	F	F

Fig. 2.5

Example 2: Is the proposition "$x = 2$ but $3 = 4$" true or false?

Solution: This is a conjunction, since *but* is also used in English to mean *both*. $x = 2$ is a propositional form; that is, we cannot tell whether it is true or false. $3 = 4$ is false; the conjunction is false by Definition (2-e).

The following compound proposition provides us with our basic tool for doing proofs. Both the definition and its truth table (see Fig. 2.6) should be studied with care.

p	q	$p \Rightarrow q$
T	T	T
T	F	F
F	T	T
F	F	T

Fig. 2.6

Definition (2-f): For any propositions p and q, the proposition **p ⇒ q** (read "p implies q," "if p then q," "p only if q," or "q if p") is false whenever p is true and q is false; otherwise it is true. The proposition $p \Rightarrow q$ is called an **implication**.

Beginners often find the provisions of the definition for $\Rightarrow$ strange. This use differs from the everyday English usage of its verbal translations. The best advice is learn it and learn it well in spite of seeming strangeness.

The two propositions p and q joined by the connective $\Rightarrow$ have special names. They are called the **hypothesis** and the **conclusion**, respectively.

Example 3:   Is the proposition "if $x = 2$, then $3x = 6$" true or false?

Solution: It is only on close inspection that we see the given sentence is really a proposition and not a propositional form.   If we substitute 2 for x, both the hypothesis $x = 2$ and the conclusion $3x = 6$ are true.   By Definition (2-f) the implication is thus true. (See also Row 1, Fig. 2.6.)   If any other number is substituted for x, both hypothesis and conclusion are false.   Thus by Definition (2-f) again the implication is true.   (See also Row 4, Fig. 2.6.) Hence the implication is true for all values of x.

Definition (2-g):   For any implication $p \Rightarrow q$, the proposition $q \Rightarrow p$ is called the **converse** of $p \Rightarrow q$.

The truth table for $q \Rightarrow p$ is displayed in Fig. 2.7.   If it does not seem correct at first, recall that in this case q is the hypothesis and p is the conclusion.

p	q	$q \Rightarrow p$
T	T	T
T	F	T
F	T	F
F	F	T

Fig. 2.7

Definition (2-h):   For any implication $p \Rightarrow q$, the proposition $\sim p \Rightarrow \sim q$ is called the **inverse** of $p \Rightarrow q$.

Definition (2-i):   For any implication $p \Rightarrow q$, the proposition $\sim q \Rightarrow \sim p$ is called the **contrapositive** of $p \Rightarrow q$.

The truth tables of these last two compounds are left to the exercises. When discussing an implication $p \Rightarrow q$, and its converse, inverse, or contrapositive, it is convenient to call the form $p \Rightarrow q$ itself the **positive**.

The following definition provides us with the last of the connectives we shall use.   The reader will note that use is made of the converse principle.

Definition (2-j):   For any propositions p and q, the proposition **p iff q** (read "p if and only if q") is the same as the conjunction $(p \Rightarrow q) \wedge (q \Rightarrow p)$.

In words, this connective is the conjunction of an implication and its converse.

We can construct the truth tables for p iff q by using the tables of Figs. 2.6 and 2.7. (See Fig. 2.8.) The last column was filled in by using Definition (2-e), the conjunction $(p \Rightarrow q) \wedge (q \Rightarrow p)$ being true only when $p \Rightarrow q$ and $q \Rightarrow p$ are both true.

p	q	$p \Rightarrow q$	$q \Rightarrow p$	p iff q
T	T	T	T	T
T	F	F	T	F
F	T	T	F	F
F	F	T	T	T

Fig. 2.8

Now note that in the two cases when p iff q is true (Row 1 and Row 4), p and q have the same truth values (both F or both T). By Axiom L-3 either of two propositions that have the same truth values may be substituted for the other.

Definition (2-k): Two propositions that have the same truth values are said to be **logically equivalent**.

A look at Figs. 2.6 and 2.7 will remind us that any implication and its converse are *not* logically equivalent in general. When an implication and its converse are logically equivalent, we say the proposition is **reversible**.

Example 4: Is the proposition "If each of two numbers is even, then their sum is even" reversible?

Solution: This implication is certainly true. The converse would be: If the sum of two numbers is even, then each of the numbers is even. Is this true in general? No, it is not. 8 is an even number, and $3 + 5 = 8$, but neither 3 nor 5 is even. Thus the converse is not true in general, and the implication is not reversible.

In an axiomatic system, the *converse* of an axiom or a theorem is not true in general. The converses must be proved separately. Axioms and theorems are *not* reversible. However, definitions *are* reversible. Hence many definitions are stated in iff form. Even when the if..., then... form is used, it is *understood* that the converse of a definition is also true.

Exercise Set

In Exercises 1 through 7, list the hypothesis and conclusion of each proposition or tell why this is not possible.

1. If x is heavier than y, then y is heavier than z.

2. $3 \cdot 5 = 15$ implies that $9 + 4 = 1$.

3. The earth is a planet $\Rightarrow$ The moon is a satellite.

4. Birds can fly $\Leftarrow$ Micky is sticky.

5. $2 + 1 = 5$ only if $3 + 4 = 7$.

6. We are happy and no one is sad.

7. Two lines are perpendicular iff they determine right angles.

In Exercises 8 through 13, determine whether the given sentences are propositional forms or propositions. If the latter, classify them as true or false according to the most obvious truth standard.

8. The sentence in Exercise 1 above.

9. The sentence in Exercise 2 above.

10. $x^2 - 4x + 3 = 0$ or $2 = 1$.

11. $x^2 - 4x + 3 = 0$ and $2 = 1$.

12. If $x^2 - 4x + 3 = 0$, then $2 = 1$.

13. The sentence in Exercise 5 above.

14. Make a truth table for $p \lor p$.

15. Make a truth table for $p \land p$.

16. Make a truth table for $p \Rightarrow p$.

17. Make a truth table for $p \lor \sim p$.

18. Make a truth table for $p \land \sim p$.

19. Make a truth table for the inverse of an implication $p \Rightarrow q$.

20. Make a truth table for the contrapositive of an implication $p \Rightarrow q$.

21. Write the converse, inverse, and contrapositive of the following propositions.
    (a) If it snows, then it is cold.
    (b) If two line segments are similar, then they are congruent.

*22. Compare the truth tables in Exercises 19 and 20 with those in Figs. 2.6 and 2.7. In the light of Definition (2-k), what conclusions can you draw?

*23. Make a truth table for the proposition $(p \land q) \Rightarrow p$.

**24. Make a truth table for the proposition $(\sim p) \lor q$. In the light of Definition (2-k), which conclusion can you draw?

2d   Rules of Inference

Recall from Section 2b that a proof is a valid argument in the form of a sequence of steps. Generally the argument is longer than the examples given in that section. In addition, we do not assume premises to be true in a proof, for it is not a study of constructions. Instead we supply a "reason" to show why each premise is true.

Some of the reasons would be known true principles from the axiomatic structure at hand. Others are principles of logic called *rules of inference*.

To allow us to make a start, the hypothesis of the proposition to be proved is also taken as true.   A proved proposition is called a **theorem**. As a convenience to the reader, certain theorems are called **corollaries** to some given theorem.   A corollary is a proposition that can be proved by an immediate application of the given theorem.

In preceding sections, truth tables have been used to establish logical principles.   In Exercise 15, Section 2b, for example, we found that $\sim(\sim p)$ and p are logically equivalent.   Using $\Leftrightarrow$ to symbolize logical equivalence, we thus have

Theorem (2d-1):   For any proposition p, $\sim(\sim p) \Leftrightarrow p$.

Example 1:   What is the correct negation of "She is not at home"?

Solution: One negation form is "It is false that she is not at home," and by Theorem (2d-1) this becomes "She is at home."

The exercises in Section 2c established the following theorems:

Theorem (2d-2):   For any implication $p \Rightarrow q$, $(\sim q \Rightarrow \sim p) \Leftrightarrow (p \Rightarrow q)$; $(q \Rightarrow p) \Leftrightarrow (\sim p \Rightarrow \sim q)$; and $(q \Rightarrow p) \nLeftrightarrow (p \Rightarrow q)$.

Theorem (2d-3): $(\sim p \lor q) \Leftrightarrow (p \Rightarrow q)$.

It is sometimes easier to prove a proposition in contrapositive form than in positive form.   Theorem (2d-2) justifies this procedure.   However, the contrapositive form makes use of negation.   As a final example of the use of truth tables as a proof device based on L-3, we prove a theorem that shows how to negate a disjunction of the type found in the conclusion of Theorem (6c-3).

Example 2:   Show that the correct negation of $p \lor q$ is $\sim p \land \sim q$.

Solution: First find the truth values of $\sim p$ and $\sim q$ by Definition (2-a), then $(\sim p) \land (\sim q)$ by Definition (2-e), $p \lor q$ by Definition (2-d), and $\sim(p \lor q)$ by Definition (2-a), and then compare.   Figure 2.9 shows that $(\sim p \land \sim q) \Leftrightarrow \sim(p \lor q)$.

p	q	$\sim p$	$\sim q$	$\sim p \land \sim q$	$p \lor q$	$\sim(p \lor q)$
T	T	F	F	F	T	F
T	F	F	T	F	T	F
F	T	T	F	F	T	F
F	F	T	T	T	F	T

Fig. 2.9

Accordingly, the negation of "the lines are parallel or they intersect" is "the lines are not parallel and they do not intersect." See the exercises for negation forms for $(p \Rightarrow q)$ and $(p \wedge q)$.

Some important rules of logic do not depend on the principle of logical equivalence. We can use truth tables in a different way to establish these principles. Suppose, for example, we know that p is true and that $p \Rightarrow q$ is true. Can we conclude anything about q? The truth table for $p \Rightarrow q$ is shown in Fig. 2.10. We are given that $(p \Rightarrow q)$ is true. Hence Row 2 is

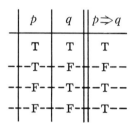

Fig. 2.10

no longer possible because of the F under $p \Rightarrow q$. We cross it out. We are also given that p is true. Hence we can also cross out Rows 3 and 4 because of the F's in the p column. Only Row 1 remains. Thus q must be true. We have proved the following theorem.

Theorem (2d-4) (*Rule of Detachment or Fundamental Rule of Inference*): If $p \Rightarrow q$ is true and if p is true, then q is true.

In the argument form used in Section 2a, the pattern of this principle appears as

(If)	$p \Rightarrow q$	(is true)
(and)	p	(is true),
(then)	q	(is true).

Generally the words in parentheses are omitted as was done in Section 2a. This is the construction of argument (3) of that section.

To see this, let

p: Polly is a zoy and
q: Polly is a vlacho.

Then the symbolic form is

$$\frac{\begin{array}{c} p \Rightarrow q \\ p \end{array}}{q.}$$

Since this is the pattern of Theorem (2d-4), the argument is valid.

Notice that the construction form of argument (4), Section 2a, is

$$p \Rightarrow q$$
$$q$$
$$\overline{}$$
$$p.$$

It was stated there that this form is not valid.   Let us see why.   Using a truth table yields Fig. 2.11.   Row 2 has a false in the $p \Rightarrow q$ column.   Therefore it is crossed out because $p \Rightarrow q$ is true.   Row 4 is crossed out because q is given true.   Now the p column still has a T in Row 1 and an F in Row 3. Thus p may be either true or false and the argument is invalid.   We can also call this form of argument *reasoning from the converse*, since we are given

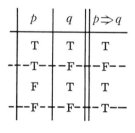

Fig. 2.11

$p \Rightarrow q$ and are asked to go from q to p.   As Theorem (2d-2) states, $(p \Rightarrow q) \not\Rightarrow (q \Rightarrow p)$, which also shows that the argument is not valid.

Additional rules of inference could be proved.   For example, Theorem (2d-2) states that $\dfrac{p \Rightarrow q}{\sim q \Rightarrow \sim p}$ is a rule of inference.   Moreover, Definition (2-e) ensures us that

$$p$$
$$q$$
$$\overline{}$$
$$p \wedge q$$

is a rule of inference.   This is, in fact, the pattern of Exercise 8, Section 2a.

If proofs were written out completely, steps involving the material at hand would be interwoven with steps requiring the use of these and other rules of inference.   Theorem (2d-4) would occur most frequently.   See the alternative proof of two steps of Theorem (3d-1) for example.

As in the complete proof of this theorem, we most often shorten our work by omitting specific mention of rules of inference.   Nevertheless, their use is implicit in all the mathematics we do.   Often we even avoid the formal style of the proof of Theorem (3d-1) and write proofs in conversational style.

Using this latter style, the proof of Theorem (2b-1) would be about as follows.   Let p be a given proposition.   We take the hypothesis as true. Therefore p must have either the value T or the value F.   In either case a contradiction results; that is, we have p both T and F by hypothesis. This is impossible by L-2, however, and since L-1 requires that p have one of the two labels, it must have the one that did not cause the contradiction. Thus the theorem is established.

Exercise Set

Write (a) the inverse and (b) the contrapositive of the implications given in Exercises 1 and 2.

1. If it is raining, then it is not snowing.
2. $2x = 3$ only if $x \neq 4$.
3. Are the inverse and contrapositive of any $p \Rightarrow q$ equivalent? Explain.
4. Are the converse and contrapositive of any $p \Rightarrow q$ logically equivalent? Explain.

In Exercises 5 through 9 let

$$p: \quad \text{The lines are parallel.}$$
$$q: \quad \text{They do not intersect.}$$

Write verbal translations of the given symbolic forms.

5. $p \wedge q$.   6. $p \Rightarrow q$.   7. $p \vee \sim q$.
8. p iff q.   9. $\sim(\sim q)$.

In Exercises 10 through 12, work out truth tables for the given symbolic form.

10. $p \vee \sim p$ (This is one way of symbolizing Axiom L-1.)
11. $\sim(p \wedge \sim p)$ (This symbolizes L-2.)
12. $\sim(\sim p \vee q)$.

In Exercises 13 through 18, write the given argument in symbolic form and determine its validity.

13. Exercise 2, Section 2a.   14. Exercise 6, Section 2a.
15. Exercise 7, Section 2a.   16. Exercise 8, Section 2a.
*17. Exercise 1, Section 2a.   *18. Exercise 5, Section 2a.
*19. *Prove:* $\sim(p \wedge q) \Leftrightarrow \sim p \vee \sim q$.
*20. *Prove:* $p \vee (q \vee r) \Leftrightarrow (p \vee q) \vee r$.
*21. *Prove:* $p \wedge (q \wedge r) \Leftrightarrow (p \wedge q) \wedge r$.
**22. Is $p \wedge (q \vee r) \Leftrightarrow (p \wedge q) \wedge r$ true? Show by truth table.
**23. *Prove:* $\sim(p \Rightarrow q) \Leftrightarrow (p \wedge \sim q)$. [*Hint:* Note Theorem (2d-3).]

chapter 3

Sets and Real Numbers

3a Fundamental Set Concepts

Let us consider for a moment the numbers

$$2, 13, -7, 29, 91, 38, -41.$$

There seems to be no particular relationship beteen any two of the numbers, no pattern in the way in which they are ordered.   In fact, they seem to be just a group of numbers picked at random.   However, this collection of numerals is right in front of our eyes.   Thus we can distinguish it from other collections.   Any collection of things that can be distinguished from others is called a **set**.

Since we have not previously defined the word "collection" in a technical sense, we cannot call the preceding sentence a formal definition.   The word "set" is most usually regarded as a primitive term in mathematics.

The symbol $\in$ is also regarded as a primitive term.   It is used in sentences such as $x \in S$, which we understand to mean that x is one of the distinguishable things in the set S.   We say that x is a **member** or **element** of the set. The symbol $\in$ we translate verbally as "belongs to," "is an element of," "is a member of," "is contained in," or just "is in."   Also, we read the sentence $S \ni x$ as "set S contains x."

Of great importance is the idea that the members of the set must be distinguishable.   We can easily give many examples of sets. We could talk about the set of people in a room, the set of books in a library, the set of all the merchandise for sale in a department store.

Note that in each of these cases it would be easy to tell which things (persons, books, articles for sale) are in the set and which are not.   In other words, we can distinguish which items are to be considered as members of the set. We often say that a set must be a *clearly defined* collection of things, where by "clearly defined" we mean that there is some rule or method whereby one can tell exactly which items are in the set and which are not.

Example 1:   Consider the set S such that S contains even whole numbers. $2 \in S$, but $3 \notin S$.   The elements of S are clearly distinguishable.

Example 2:   Consider the set P such that P contains the prettiest states in the Union.   Is California or New York in the set?   Clearly, it is impossible to determine the answer.   It is a matter of opinion. P is *not* a well-defined set.

Another aspect of distinguishability is important.   We agree that each element in a set must have a property that will distinguish it from other elements of the same set.

Example 3:   The set $S = \{$George Washington, General Grant, the first president of the U.S.$\}$ is considered to have only two elements, for only two distinguishable persons are contained in it.

If the elements of a set are arranged in some order so that they are countable one by one until we reach a last element, then the set is called a **finite set**. If, no matter how far we count, there is always at least one more element to be counted, we call the set **infinite**.   Thus the set whose elements are $\square$, $\triangle$, $\square$ is finite and the set whose elements are all the natural numbers $1,2,3,\ldots$ is infinite.   The symbol $\ldots$ stands for the words "and so on" and means that we are to continue to list elements in a similar manner.   (In this book we shall consider that "a similar manner" means that we are to use the most obvious pattern we can imagine.)

If a set contains no elements, it is called the **null** set or **empty** set.   The null set is represented by the symbol $\emptyset$.

We shall use braces $\{\ \}$ and capital letters $A,B,C,$etc. to indicate a set. Thus the expression

$$S = \{1,2,3,4\}$$

means a set whose elements are the numbers 1, 2, 3, and 4.   This notation for a set such as S is called **roster** notation because an actual list of the elements is given.

The symbol $\{x \mid p(x)\}$ is read: The set of all x such that the propositional form (open sentence) $p(x)$ is true.   This is called **set-builder** notation.

Since $p(x)$ is to be true, $S = \{x \mid p(x)\}$ is the **solution set** for $p(x)$.

Example 4: $\{x \mid x + 1 = 4\} = \{3\}$ is the solution set for the open sentence $x + 1 = 4$.   Because $3 + 1 = 4$ is true, the set $\{3\}$ must be the same as the set $\{x \mid x + 1 = 4\}$.

Example 5:   Is the number 8 an element of the set $\{x \mid 3x + 1 = 7\}$?

Solution: When we substitute 8 for x in the open sentence $3x + 1 = 7$, we get either a true sentence or a false sentence.   If the sentence is true, then $8 \in \{x \mid 3x + 1 = 7\}$.   If the sentence is false, then $8 \notin \{x \mid 3x + 1 = 7\}$.

Since upon substitution of 8 for x we get the sentence $25 = 7$, which is false, we know then that $8 \notin \{x \mid 3x + 1 = 7\}$.

Definition (3-a): If the elements of two sets are paired in such a way that each element of the first set is associated with one and only one element of the second set and each element of the second set is associated with one and only one element of the first set, the sets are said to be in a **one-to-one-correspondence.**

The sets $\{2,3,5\}$ and $\{9,11,13\}$ can be associated in the manner

$$\{2,3,5\}$$
$$\updownarrow \ \updownarrow \ \updownarrow$$
$$\{9,11,13\}$$

and we say the sets are in one-to-one correspondence.

We should note here that a one-to-one correspondence between sets does not mean that the elements of the sets must be similar in nature. We could very well have a one-to-one correspondence between the set of boats on a lake and a finite set of natural numbers.

Definition (3-b): If two sets are in one-to-one correspondence, they are said to be **equivalent.**

The sets $\{\varDelta,\beta,5\}$ and $\{$coat, up, small$\}$ can be put in a one-to-one correspondence. For example,

$$\{\varDelta,\beta,5\}$$
$$\updownarrow \ \updownarrow \ \updownarrow$$
$$\{\text{coat, up, small}\}$$

By Definition (3-b) these sets are equivalent. We immediately see that the equivalence of sets does not necessarily mean that the corresponding elements of the two sets are identical or equal.

Definition (3-c): Two sets are **equal** iff they have exactly the same elements.

Example 6: $\{2,4,-5\} = \{4,2,-5\} = \{-5,4,2\}$.

Definition (3-d): A set B is a **subset** of a set A (or B is **included in** A) iff every element of B is also an element of A. We write $B \subset A$.

Example 7: Consider $A = \{1,2,3,4\}$ and $B = \{3,4\}$. Since $3 \in A \wedge 4 \in A$, B is a subset of (is included in) A.

It turns out that the null set is a subset of every set and that a set is a subset of itself; that is, $A \subset A$ and $\emptyset \subset A$ for all sets A.

Example 8: What are the subsets of $\{2,3,4\}$?

Solution: The subsets are $\emptyset$, $\{2\}$, $\{3\}$, $\{4\}$, $\{2,3\}$, $\{2,4\}$, $\{3,4\}$, $\{2,3,4\}$.

In the following exercises, reference is made to different sets of numbers. The following *intuitive* description can be used for these sets.

The set N of *natural numbers* is the set $\{1,2,3,4,5,\ldots\}$ of the usual counting numbers. The set Z of *integers* is the set $\{\ldots,-3,-2,-1,0,1,2,3,\ldots\}$ of positive and negative whole numbers and 0. The set Q of *rational numbers* is the set of fractions having whole numbers as numerator and denominator.

Exercise Set

Using braces, list the elements of the sets in Exercises 1 through 5.

1. The set of all natural numbers.

2. The set of first four odd natural numbers.

3. The set of all integers greater than -10 and less than 2.

4. The set of odd integers.

5. The set of even integers.

6. Indicate all possible one-to-one correspondences between the two equivalent sets $\{1,2,3\}$ and $\{\square,\triangle,\square\}$.

7. Which of the following sets are equivalent?
   $A = \{1,2,3\}$, $B = \{4,5,6\}$, $C = \{7,8,9,10\}$,
   $D = \{-4,2\}$, $E = \{\square,\triangle\}$, $F = \{\alpha,\beta,\gamma,\delta\}$,
   $G = \{1,2,3,1,2,3\}$.

8. Which of the following sets are equal?
   $A = \{1,2,3\}$, $B = \{4,5,6\}$, $C = \{\alpha,\beta,\gamma\}$,
   $D = \{2,1,\alpha\}$, $E = \{\gamma,\beta,\alpha\}$, $F = \{6,4,5\}$,
   $G = \{1,2,3,\alpha,\beta,\gamma\}$, $H = \{1,\alpha,2,\beta,3,\gamma\}$, $I = \{4,4,5,5,6\}$.

List the subsets of the sets in Exercises 9 through 14.

9. $A = \{1,2\}$.

10. $A = \{0,1\}$.

11. $A = \{a,\beta\}$.

12. $A = \{\delta\}$.

13. $A = \{0,1,2,3\}$.

14. $A = \{-1,1,\alpha\}$.

Indicate whether the sets in Exercises 15 through 20 are infinite, finite, or empty finite sets.

15. $A = \{1,2,3,4,\ldots\}$.

16. $A = \{$all numbers between 0 and 1$\}$.

17. $A = \{$all natural numbers less than 99$\}$.

18. $A = \{$the pink elephants in your home$\}$.

19. $A = \{\ldots-3,-2,-1,0,1,2,3,\ldots\}$.

20. $A = \{$all the trees in the world$\}$.

21. If two sets are equivalent, are they equal? If two sets are equal, are they equivalent?

22. Use set-builder notation to describe the following sets.
    (a) All positive integers less than 10.

(b) All natural numbers greater than 5.
(c) Solution set of $x = 3$.
(d) All the values of x greater than or equal to -2.
(e) All the grains of sand in Mexico.
(f) All the fish that are fat and red.

3b   Set Operations

When investigating two sets, we find there are several combination possibilities for the elements.   If we consider the sets

(1) $A = \{0,1,2\}, \quad B = \{1,2,3\}, \quad C = \{3,4,5\},$

we see that the sets A and B have the elements 1 and 2 in common.   The
sets B and C have the element 3 in common.   The sets A and C have no
elements in common.   Certainly we could have sets $D = \{1,2\}$ and $E = \{3\}$.
We also remember that the null set has no elements.   These ideas lead us
to the following definition.

Definition (3-e):   The **intersection** of two sets A and B is a set C such that
the elements of C are those and only those elements common to A and B.
We say A intersection B equals C and write $A \cap B = C$.

Referring to the sets (1), we can now write $A \cap B = \{1,2\}$ and $B \cap C =$
$\{3\}$.   What about $A \cap C$? A and C have no elements in common, but
Definition (3-e) requires that $A \cap C$ equal a set.   Hence we call upon the
set that contains no elements, that is, the null set.   Thus

$$A \cap C = \emptyset.$$

Definition (3-f):   Two sets A and B that have no elements in common
(i.e., $A \cap B = \emptyset$) are said to be **disjoint**.

Referring to the sets (1) once again, we know that the given elements
could be combined to form a set $F = \{0,1,2,3\}$ or a set $G = \{1,2,3,4,5\}$.
The following definition gives us a means of forming such sets.

Definition (3-g):   The **union** of two sets A and B is a set C such that the
elements of C are those and only those elements that belong to A or to B
or to both A and B.   We say A union B equals C and write $A \cup B = C$.

Now $F = \{0,1,2,3\} = A \cup B$ and $G = \{1,2,3,4,5\} = B \cup C$.   Referring to
(1) again, we also have $A \cup C = \{0,1,2,3,4,5\}$.

Example 1:   Listing each *symbol* of $A \cup B$ from (1), we obtain $A \cup B =$
$\{0,1,1,2,2,3\}$.   By Definition (3-c) we know that $\{0,1,1,2,2,3\} = \{0,1,2,3\}$.
Thus $A \cup B = F$.

Definition (3-h):   A **constant** is a symbol that stands for exactly one element of a given set.

Example 2:   If $\omega \in S$ and if $\omega = 3$, then ω is a constant.

Example 3:   If $p \in M$ and if $M = \{1\}$, then p is a constant.   In fact, $p = 1$.

Example 4:   If $q \in S$ and $S = \{1,2,3\}$, then q is not a constant, for S contains more than one element.   Thus q is 1, 2, or 3; that is, q is a *variable*.

Definition (3-i):   A **variable** is a symbol that stands for any element of a set.

Exercise Set

In Exercises 1 through 8, find (a) the intersection and (b) the union of the given pairs of sets.

1. $\{1\}$ and $\{2\}$.
2. $\{0\}$ and $\{0,1\}$.
3. $\{-2,3,4\}$ and $\{-1,5,6\}$.
4. {natural numbers} and $\{2,4,6,8,\ldots\}$.
5. {odd integers} and {even integers}.
6. {odd integers} and {natural numbers}.
7. {negative integers} and $\{-1\}$.
8. $\{\alpha,\beta,\gamma\}$ and $\{2\alpha,2\beta,2\gamma\}$.
9. Justify the proposition $p = 1$ in Example 3.
10. Which sets in each of Exercises 1 through 8 are disjoint?

In Exercises 11 through 18, use $A = \{1,2,3\}$, $B = \{4,5,6\}$, $C = \{3,4\}$ to find the given set.

11. $A \cup B$.
12. $A \cap C$.
13. $A \cap B$.
14. $A \cup C$.
15. $A \cap (A \cap C)$.
16. $A \cup (A \cap C)$.
17. $A \cup (B \cap C)$.
18. $(A \cup B) \cap (A \cup C)$.

If $A = \{1\}$, $B = \{1,2\}$, $C = \{1,2,3\}$, state whether p is a constant, a variable, or neither if p is an element of the sets given in each of Exercises 19 through 26.

19. $p \in (A \cup B)$.
20. $p \in (A \cap C)$.
21. $p \in (B \cup C)$.
22. $p \in A$.
23. $p \in [A \cup (B \cup C)]$.
24. $p \in (B \cap C)$.
25. $p \in [(A \cup B) \cup (A \cap C)]$.
26. $p \in [A \cap (B \cup C)]$.

3c   The Real Numbers

In Section 1b we saw that one aspect of a modern treatment of geometry is the use of number properties to establish geometric facts.

In progressing through school a student learns a vast array of number facts.   The rules for handling constants such as 2, 0, and $\frac{5}{2}$ are developed early.   Roughly speaking, the study of properties of such number constants is called arithmetic.   Later, number sentences containing one or more variables are considered.   This study has traditionally been called algebra.

In both cases, many of these number concepts are learned so early that high school and college students often seem to regard them as part of their natural environment.   Actually, the algebra of numbers is just as much a logical structure as any other branch of mathematics.   By this we mean that some of the basic general properties of numbers could be used as axioms from which all their other properties are derived.

Another fact that the student must recognize is that we make use of several different sets of numbers in mathematics.   Some of these were described in Section 3a.   The natural numbers N are useful in counting.   However, natural numbers are not sufficient for keeping track of temperature and football yardage.   For these tasks we use the set Q of rational numbers which contains negative numbers and fractions.   The set of numbers we use for geometry is called the set of *real* numbers.   The word *real* in this use must be regarded simply as a label.   It has none of its everyday meaning as contrasted with such terms as "unreal" or "nonexistent."   *At this point it is our purpose to specify the properties that make the set of reals so useful in the study of geometry.*

If the algebra of numbers is a logical system, what principles are important enough to be stated as axioms?   Let us explore this matter by considering some familiar examples.

Factoring is important in algebra.   The sentence

(1) $$2(x + y) = 2x + 2y$$

expresses a well-known factoring fact.   Would it make a suitable axiom for numbers?   We note that one of the three symbols in (1) is a constant.   The sentence

(2) $$3(x + y) = 3x + 3y$$

is similar to (1).   In fact, we see that they are the same except that one constant has been replaced by another.   Would the sentence (1) still be true if any other constant were written in place of the constant 2?   If we find no constant for which it would be false, we can use a variable in place of the constant 2.   Then the sentence would read

(3) $$z(x + y) = zx + zy.$$

If we understand that this proposition is to be true for all x, for all y, and for all z, then this is a much more general statement than (1) or (2) because it includes both of these constants and infinitely many others in one sentence. (3) is called the *distributive property of multiplication over addition*. Perhaps the expressions "clearing parentheses," often used when reading (3) from left to right, or "taking out a common factor," often used when reading it from right to left, are more familiar.

Throughout our work with numbers, one fact that should seem important is that when two arithmetic numbers are added or multiplied, we always get an *answer*. This answer is obvious in a case like $2 + 3$. We can "see" that it is 5. The particular number that is equal to $5280 \times \frac{2}{7}$ is by no means so readily obtained. Yet we are certain that an arithmetic number x does exist such that $5280 \times \frac{2}{7} = x$. Generalizing again, we say that for any real numbers a and b,

(4)   a real number x exists such that $a + b = x$

and

(5)   a real number y exists such that $a \cdot b = y$.

These are called *closure* properties, and we say that the set of real numbers is *closed* under addition and multiplication.

Recall that some number sets are *not* closed under familiar operations. The set of natural numbers is not closed under subtraction, for example. To see this, we ask ourselves "Is there a natural number x such that $x = 2 - 5$?" No such x exists. Stated in terms of addition, we can say that there is no natural number x such that $2 = 5 + x$. Thus one of the most important properties of real numbers is that for any real numbers a and b, in that order,

(6)   a real number x exists such that $a = b + x$.

Similarly, for multiplication, we have the property that for any real numbers a and nonzero b, in that order,

(7)   there is a real number x such that $a = b \cdot x$.

Statements (6) and (7) are called respectively the *solvability* properties for addition and multiplication.

The requirement that b is to be nonzero in (7) is easily explained. Suppose one were to try to find x corresponding to $a = 3$ and $b = 0$. We would have $3 = 0 \cdot x$. Because of the fact that $0 \cdot x = 0$ for all x, the contradictory statement $3 = 0$ would result. Thus we must have $b \neq 0$ in (7).

Very early the reader learned that $2 + 3 = 3 + 2$ and that $7 \times 5 = 5 \times 7$. These are illustrations of the general properties

(8) $x + y = y + x$

and

(9)
$$x \cdot y = y \cdot x$$

for all real numbers x and y. Statements (8) and (9) are called the *commutative* properties for addition and multiplication, respectively. In effect, they state that the order of adding and multiplying real numbers does not affect the final sum or product.

Another important pair of number properties is concerned with what is often called "shifting parentheses." For example, we know that $(7 + 2) + 13 = 7 + (2 + 13)$ and $(\frac{1}{2} \times 4) \times 5 = \frac{1}{2} \times (4 \times 5)$ are both true. Stated generally, we have

(10)
$$(x + y) + z = x + (y + z)$$

and

(11)
$$(x \cdot y) \cdot z = x \cdot (y \cdot z)$$

for all real numbers x, y, z. Statements (10) and (11) are called the *associative* properties for addition and multiplication, respectively. In effect, they state that the grouping of terms and factors does not affect the final sum or product.

Another early learned number skill is handling equations. If we have the equation $x + 3 = 7$, for example, one adds -3 to each side to obtain $x = 4$. Stated generally, the properties used are

(12)
$$\text{if } a = b \text{ and if } c = d, \text{ then } a + c = b + d$$

and

(13)
$$\text{if } a = b \text{ and if } c = d, \text{ then } a \cdot c = b \cdot d$$

for all real numbers a, b, c, and d. Properties (12) and (13) are called *uniqueness of sum* and *uniqueness of product*, respectively.

In this discussion we have been calling on past experience by using particular numbers to illustrate important properties. In a formal statement of real number properties, definite provision would have to be made for some particular numbers. The numbers 0 and 1 are especially important. The following statement delineates the essential properties of these two numbers.

(14) Unique real numbers 0 and 1 exist such that
$$x = x + 0 \quad \text{and} \quad x = x \cdot 1 \quad \text{and} \quad 0 \neq 1$$

for all real numbers x. The restriction $0 \neq 1$ guarantees that the set of real numbers is infinite rather than finite, although this fact will not be established directly in this book.

The preceding properties have all been concerned with how addition and multiplication of real numbers act relative to equality. It is also important to specify how addition and multiplication act relative to the relation $<$. This relation is called an *order* relation.

Two symbols are used for order: $<$ reads "less than"; $>$ reads "greater than." Previous experience will assure us, for example, that $2 < 3$ and $-\frac{7}{3} < 0$. Note that we could also write $3 > 2$ and $0 > -\frac{7}{3}$. We *regard* $a < b$ *and* $b > a$ *as equivalent statements.* Note also that $a > 0$ can be read "a is positive" and $a < 0$ as "a is negative."

We know that since $3 > 2$ is true, $3 < 2$ and $3 = 2$ are both false. Stated generally, we have

(15)   exactly one of $a < b$, $a > b$, $a = b$

               is true for all real numbers a and b.

Statement (15) is called the *trichotomy* property.

Recall that if $\frac{1}{2} < x$ and $x < 3$, then $\frac{1}{2} < 3$ is also true. In general terms,

(16)   if $a < b$ and $b < c$, then $a < c$

for all real numbers a, b, and c. (16) is called the *transitive* property of $<$.

Let us return to the question of how to specify properties of addition and multiplication relative to $<$. We know that $\frac{3}{2} + 3 < 5 + 3$ and that $\frac{3}{2} \times 3 < 5 \times 3$. Is it also true that $\frac{5}{2} + (-3) < 7 + (-3)$ and $\frac{5}{2} \times (-3) < 7 \times (-3)$? Simplifying the first, we obtain $-\frac{1}{2} < 4$, which is true. Simplifying the second, we obtain $-\frac{15}{2} < -21$, which is false. That is, order is disturbed when multiplying by a negative number. It is easy to find examples to show that multiplication by 0 also changes order. (See Exercise 1.) The preceding facts are stated generally as

(17)   if $a < b$, then $a + c < b + c$;

               if $a < b$ and $c < 0$, then $a \cdot c > b \cdot c$,

and

(18)   if $a < b$ and $c > 0$, then $a \cdot c < b \cdot c$

for all real numbers a, b, and c.

Illustrations of the more important of these principles follow.

Example 1:   Is $5 + \sqrt{3}$ a real number?

Solution: Yes, this is true by closure (5). A decimal approximation of this number is 6.73.

Example 2:   Is there a real number x such that $\sqrt{18} = x\sqrt{2}$?

Solution: Yes, this is true by solvability property (7). $x = 3$.

Example 3:   Does $3(7) = 6 + 15$?

Solution: Yes, $3(7) = 3(2 + 5)$ and then $3(2 + 5) = 3 \cdot 2 + 3 \cdot 5$ by distributive property (3). Since $3 \cdot 2 = 6$ and $3 \cdot 5 = 15$, we have $3(7) = 6 + 15$.

Example 4:   Is the set $S = \{$odd whole numbers$\}$ closed under addition?

Solution: No.   *Counterexample:* $3 \in S$ and $7 \in S$ but $(3 + 7) \notin S$.   If the closure property held in S, we would have to have $(a + b) \in S$ for all $a \in S$ and $b \in S$.

Exercise Set

1. Show by example that multiplying both sides of a true $<$ sentence by zero makes it false.

2. Explain how (7) guarantees closure of the reals under division by a nonzero divisor.

State the property of the real numbers which justifies each of the propositions in Exercises 3 through 13.   (Symbols for particular fractions, whole numbers, or surds are to be taken as real numbers.)

3. $x \not> 3$ and $x \neq 3$; therefore $x < 3$.

4. $(x + \frac{3}{5})$ is a real number where x is a real number.

5. $x \cdot (x + y) = (x + y) \cdot x$ where $x,y,(x + y)$ is a real number.

6. $3 + 4 = 4 + 3$.

7. $4 + (\sqrt{2} + 5) = (4 + \sqrt{2}) + 5$.

8. $\sqrt{7} \cdot [3 \cdot (-\frac{4}{5})] = [\sqrt{7} \cdot 3] \cdot (-\frac{4}{5})$.

9. $(x = 2 \wedge y = 3) \Rightarrow x \cdot y = 2 \cdot 3$ where x,y are each real numbers.

10. $(a = b) \Rightarrow (2a = 2b)$ where a,b are each real numbers.

11. A real number exists such that $2 = -3 + x$.

12. $(a = b) \Rightarrow (a + c = b + c)$ where a,b,c are each real numbers.

13. A real number exists such that $4 = -\frac{3}{5}x$.

14. Make a verbal restatement of the principle stated in Exercise 12.

Which of the sets in Exercises 15 through 18 is closed under the given operation? Give an example in each case.

15. $S = \{$odd whole numbers$\}$ under multiplication.

16. $M = \{$even whole numbers$\}$ under addition.

17. $T = \{0\}$ under (a) addition, (b) multiplication, (c) subtraction, (d) division.

18. $V = \{1\}$ under (a) addition, (b) multiplication.

19. Using the symbols N, Z, and Q for the natural numbers, integers, and rationals, respectively, list the sets that are closed under (a) addition, (b) subtraction, (c) multiplication, (d) division.

20. Which of the operations, if any, tested in Exercise 19 are not commutative? Give examples.

21. Which of the operations, if any, listed in Exercise 19 are not associative? Give examples.

3d   Real Number Axioms

The basic properties of the real numbers examined in the preceding section will now be stated as axioms. We shall use the script capital $\mathscr{R}$ as a special symbol for the set of real numbers.

Since we use the $=$ relation constantly with elements of $\mathscr{R}$, we state its important properties first.

E-1: $\forall x,\ x = x$. That is, any number equals itself. (This is called the **reflexive property** of equality.)

E-2: $\forall x,y$, if $x = y$, then $y = x$. (This is called the **symmetric property** of equality.)

E-3: $\forall a,b,c$, if $a = b$ and if $b = c$, then $a = c$. (This is called the **transitive property** of equality.)

The properties of the set $\mathscr{R} = \{a,b,c,\ldots\}$ are determined by the following axioms. Our primitive terms are $+$, $\times$, $<$, and the set $\mathscr{R}$ itself. We are also including logic and the properties of sets among our premises.

R-1: $\forall (a,b) \in \mathscr{R}$, $\exists x \in \mathscr{R}$ such that $a + b = x$. **Closure** of $\mathscr{R}$ under $+$.

R-2: $\forall (a,b) \in \mathscr{R}$, $a + b = b + a$. **Commutativity** of $+$ in $\mathscr{R}$.

R-3: $\forall a,b,c \in \mathscr{R}$, $(a + b) + c = a + (b + c)$. **Associativity** of $+$ in $\mathscr{R}$.

R-4: $\forall a,b,c,d \in \mathscr{R}$, if $a = b$ and if $c = d$, then $a + c = b + d$. **Uniqueness of sum** in $\mathscr{R}$.

R-5: $\forall (a,b) \in \mathscr{R}$, $\exists x \in \mathscr{R}$ such that $a = b + x$. **Solvability** relative to $+$ in $\mathscr{R}$.

R-6: There are unique numbers $0, 1 \in \mathscr{R}$ such that $a = a + 0$ for $\forall a \in \mathscr{R}$, and $a = a \cdot 1$ for $\forall a \in \mathscr{R}$ and $0 \neq 1$.

R-7: $\forall (a,b) \in \mathscr{R}$, $\exists x \in \mathscr{R}$ such that $a \cdot b = x$. **Closure** of $\mathscr{R}$ under $\times$.

R-8: $\forall (a,b) \in \mathscr{R}$, $a \cdot b = b \cdot a$. **Commutativity** of $\times$ in $\mathscr{R}$.

R-9: $\forall a,b,c \in \mathscr{R}$, $(a \cdot b) \cdot c = a \cdot (b \cdot c)$. **Associativity** of $\times$ in $\mathscr{R}$.

R-10: $\forall a,b,c,d \in \mathscr{R}$, if $a = b$ and if $c = d$, then $a \cdot c = b \cdot d$. **Uniqueness of product** in $\mathscr{R}$.

R-11: $\forall (a,b) \in \mathscr{R}$ such that $a + b \neq a$, $\exists x \in \mathscr{R}$ such that $a = b \cdot x$. **Solvability** relative to $\times$ in $\mathscr{R}$.

R-12: $\forall a,b,c \in \mathscr{R}$, $a \cdot (b + c) = (a \cdot b) + (a \cdot c)$. **Distributivity** of $\times$ over $+$ in $\mathscr{R}$.

R-13: $\forall (a,b) \in \mathscr{R}$, one and only one of the following is true: $a < b$, $a > b$, $a = b$. **Trichotomy** property.

R-14: $\forall a,b,c \in \mathscr{R}$, if $a < b$ and $b < c$, then $a < c$. **Transitivity** of $<$ in $\mathscr{R}$.

R-15: $\forall a,b,c \in \mathscr{R}$, if $a < b$, then $a + c < b + c$.

R-16: $\forall a,b,c \in \mathscr{R}$, if $a < b$ and $c > 0$, then $a \cdot c < b \cdot c$.

The last of the sequence of axioms for $\mathscr{R}$ will be listed by name only.

R-17: The Axiom of Completeness.

Any set of things having properties R-1 through R-12 is called a *field*. Axioms R-13 through R-16 are called *order* axioms.   Any set for which R-1 through R-16 all hold true is called an *ordered field*.

Any set of things for which all *seventeen* properties hold is called a **complete ordered field**.   Thus the set of real numbers is a complete ordered field. Further discussion of all of these axioms can be found under the heading *Fields* in a variety of mathematics books.

The completeness property is an important one.   It guarantees, for example, that numbers like $\sqrt{2}$ exist in $\mathscr{R}$.   However, any accurate statement of the principle would be complicated beyond usefulness for our study of geometry.   For this reason we shall make only informal use of this axiom in all that follows.   Reasonably elementary discussions of the principle can be found in several works.*

The reader unfamiliar with a formal statement of real number properties could well spend a little more time with the existence axioms (R-1, R-5, R-7, and R-11) than the other axioms.   More specific mention will be made of these in connection with arguing for the existence of basic geometric entities.

In addition to the axioms themselves, still other properties of the real numbers will be used as we construct geometry.   These are definitions and theorems that the reader has studied in a first course in algebra.   A few are listed here as examples.   Others will be introduced in the succeeding chapters as needed.

The important thing is to understand what each theorem or definition says. Hence it is vital to make verbal restatements and to write out numerical examples to illustrate each of the properties stated.

Since we make such a significant use of real number properties, it is instructive to look at the proof of a familiar number fact as an example of proof construction.   Hence the following theorem is given with its proof.

Theorem (3d-1): $\forall a \in \mathscr{R}, a \cdot 0 = 0$.

Example 1:   We know that $\sqrt{5} \in \mathscr{R}$; hence by this theorem $\sqrt{5} \cdot 0 = 0$. A verbal restatement is "The product of any real number and zero is zero."

Before starting the actual proof, recall from Chapter 2 that this proposition can be restated in strict implication form as $(a \in \mathscr{R}) \Rightarrow (a \cdot 0 = 0)$.   The proposition can now be read, "If a is a real number, then $a \cdot 0 = 0$."   Note also that $a \in \mathscr{R}$ is the hypothesis of the implication and $a \cdot 0 = 0$ is its conclusion.

Proofs of theorems are written in several different forms in mathematics. In advanced work, proofs are often simply sketched out and the reader is

---

* Edwin F. Beckenbach, Irving Drooyan, and William Wooton, *College Algebra*, Belmont, Calif.: Wadsworth Publishing Company, 1964, pp. 33, 34.   Daniel E. Dupree and Frank L. Harmon, *Modern College Algebra*, Englewood Cliffs, N.J.: Prentice-Hall, 1965, Sec. 3.5.   G. C. Witter, *Mathematics, The Study of Axiom Systems*, New York: Blaisdell Publishing Company, 1964, pp. 80ff.

left to fill in many gaps. However, the beginner is unlikely to appreciate the fact that the basic principles of the system (i.e., axioms and definitions) must be learned quickly and well. This stumbling block, together with his obvious need to learn both what to look for in a proof and how to look for it, makes it advisable to include more detail at the beginning. This we shall do.

The most easily read layout for a proof is the so-called "formal" style. This form of stating a proof takes more time and space than others, but it has the advantage that all the parts of the argument are displayed in one framework so as to minimize the difficulties of understanding. This traditional format uses two columns. The left column contains the assertions in the argument. Each such assertion is either to be the hypothesis of the theorem or a proposition that can be immediately shown to be true. In the right column we give the reason why the corresponding assertion in that step must be considered true. Hence each "reason" will be an axiom, a definition, or a previously proved theorem; no other "reasons" may ever be used. To shorten the work, we most often use the reference number for the known true reason instead of writing it out completely.

Now let us display the proof of our theorem.

PROOF

Given: $a \in \mathscr{R}$.
To Prove: $a \cdot 0 = 0$.

Statements	Reasons
1. $a \in \mathscr{R}$ (i.e., a is a real number).	1. Hypothesis
2. $a = a + 0$.	2. R-6
3. $0 \in \mathscr{R}$.	3. R-6
4. $(a + 0) \in \mathscr{R}$.	4. R-1
5. $a = a$.	5. E-1
6. $a \cdot a = a(a + 0)$.	6. R-10
7. $a(a + 0) = a \cdot a + a \cdot 0$.	7. R-12
8. $a \cdot a,\ a(a + 0),\ a \cdot 0 \in \mathscr{R}$.	8. R-7
9. $(a \cdot 0 + a \cdot 0) \in \mathscr{R}$.	9. R-1
10. $a \cdot a = a \cdot a + a \cdot 0$.	10. E-3 (from Steps 6 and 7)
11. $a \cdot 0 = 0$.	11. R-6
Q.E.D.	

The reader should not allow the Q.E.D. at the end to be frightening. The letters stand for the Latin phrase *quod erat demonstrandum*, which means approximately "which was to be shown." It is a traditional way a mathematician has of staging a little celebration at the completion of his job. In addition, it is one way to assert that the last statement in the proof, the conclusion of the theorem, is implied by the axioms of the system.

On reading through this proof it may not be obvious how the rules of formal logic are being used. True, the theorem itself is stated as an implication, but the use of conjunction and of the Rule of Detachment, for example, is not explicitly shown. Let us write out the first two steps above in a form to show use of the latter.

1a. $a \in \mathcal{R}$.	1a. Hypothesis
1b. If $a \in \mathcal{R}$, then $a = a + 0$.	1b. R-6
2. $a = a + 0$.	2. Rule of Detachment (2d-4)

Similarly, all the rest of the argument could be constructed making direct use of logical principles. Even when the shortened form is used, the reader should practice thinking through the steps in logical detail.

In a course of higher algebra, even some of the steps shown above would be omitted by leaving out the direct use of closure properties and the properties of equality. As our work in geometry proceeds, we shall also allow ourselves to write shortened proof forms.

In quoting the principles that follow, each literal symbol stands for a real number. In addition, each variable is *universally quantified* unless otherwise stated. Recall, too, that $a > b$ is another way of writing $b < a$. Also, we shall use the symbol $\therefore$ to mean "therefore."

Theorem (3d-2): $a \cdot b = 0$ if $(a = 0) \vee (b = 0)$.

Theorem (3d-3): If $a < b$, there is a $c \in \mathcal{R}$ such that $a < c < b$.

Theorem (3d-4): For $a,b,c,r \in \mathcal{R}$ and $0 < r < 1$, $a < c < b$ iff $c = a + r(b - a)$.

Definition (3-j): If $a^n = b$, then a is called **an nth root** of b.

Notice that even the language of this definition implies that in general more than one nth root exists.

Example 2: $(-2)^2 = 4$. $\therefore$ -2 is a second (square) root of 4. Also, $2^2 = 4$. $\therefore$ 2 is also a square root of 4.

Definition (3-k): For $b > 0$ and $a^2 = b$, a is called **the principal square root** of b iff $a \geq 0$. We use the symbols $a = \sqrt{b}$ or $a = b^{1/2}$ for the principal square root.

We often say *the* square root of a when we write $\sqrt{a}$ because it is understood that there is *only* **one** *such root*. The reader should realize that the restriction $a \geq 0$ means that the principal square root is a nonnegative number.

Example 3: $\sqrt{4} = 2$ and $4^{1/2} = 2$. Note that -2 is *not* the principal square root of 4.

Theorem (3d-5): $\forall(a > 0$ and $b > 0)$, if $a = b$, then $\sqrt{a} = \sqrt{b}$.

Definition (3-1): $|a| = \begin{cases} a & \text{if} \quad a > 0. \\ 0 & \text{if} \quad a = 0. \\ -a & \text{if} \quad a < 0. \end{cases}$

Example 4: $-3 < 0.$ $\therefore |-3| = -(-3) = 3.$

Theorem (3d-6): $\sqrt{a^2} = |a|$.

Theorem (3d-7): $\forall(a > 0$ and $b > 0)$, if $a^2 = b^2$, then $|a| = |b|$.

Theorem (3d-8):   For any $a,b,c \in \mathcal{R}$ such that $c < b < a$ there are $r,s \in \mathcal{R}$, $r > 0$, and $s > 0$ such that $|b - a| = r|c - a|$, $|c - b| = s|c - a|$, and $r + s = 1$.

Exercise Set

1. Quote the contrapositive of Axiom E-2.

2. Is $\forall a,b,c \in \mathcal{R}$, $(a \neq b \wedge b \neq c) \Rightarrow (a \neq c)$ a true proposition?   Give an example.

3. If we know that $(x - 3)\sqrt{x^2 - y^2} = 0$ and that $x^2 - y^2 \neq 0$, what can we determine about x?   Explain.   If we do *not* know that $x^2 - y^2 \neq 0$, what can we determine about x?   See Theorem (3d-2).

4. Is it true that if $-3x < 6$, then $x > -2$?   Explain.

5. Is $|-5 + 3| = 2$ true?   Explain.

6. Is it true that $a^2 = -a^2$?   Explain.

7. Find x if $x = \sqrt{(-3)^2}$.

8. Is $\forall a, 0 + a = 0$ true?   If not, change the proposition in two ways to make it true.   Change one symbol only.

9. Is $\dfrac{a^2}{(a - a)} = a$ true?   Explain.

10. For $a = -2$, $b = 3$, and $c = 5$, find the numbers s and r whose existence is guaranteed by Theorem (3d-8).

11. Give an example to show why the restriction in the statement of Theorem (3d-7) is needed.

12. Could we restate R-16 as $\forall a,b,c \in \mathcal{R}$ such that $c \geq 0$, $(a < b) \Rightarrow (a \cdot c < b \cdot c)$?   Explain.

13. Make verbal restatements of the following properties of $\mathcal{R}$.
    (a) R-2 and R-8 together.
    (b) R-3 and R-9 together.
    (c) R-4 and R-10 together.
    (d) R-12, once reading left to right, once reading right to left.

14. Rewrite R-13 to and including R-16 using nonverbal symbols for exclusive disjunction, implication, and the other logical connectives where applicable.

15. What would be the situation for $\mathscr{R}$ if Axioms R-13 to R-16 were omitted? (*Hint:* Think of the number line.)

16. Translate each axiom completely into verbal form; that is, read "there is a real number x" for "$\exists x \in \mathscr{R}$"; "for each real number a and for each real number b" for "$\forall a,b \in \mathscr{R}$"; "for each ordered pair of real numbers" for "$\forall (a,b) \in \mathscr{R}$," and so on.

17. Give an illustration of each of the preceding theorems using familiar constants.

18. Write out verbal restatements of each of the theorems and definitions above.

chapter 4

Coordinate Systems

4a Geometry with Coordinates

Everyone knows that geometry deals with points and lines. Sometimes we tend to forget how closely the subject is connected with the idea of numbers. The word *geometry* comes from Greek words meaning "earth measurement." When we measure anything from jam to interplanatory distance, we use a *number* to express the quantity of the thing measured.

The main characteristic of the analytic method of developing geometry is that it makes direct use of numbers to help establish geometric facts. The principal tool required by the analytic method is a coordinate system. Exactly what is a coordinate system? To answer this question, at least in part, let us look at some applications of geometry.

It is true, as stated previously, that any branch of mathematics is an abstract science which need not have any application in particular to excuse its existence. It is equally true that the most fruitful mathematical ideas have been suggested by observing patterns in one's surroundings.

A football field is a common sight. Measurement is, of course, very much a part of both the game and the field on which it is played. Let us examine the way in which measurement is used in this instance. Along the sideline regular intervals are marked off. At the end of each interval, a marker showing a number is set down so that the effect is about as shown in Fig. 4.1.

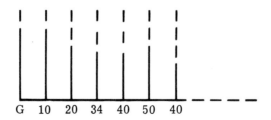

Fig. 4.1

Now it is possible to use the geometric concept of measurement to chart the progress of the teams up and down the field.

The effectiveness of this system is due to the ordered association of numbers with particular spots on the sideline. That is, a single measurement scale has been constructed along the side of the field. This association of numbers with locations is the essential feature of the coordinate idea.

A single measurement scale of the type found along the side of a football field has definite limitations. Can we chart the movement of teams from side to side for example? Such a measurement is admittedly not important in football, but in other applications it would be useful to measure in two or more directions.

Imagine yourself trying to locate a spot P on a map. If you were told simply that P lies between 20 and 19 in Fig. 4.2, how easy would it be to locate

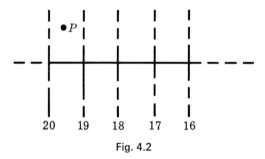

Fig. 4.2

the spot? What if P were *below* the scale line? It could be, as far as the given information tells us.

To locate the spot more exactly, we need some way of limiting its position vertically. A set of "lines" crossing the vertical ones would certainly be helpful.

If we are now told that P lies between 20 and 19 horizontally and between 42 and 43 vertically, it is obviously easier to locate the spot. This is essentially the same idea that is used when one person tells another that a certain checker piece is located five squares over and six squares up from a corner of the board. In each case two intersecting measurement scales are used.

To make measurement of location even easier, we could now make finer divisions of the scales so as to use fractions. This is the plan used in quoting longitude and latitude in minutes and seconds instead of solely in degrees.

Now let us determine the essential mathematical characteristics of this coordinate method of finding locations and making measurements. Notice that (i) two sets of lines are used, one horizontal and one vertical, as in Fig. 4.3. Furthermore, (ii) each vertical line intersects each horizontal line.

Is this enough? What if some of the vertical lines were to intersect each other? Then it would certainly be difficult, if not impossible, to tell which number is associated with a particular line. We must be certain that (iii)

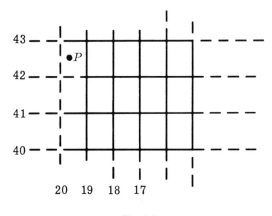

Fig. 4.3

no horizontal line intersects another horizontal line and similarly for the vertical case.

If you were asked to find the actual spot located by the numbers 19 and 42 in Fig. 4.3, it would be necessary to know that the associated lines actually intersect.   On the surface of a page, they cannot help but intersect, but mathematics does not deal with surfaces of pages.   We must be *mathematically* certain that (iv) each horizontal line intersects each vertical line and that they intersect exactly once.   As shown in our football field and map examples, we also want to make certain that (v) the desired number correspondences can be made.

Properties (i) through (v) are what a coordinate system should be like intuitively.   It is now up to us to state some suitable axioms that give us a geometric coordinate system with these intuitive properties.   However, we must always remember to state our axioms and build our geometry in a precise and logical manner.   The remainder of this book is dedicated to that task.

Exercise Set

1. List some examples of single measurement scales used in everyday situations.

2. What is the essential property of both real numbers and letters that makes it possible to use them as markers on a scale to locate position?

3. List some examples of intersecting measurement scales used in everyday situations.

4. Would a coordinate grid system have to make use of lines we usually call "straight" in order to be useful?   (*Hint:* Think of a globe.)   Give some examples.

4b Axioms for Euclidean 2-Space

We have stated at several points that the analytic method employs the properties of real numbers to establish geometric facts. Here, then, we are taking the properties of real numbers detailed in Chapter 3 as given. In addition, we are considering set properties to be at our disposal. The following set of axioms utilizes each of these theories to establish a coordinate system having the properties discussed in the preceding section.

Primitive terms: *Points;* sets of points called *loci*; particular loci called *grid loci.*

A-1: For any subset of the real numbers there is a locus whose points are in one-to-one correspondence with the numbers in that subset.

A-2: At least one grid locus exists.

A-3: The points in each grid locus are in one-to-one correspondence with the entire set of real numbers.

A-4: Any point in one grid locus is also in exactly one other grid locus and is the only point in their intersection.

A-5: If each of a pair of grid loci intersects a third grid locus, then the given pair has no common point.

If $\mathscr{L}_1$ and $\mathscr{L}_2$ are intersecting grid loci, then the set of grid loci having a common point with $\mathscr{L}_2$ will be called class H. The set of grid loci having a common point with $\mathscr{L}_1$ will be called class V. Figure 4.4 illustrates this arrangement. Using these names, we now complete the set of axioms.

A-6: Each grid locus of class H has exactly one point in common with each grid locus of class V.

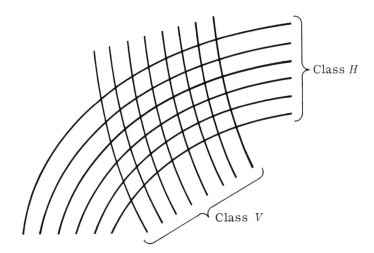

Class H

Class V

Fig. 4.4

A-7: If any point P is not in a given grid locus, then it is in a grid locus that intersects the given one.

4c Interpreting the Axioms

In order to clarify our logical system and give us some means of visualization, we often construct what we call *models*. These are physical representations that approximate what we have been constructing mathematically. Certainly a point for us is a "dot" that a pencil point makes, and a line is a mark that a pencil creates when pulled along a sheet of paper. Thus we will use these marks on a piece of paper as our "model." Since, however, we want to be very general, we should not necessarily make our lines "straight" as we intuitively think of the word. This would be a special kind of a line that might have special properties. Remember, we want to keep our model as general as possible.

It is important to note some of our conventions for notation and terminology. As used in the axioms and elsewhere, the preposition *in* is simply a short synonym for the set terms *an element of*, *belongs to*, and *contained in*. Whenever a point P has been mentioned previously and we then find that some locus $\mathscr{L}$ contains P ($\mathscr{L} \ni P$), we often say that $\mathscr{L}$ is *on P*. Occasionally we may even use the traditional term $\mathscr{L}$ *passes through P*.

To avoid some technical difficulty, whenever we use the word *intersect* relative to loci, we shall mean that the intersection is *nonempty* unless specifically stated otherwise. The terms *common point*, *point in common*, and *point of intersection* of two loci are all used to indicate that a given point is an element of the intersection of the loci. That is, if P is the point and $\mathscr{L}_1$ and $\mathscr{L}_2$ are the loci, then $\mathscr{L}_1 \cap \mathscr{L}_2 = \{\dots, P, \dots\}$. Also, if $P \in \mathscr{L}$ and $P \in \mathscr{M}$, we often say that $\mathscr{L}$ and $\mathscr{M}$ intersect *at P*. If two points P and Q have been mentioned previously and it is found that a locus $\mathscr{L}$ contains both (i.e., $\mathscr{L} \ni P \wedge \mathscr{L} \ni Q$), we often say that $\mathscr{L}$ *joins P and Q*.

When we make models of geometric problems, it is useful to use two other terms, namely *cuts* and *meets*. Figure 4.5 illustrates the use of these words. Note that when $\mathscr{L}$ meets $\mathscr{M}$ at P, there are no points in $\mathscr{L}$ beyond P.

We are now working with the concepts named by the primitive terms *point*, *locus*, and *grid locus*. Since we accept the existence of real numbers (and all their properties), Axiom A-1 requires that both points and loci exist. Axiom A-2 requires specifically that a grid locus exists.

Example 1: $\{1,4\} \subset \mathscr{R}$; therefore a set of points, that is, a locus $\{P,Q\}$ exists and has the property that $P \leftrightarrow 1$ and $Q \leftrightarrow 4$ or that $Q \leftrightarrow 1$ and $P \leftrightarrow 4$ by Axiom A-1 and the definition of one-to-one correspondence.

Example 2: $\mathscr{R} \subset \mathscr{R}$; therefore Axiom A-1 requires the existence of at least one locus whose points are in one-to-one correspondence with the real numbers.

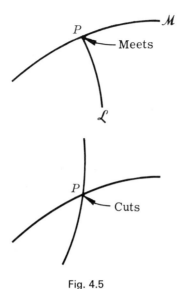

Fig. 4.5

We must not make the mistake of assuming that just any locus whose points are in one-to-one correspondence with the real numbers is a grid locus. Axiom A-3 does state that any grid locus has this property of set equivalence to $\mathscr{R}$. The converse of the axiom would indeed require that any such locus be a grid locus, but in Chapter 2 we saw that the converse of an axiom is not necessarily true.

Example 3:   Let P be a point in a grid locus $\mathscr{L}_1$.   By Axiom A-4 there is a grid locus $\mathscr{L}_2$ that intersects $\mathscr{L}_1$ at P.   Is P the only point of intersection in $\mathscr{L}_1$ and $\mathscr{L}_2$?   Yes, it must be the only one, for the axiom states that any point in one grid locus is also in *exactly* one other grid locus.   Figure 4.6 illustrates this example.

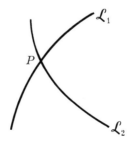

Fig. 4.6

Example 4:   Let grid loci $\mathscr{L}_2$ and $\mathscr{L}_3$ each intersect grid locus $\mathscr{L}_1$ at points P and Q, respectively.   (See Fig. 4.7.)   By Axiom A-4 we know that

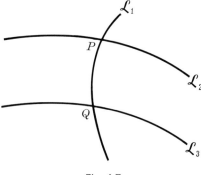

Fig. 4.7

each of these intersections contains exactly that single point.   Axiom A-5 requires that $\mathscr{L}_2$ and $\mathscr{L}_3$ have no point of intersection.   For the same reason, any grid locus that has a point in common with either $\mathscr{L}_2$ or $\mathscr{L}_3$ cannot intersect $\mathscr{L}_1$.

Example 5:   Let grid locus $\mathscr{L}_1$ have common points P and Q with loci $\mathscr{L}_2$ and $\mathscr{L}_3$, respectively.   Let grid locus $\mathscr{L}_4$ intersect $\mathscr{L}_2$ at R.   By Axiom A-6 we know that $\mathscr{L}_4$ and $\mathscr{L}_3$ must also have a common point, say S.   Figure 4.8 illustrates this example.

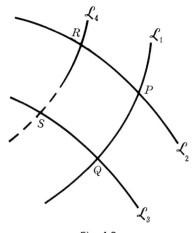

Fig. 4.8

Example 6:   Consider the grid locus $\mathscr{L}_1$ and the point P not in $\mathscr{L}_1$. Axiom A-7 requires that a grid locus $\mathscr{L}_2$ exist such that $P \in \mathscr{L}_2$, and that the intersection of $\mathscr{L}_1$ and $\mathscr{L}_2$ be nonempty.   That is, $\mathscr{L}_1$ and $\mathscr{L}_2$ intersect on at least one point.   By Axiom A-4, however, we know that $\mathscr{L}_1$ and $\mathscr{L}_2$ intersect at exactly one point.   (See Fig. 4.9.)

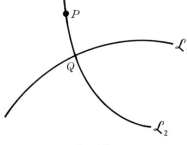

Fig. 4.9

Exercise Set

1. State the converse of Axiom A-3. (*Hint:* First change the statement of the axiom to the if-then form.)

2. Which of the axioms for real numbers guarantees that at least one locus exists?

3. In Example 3, how does Axiom A-4 guarantee that there is a point in the intersection of $\mathscr{L}_1$ and $\mathscr{L}_2$?

4. Do the axioms allow the correspondence

$$\mathscr{L} = \{\ldots,P,Q,R,\ldots\}$$
$$\mathscr{R} \supset \{\ldots,1,2,3,4,\ldots\}$$

where $\mathscr{L}$ is a locus, $\mathscr{R}$ is a set of real numbers, and P, Q, and R are points?

5. Illustrate with a model the situation described by $P \in \mathscr{L}_1$ and $Q \in \mathscr{L}_2$ and $P = Q$. Is more than one model possible?

6. Illustrate with a model at least two interpretations of Axiom A-5.

7. Recalling the definition of a number line given in algebra, explain the difference between a number line and a grid locus.

8. Would the latitude lines on a sphere satisfy the requirements described in the axioms for grid loci?

9. On a sheet of paper make two "dots" with a pencil. Using these as points and the mark a pencil makes as it moves along the paper as a grid locus, illustrate as many different models as you can of the axioms.

*10. Restate Axioms A-4 to A-7 in set notation.

4d Properties of the Grid System

The axioms have provided for the existence of particular points and sets of points called grid loci. We shall refer to this collection of points and loci as a *grid system*.

In studying our axioms, we cannot find direct answers to all the questions we might ask.   We are not told directly, for example, whether only one grid system exists or how many grid loci each point is contained in.   Furthermore, we are not told how many points a grid locus contains.   We now state these properties as formal propositions and construct a proof for each.

Theorem (4d-1):   A grid locus is infinite.

PROOF

By Axiom A-2, a grid locus exists.   By Axiom A-3, the points in a grid locus are in one-to-one correspondence with $\mathscr{R}$; that is, there are as many distinct points in a grid locus as there are distinct numbers in $\mathscr{R}$.   We classify the numbers in $\mathscr{R}$ as infinite.   Therefore the points in a grid locus are infinite. Thus the theorem is established.

Theorem (4d-2):   There are an infinite number of grid loci in a grid system

PROOF

We know that a grid locus is a set of points and, by Theorem (4d-1), that set is infinite.   Axiom A-4 states that each point in our grid locus is in exactly one other grid locus.   This gives us infinitely many grid loci, each intersecting the first grid locus.   Repeating this argument for one of the new grid loci, we establish that there are an infinite number of grid loci.

Theorem (4d-3) and the one that follows are both proven by *contradiction*. This technique of proof involves the principle of assuming the contrary (or negative) of the conclusion of the proposition to be proven and then deducing some proposition we know to be false.   (See Exercise 3.)

Theorem (4d-3):   All grid loci are included in one grid system.

The proof of this theorem is omitted.   It can be found, however, in the Appendix.

Even though we have shown that our grid loci are infinite, we still have no direct guarantee that all points are contained in some grid locus.   However, Examples 1 and 6, Section 4c, indicated that each point is in exactly two loci. The following theorem establishes this fact.

The student should recall at this point that the term *exactly one* stands for the conjunction *one and only one*.   We are actually stating: *Each point is in at least two grid loci and* ($\wedge$) *each point is in at most two grid loci*.   Each part of the conjunction must be proved true separately.

Recalling our discussion of class H and class V, we see that each of these classes is infinite by Theorem (4d-2). By Theorem (4d-3) the sets H and V contain all the grid loci, but are there points that are not in set H or in set V? The following theorem answers this question.

Theorem (4d-4): Each point is in exactly two grid loci.

PROOF

Consider a point P. By Axiom A-7, P is either in some grid locus $\mathscr{L}_1$ or in some grid locus that intersects $\mathscr{L}_1$. Let us say that it is in grid locus $\mathscr{L}_1$. Axiom A-4 requires that there also be an $\mathscr{L}_2$ on P. Hence P is in at least two grid loci. The case where $P \notin \mathscr{L}_1$ is left to the exercises.

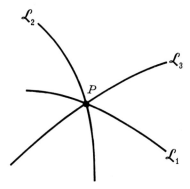

Assume there is a grid locus $\mathscr{L}_3$ that also contains P. Now both $\mathscr{L}_2 \cap \mathscr{L}_1 \neq \emptyset$ and $\mathscr{L}_3 \cap \mathscr{L}_1 \neq \emptyset$. Hence Axiom A-5 requires that $\mathscr{L}_2 \cap \mathscr{L}_3 = \emptyset$. This is a *contradiction*, since $P \in \mathscr{L}_3$ by our assumption. Thus the theorem is established.

Definition (4-a): All the points established by Axioms A-1 through A-7 will be called **2-space**.

Exercise Set

1. Is it true that each point in 2-space is in at least one grid locus? Explain.

2. Finish the proof of Theorem (4d-2).

3. Explain the use of the method of contradiction in Theorem (4d-4).

4. Complete the proof of Theorem (4d-4).

5. In Section 4b replace A-3 with the following: "The points in each grid locus are in one-to-one correspondence with the set $\{1,2\}$." Assume that A-4 still holds.

(a) Is Axiom A-5 now applicable? Explain.

(b) Are Axioms A-5 and A-6 applicable? Explain.

(c) Are Theorems (4d-3) and (4d-4) applicable? Explain.

(d) Draw a model of the system. Can more than one model be created?

6. Rework Exercise 5 replacing the given set with the set {1,2,3}.

7. Rework Exercise 5 replacing the given set with the set {1,2,3,4}.

8. Using the language of implication ($p \Rightarrow q$), discuss proof by contradiction.

4e   Constructing Coordinate Systems

As a first step in construction of a useful coordinate system, let us consider a *monocoordinate* system. This is a system in which it would be important to consider number correspondences to the points in only one locus having the properties of our grid loci.

A grid locus $\mathscr{L}$, by Theorem (4d-1), has infinitely many points. By Axiom A-3, we know that each point has exactly one real number associated with it. Thus let points P and Q be associated with real numbers u,v, respectively, as shown in Fig. 4.10.

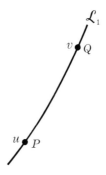

Fig. 4.10

Now suppose this particular numbering system involving u and v is not the point-number association that we want. For example, we may want zero associated with point P.

To obtain this new point-number association, we proceed as follows. Since we have P associated with u, we shall add to every real number the additive inverse of u. This will determine a new one-to-one correspondence between the points in a grid locus and the real numbers. The number associated with P is now

(1) $$u + (-u) = 0.$$

Thus we have, as in Fig. 4.11,

(2) $P \leftrightarrow 0.$

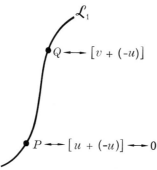

Fig. 4.11

Using similar procedures, we can change the point-number correspondence of other grid loci as the need arises.

We now consider any grid locus $\mathscr{L}_1$ and any point $A \in \mathscr{L}_1$. By Axiom A-3 there is a one-to-one correspondence between the points contained in $\mathscr{L}_1$ and the real numbers in $\mathscr{R}$. Thus we have a number $r \in \mathscr{R}$ corresponding to the point A in $\mathscr{L}_1$. Axiom A-4 guarantees that there is a second grid locus $\mathscr{L}_2$ that contains the point A. Applying Axiom A-3 again, we have a one-to-one correspondence between the real numbers and the points in $\mathscr{L}_2$. However, this second correspondence for $\mathscr{L}_2$ may have assigned to the point A a number s such that $s \neq r$. Figure 4.12 illustrates the situation.

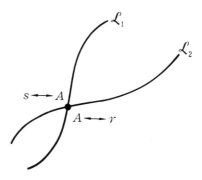

Fig. 4.12

We now make a new point-number correspondence in the same way that we did to obtain the correspondences of statements (1) and (2) above. That is, we wish to associate the point A with the number zero in the point-number correspondences for both grid loci $\mathscr{L}_1$ and $\mathscr{L}_2$. Thus in the case of point A and $\mathscr{L}_1$, we add the additive inverse of r to every real number of $\mathscr{R}$, and in the case of point A and $\mathscr{L}_2$, we add the additive inverse of s to every real number of $\mathscr{R}$.   This yields

$$r + (-r) = 0 \leftrightarrow A \in \mathscr{L}_1$$
$$s + (-s) = 0 \leftrightarrow A \in \mathscr{L}_2$$

and $$\mathscr{L}_1 \cap \mathscr{L}_2 = A.$$

Figure 4.13 shows this new number and point correspondence.   We shall, temporarily, call the loci $\mathscr{L}_1$ and $\mathscr{L}_2$ *reference loci*.

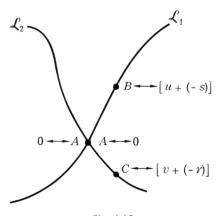

Fig. 4.13

For each point $A, B, C, \ldots$ in $\mathscr{L}_1$, there is a real number associated with it. That is,

(3) $$A \leftrightarrow 0, \quad B \leftrightarrow b, \quad C \leftrightarrow c, \quad \ldots$$

The numbers $0, b, c, \ldots$ are now associated with *ordered pairs of real numbers* such that the first number of the ordered pair is the real number to which it is being associated and the second number of the ordered pair is zero.   Thus we have from statement (3) the point-ordered pair correspondences

(4) $$0 \leftrightarrow (0,0), \quad b \leftrightarrow (b,0), \quad c \leftrightarrow (c,0), \quad \ldots$$

Note that (4) will be a one-to-one correspondence.   Since the transitive property holds for one-to-one correspondences, we conclude from (3) and (4) that we have the one-to-one correspondence

$$A \leftrightarrow (0,0), \quad B \leftrightarrow (b,0), \quad C \leftrightarrow (c,0), \quad \ldots$$

In a similar fashion, the points $A, B', C', \ldots$ in $\mathscr{L}_2$, are associated with ordered pairs of real numbers having zero as their first number.   That is,

$$A \leftrightarrow (0,0), \quad B' \leftrightarrow (0,b'), \quad C' \leftrightarrow (0,c'), \quad \ldots$$

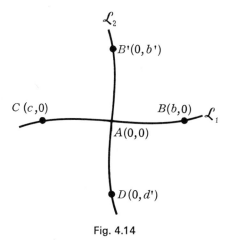

Fig. 4.14

Figure 4.14 illustrates the two reference loci and some representative points. We now make some definitions that will provide us with some new notation and terminology.

Definition (4-b): The first element of each ordered pair of real numbers associated with a point is called the **abscissa** of the point.

Definition (4-c): The second element of each ordered pair of real numbers associated with a point is called the **ordinate** of the point.

Definition (4-d): Either the abscissa or the ordinate of a point is called a **coordinate** of the point.

Definition (4-e): The grid locus, each of whose points has ordinate equal to zero, is called the **x axis** and symbolized $\overleftrightarrow{OX}$.

Definition (4-f): The grid locus, each of whose points has abscissa equal to zero, is called the **y axis** and symbolized $\overleftrightarrow{OY}$.

Definition (4-g): The point of intersection $(0,0)$ of the x and y axes is called the **origin**.

We need to make a few drawing conventions at this point. As we may have come to realize, various interpretations of our axioms are possible. To agree with these possibilities, our grid loci have been illustrated by a variety of curves. We have, however, constantly assumed in our drawings that it would be possible to interpret them as what we call "continuous" or "unbroken" curves or lines. Although nothing as yet guarantees that they will have this important property, for convenience we shall continue to use this interpretation. In Chapter 5 we shall find that it is a reasonable one.

Axiom A-4 requires that there be grid loci on each point in $\overleftrightarrow{OX}$, not just $\overleftrightarrow{OY}$ on point O.   Similarly, there must be grid loci on each point in $\overleftrightarrow{OY}$, not just $\overleftrightarrow{OX}$ on O.   Figure 4.15 illustrates some other possible grid loci.   At this point two additional definitions become useful.

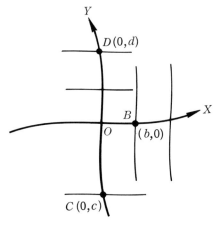

Fig. 4.15

Definition (4-h):   Each grid locus that intersects $\overleftrightarrow{OX}$ is called a **vertical grid locus**.

Definition (4-i):   Each grid locus that intersects $\overleftrightarrow{OY}$ is called a **horizontal grid locus**.

These definitions are acceptable, for Axiom A-5 rules out any possible contradictions.   Why?

Note that the words *horizontal* and *vertical* have been defined mathematically.   Since our drawing convention makes them look horizontal and vertical, it does not mean they must be drawn this way.   (For some purposes in mathematics, it is more convenient to have $\overleftrightarrow{OY}$ drawn left-to-right.)

We now associate each vertical grid locus $\mathscr{L}_V$ with the number corresponding to the point of intersection of $\overleftrightarrow{OX}$ and $\mathscr{L}_V$.   Similarly, we associate each horizontal grid locus $\mathscr{L}_H$ with the number corresponding to the point of intersection of $\overleftrightarrow{OY}$ and $\mathscr{L}_H$.   For example, if the number associated with $D \in \overleftrightarrow{OX}$ is

$$D \leftrightarrow (d,0) \leftrightarrow d$$

and if

$$\overleftrightarrow{OX} \cap \mathscr{L}_V = D,$$

then

$$\mathscr{L}_V \leftrightarrow d.$$

Figure 4.16 illustrates this one-to-one correspondence between vertical grid loci and the real numbers and horizontal grid loci and the real numbers.

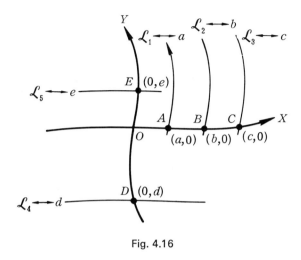

Fig. 4.16

Axiom A-6 requires that each horizontal grid locus intersect each vertical grid locus in one and only one point as in Fig. 4.17. To each of these points

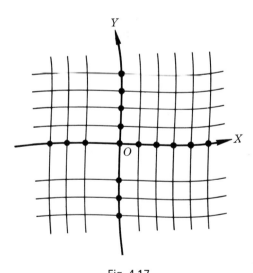

Fig. 4.17

of intersection, we shall associate an ordered pair of real numbers such that the abscissa of the ordered pair is the number associated with the vertical intersecting grid locus and the ordinate of the ordered pair is the number associated with the horizontal intersecting grid locus. Thus if we have two grid loci $\mathscr{L}_V$ and $\mathscr{L}_H$ such that

$$\mathscr{L}_V \leftrightarrow a$$
$$\mathscr{L}_H \leftrightarrow b,$$

and if

$$\mathscr{L}_H \cap \mathscr{L}_V = E,$$

then we obtain the point-ordered pair correspondence

$$E \leftrightarrow (a,b).$$

Figure 4.18 illustrates the nature of the grid system as we have developed it thus far. We note that no two points will have the same coordinate.

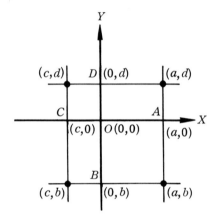

Fig. 4.18

If we let x stand as a variable for any of the abscissas of points and let y stand as a variable for any of the ordinates of points, the number pair associated with any point in general can be written (x,y). Thus the number pair $(x,0)$ is associated with a point in the x axis and the number pair $(0,y)$ is associated with a point in the y axis. We shall label points with the traditional capital letters and say that an ordered pair (x,y) is associated with a particular point. For convenience, however, we shall sometimes refer to the point (x,y).

Each horizontal grid locus intersects $\overleftrightarrow{OY}$ by definition. We recall that these points of intersection are $(0,b)$. Other points in the grid locus are of the type (x,b) by the construction above. Thus we can say that each horizontal grid locus is a set $\{(x,y) \mid y = b\}$. Following a similar argument, each vertical grid locus is a set of points $\{(x,y) \mid x = a\}$, where a is the abscissa of its intersection with $\overleftrightarrow{OX}$.

We now state these conclusions as theorems.

Definition (4-j): Two *points* $A(x_1,y_1)$ and $B(x_2,y_2)$ are *equal* iff $x_1 = x_2$ and $y_1 = y_2$.

Theorem (4e-1): A horizontal grid locus is a set $\{(x,y) \mid y = b\}$, where b is the ordinate of its point of intersection with $\overleftrightarrow{OY}$.

Theorem (4e-2): A vertical grid locus is a set $\{(x,y) \mid x = a\}$, where a is the abscissa of its point of intersection with $\overleftrightarrow{OX}$.

Based on the construction leading up to the situation illustrated in Fig. 4.18 and these two theorems, we have the following useful fact.

Theorem (4e-3): Every open sentence $p(x,y)$ determines a set of ordered pairs of real numbers that corresponds to a locus of points, and each locus of points corresponds to a set of ordered pairs of real numbers that is the solution set of some *open sentence* $q(x,y)$.

Exercise Set

1. What are the abscissas of the following points? The ordinates? $(2,-8)$, $(3,0)$, $(6,1)$, $(0,4)$, $(-2,-2)$.

2. How do we know that the ordinate and the abscissa of each point are unique?

3. Is $\overleftrightarrow{OX}$ a horizontal grid locus, a vertical grid locus, or neither? Why? Discuss $\overleftrightarrow{OY}$ similarly.

4. Are all possible ordered pairs of real numbers now associated with inter-sections of grid loci in our system? Why?

5. Is $\{-5,1\} = \{1,-5\}$? Is $(-5,1) = (1,-5)$? Is $\{(-5,1)\} = \{(1,-5)\}$?

6. Explain the statement following Definition (4-i).

7. Draw a grid system locating the integers on $\overleftrightarrow{OX}$ and $\overleftrightarrow{OY}$ such that the point associated with zero on both $\overleftrightarrow{OX}$ and $\overleftrightarrow{OY}$ corresponds to the point of inter-section of $\overleftrightarrow{OX}$ and $\overleftrightarrow{OY}$. On such a system locate the following ordered pairs of real numbers.

(a) $(3,2)$	(b) $(6,-1)$	(c) $(2,0)$
(d) $(-3,2)$	(e) $(-3,-1)$	(f) $(0,0)$
(g) $(8,-3)$	(h) $(-4,0)$	(i) $(0,3)$
(j) $(-2,1)$	(k) $(1,1)$	(l) $(-3,-1)$

8. In Exercise 7, must the "spacing" between the points associated with the integers always be the same on both axes? On the same axis?

*9. Prove Theorem (4e-1).

*10. Prove Theorem (4e-2).

4f   A Distance Function

We now have a coordinate system with at least some of the properties of grid systems used by surveyors or map makers.   In such systems, however, the grid lines are usually *straight* and they usually meet each other at *right angles.*

An important reason why a grid system is such a useful tool of surveyors and others is that a concept of *distance* can be easily expressed as a real number in terms of coordinates.   For this reason, defining a distance relation would seem to be one of the most effective ways to increase the usefulness of our geometric model.   To help determine what *a reasonable* definition of distance would be, we ask ourselves what we mean by the term in everyday usage.   The answer turns out to be harder than it looks at first.   After some reflection we see that distance means several different things.

In traveling from San Francisco to Boston, for example, the number called "distance" would depend on the route used.   If you measure the "straight-line" distance between the two cities on a flat map, or along a great circle route on a globe, you would get a distance different from that measured by the speedometer in your automobile.   In everyday usage, we use expressions such as "along the river" or "as the crow flies" to help us distinguish among some of these possibilities.

What are some of the features these different distances have in common? Perhaps most important, a number called distance is associated with a pair of points.   In each case this number is *nondirectional.*   That is, along the same route it makes no difference as to the distance whether we start in San Francisco or in Boston.   In each case we think of a *nonnegative number.*

The major difference between these various distance concepts is the way in which the number to be associated with the two points is determined.   In each case the number depends on the choice of a *particular path* between the two points.   It also depends on the *particular unit* used.   For example, a distance of 5 when measured in inches would be about 12.7 when measured in centimeters.

Which of the various kinds of distances do we want to use for our work in geometry?   Since we are building Euclidean geometry, we shall use the same one Euclid used.   This is the *straightedge*, or ruler in our everyday world.

To summarize, we want to associate a particular nonnegative real number with each pair of points in our grid system.   The association should be made in such a way that the number can be used to represent everyday straight-line distance.   Finally, it should be independent of the direction of measurement between the points.   We also want to develop our distance using a function that associates one and only one real number with each pair of points.   In any given application this real number can then be multiplied by an appropriate factor to permit its use with the chosen unit.   We shall call the real number associated with a pair of points in our grid system the *unscaled distance* and the number converted for use with a specific unit the *scaled distance*.

Since each point in our grid system is associated with an ordered pair of real numbers, it would seem reasonable that the desired distance function should be specified as a formula given in terms of coordinates of points.

We now make our definition, being sure to prove that all three of the properties we are concerned about are true. That is, we shall prove (i) that the number always exists for any two points, (ii) that it is independent of direction, and (iii) that this distance has the desired straight-line property. Because (ii) is not immediately obvious relative to points in our grid system, we first state the definition to give us the distance from A to B.

Definition (4-k): The **unscaled distance** from $A(x_1, y_1)$ to $B(x_2, y_2)$ is the real number $d = (AB) = \sqrt{(x_2 - x_1)^2 + (y_2 - y_1)^2}$.

We immediately note that d is a nonnegative real number. To prove property (i) above, we note that the coordinates x_1, x_2, y_1, and y_2 are real numbers by Definitions (4-c) and (4-d). Hence $x_2 - x_1$ and $y_2 - y_1$ are real numbers. Since $a^2 \geq 0$ for any $a \in \mathcal{R}$, $(x_2 - x_1)^2$ and $(y_2 - y_1)^2$ are real numbers. In addition, we have $(x_2 - x_1)^2 + (y_2 - y_1)^2 \geq 0$. Since $\sqrt{a} \in \mathcal{R}$ for any $a \geq 0$, d is always a real number for any $A(x_1, y_1)$ and $B(x_2, y_2)$. This proves (i).

To prove property (ii) above, we need to show that $(AB) = (BA)$ for $A(x_1, y_1)$ and $B(x_2, y_2)$.

Theorem (4f-1): $(AB) = (BA)$ for any points $A(x_1, y_1)$ and $B(x_2, y_2)$.

We are given the points $A(x_1, y_1)$ and $B(x_2, y_2)$.

$$(AB) = \sqrt{(x_2 - x_1)^2 = (y_2 - y_1)^2}$$

by Definition (4-k). We know that $(x_2 - x_1)^2 = (x_1 - x_2)^2$ and $(y_2 - y_1)^2 = (y_1 - y_2)^2$ because $(a)^2 = (-a)^2$ for any $a \in \mathcal{R}$. Hence

$$\sqrt{(x_2 - x_1)^2 + (y_2 - y_1)^2} = \sqrt{(x_1 - x_2)^2 + (y_2 - y_1)^2}.$$

Now the right side is simply (BA) by Definition (4-k). Thus $(AB) = (BA)$ by the axioms of equality, and the theorem is established.

The fact that we have this theorem means we can associate the number called unscaled distance with two points without regard to direction. It is useful to modify Definition (4-k) in such a way that we omit any reference to direction and simply talk about the distance between two points.

Definition (4-l): The **unscaled distance** between two points $A(x_1, y_1)$ and $B(x_2, y_2)$ is the real number $d = (AB) = (BA) = \sqrt{(x_1 - x_2)^2 + (y_1 - y_2)^2}$.

We shall consider part (iii) above in Section 6d.

Example 1: Find the unscaled distance between the points $A(-2, 1)$ and $B(1, 3)$.

Solution: Using Definition (4-l) we have

$$(AB) = \sqrt{(-2 - 1)^2 + (1 - 3)^2}$$
$$= \sqrt{(-3)^2 + (-2)^2}$$
$$= \sqrt{9 + 4}$$
$$= \sqrt{13}.$$

Example 2:   Find the unscaled distance between the points $C(0,1)$ and $D(3,-1)$.

Solution:

$$(CD) = \sqrt{(3 - 0)^2 + (-1 - 1)^2}$$
$$= \sqrt{3^2 + (-2)^2}$$
$$= \sqrt{9 + 4}$$
$$= \sqrt{13}.$$

Another existence question is whether there is always some point (x,y) corresponding to a given distance d and a given point (x_1,y_1).

Example 3:   Find coordinate a if the distance between the points $(a,-2)$ and $(8,6)$ is 10.

Solution: Using the definition of distance and assuming that such an a exists in $\mathscr{R}$, we may write

$$10 = \sqrt{(a - 8)^2 + (-2 - 6)^2}$$
$$= \sqrt{(a - 8)^2 + (-8)^2}.$$

Using the properties of $\mathscr{R}$, we square both sides and obtain

$$100 = (a - 8)^2 + (-8)^2$$
$$100 = (a - 8)^2 + 64$$
$$36 = a^2 - 16a + 64.$$

Simplifying this, we have

$$0 = a^2 - 16a + 28.$$

Factoring (or we may use the quadratic formula at this point), we get

$$0 = (a - 14)(a - 2)$$
$$2 = a$$
$$14 = a.$$

We obtain two results for a, since the point $(a,-2)$ could be on either side of $(8,6)$ on the line containing the two points.

This example leads to the following theorem.

Theorem (4f-2):   If d is a nonnegative real number and if (x_1,y_1) is a fixed point, then there is a point (x,y) such that d is the distance between (x_1,y_1) and (x,y).

PROOF

We are given a real number $d \geq 0$ and a point (x_1, y_1). Since $d \in \mathscr{R}$, $d/\sqrt{2} \in \mathscr{R}$. Why? By closure, we have $x, y \in \mathscr{R}$ such that $x = x_1 + d/\sqrt{2}$ and $y = y_1 + d/\sqrt{2}$. By definition of subtraction, $x - x_1 = d/\sqrt{2}$ and $y - y_1 = d/\sqrt{2}$. Squaring yields $(x - x_1)^2 = d^2/2$ and $(y - y_1)^2 = d^2/2$. Adding, we obtain $(x - x_1)^2 + (y - y_1)^2 = d^2$. Since $d \geq 0$, we may take the square root of both sides, obtaining $\sqrt{(x - x_1)^2 + (y - y_1)^2} = d$. Thus the theorem is established.

We now return to the ideas of distance and measurement. We want to be able to express a given distance as the number of accepted units, such as inches, miles, meters, or other arbitrary *length*, between two points. In graphical work with distance, we must also realize that the scale used will be a factor in determining the particular real number to stand for a given measured *length*.

Definition (4-m): The **scaled distance** between two points is the number kd, where d is the unscaled distance and k is a real number constant that depends on the unit of measure and the scale used.

Example 4: Let $kd = 1$ mile and let $d = 1$. Thus $k = 1$ and the scale is one-to-one.

Example 5: Let *length* be measured in some arbitrary units such as cocoa cans and let 1 unscaled unit represent a *length* of 4 cocoa cans. Then $k \cdot 1 = 4$ or $k = 4$. Now a length of 10 cocoa cans would correspond to an unscaled distance d such that $4d = 10$. Therefore $d = \frac{5}{2}$. That is, the length of 10 cocoa cans would be scaled to $\frac{5}{2}$ integral units on a graph.

Example 6: Consider the points $(-2, 1)$ and $(1, 5)$. Let the distance between them represent 2 inches. Then we have 2 inches $= kd = k\sqrt{(-2 - 1)^2 + (1 - 5)^2} = 5k$ inches. Therefore $k = \frac{2}{5}$.

Except when specific units of length are given, we shall mean the unscaled distance d when we use the word distance.

Exercise Set

Find the distance between the following points and the origin $(0,0)$.

1. $(3, -4)$.   2. $(0, -7)$.   3. $(2, 0)$.   4. $(-132, -55)$.

Find the distance between the following pairs of points.

5. $(-3, 1)$ and $(2, -5)$.   6. $(-7, 0)$ and $(44, 68)$.

7. $(-\sqrt{2}, \sqrt{7})$ and $(\sqrt{2}, -\sqrt{7})$.   8. The origin and $(0,0)$.

In the following exercises, determine (a) the unscaled distance, or (b) the scaled distance, or (c) the scale k. Use Definition (4-m).

9. $d = 4$, $k = 3$ miles per integral unit.

10. Scaled distance is 18 feet, $d = 3$.

11. Scaled distance is 24 inches, $k = 6$ inches.

12. $k = 6$ pounds per integral unit and $d = 3$.

13. $d = 3$ and scaled distance is 1 centimeter.

14. $k = 2$ feet per integral unit and unscaled distance is 6.

In the following exercises, find the missing coordinate, where d is the distance between the two points. Note that there will be two answers. See Example 3.

15. $(5,a)$, $(1,4)$; $d = 5$.   16. $(-4,\sqrt{11})$, $(1,a)$; $d = 6$.

17. $(a,3)$, $(5,2)$; $d = \sqrt{2}$.   18. $(3,4)$, $(a,4)$; $d = 1$.

*19. If the *length* between $(-4,1)$ and $(-2,y_2)$ is 4 miles and $k = 2/\sqrt{5}$, what is the unscaled distance?

*20. Rewrite Theorem (4f-2) in formal style.

*21. Justify the various steps in the argument following Definition (4-k) by quoting properties of $\mathscr{R}$ from Chapter 3.

4g Grid Loci and Distance

In the following theorem a simpler expression is formed for the distance between two points in the same grid locus.

Theorem (4g-1):   The distance between any two points (i) in a horizontal grid locus is $|x_2 - x_1|$ and (ii) in a vertical grid locus is $|y_2 - y_1|$.

PROOF

Given: [Part (ii)], $P(x_1,y_1)$ and $Q(x_2,y_2)$ in vertical grid locus $\mathscr{L}$.
To Prove: $(PQ) = |y_2 - y_1|$.

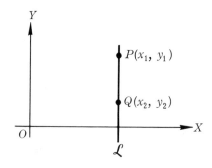

1. $P(x_1,y_1)$ and $Q(x_2,y_2)$ are in vertical grid locus $\mathscr{L}$.	1. Hypothesis
2. $\mathscr{L}$ intersects $\overset{\leftrightarrow}{O}X$.	2. Definition (4-h)
3. Let $\mathscr{L} \cap \overset{\leftrightarrow}{O}X = \{(a,0)\}$.	3. Definition (4-e)
4. $x_1 = x_2 = a$.	4. Theorem (4e-2)
5. (PQ) $= \sqrt{(x_2 - x_1)^2 + (y_2 - y_1)^2}$.	5. Definition (4-l)
6. (PQ) $= \sqrt{(a - a)^2 + (y_2 - y_1)^2}$.	6. Substitution
7. $(PQ) = |y_2 - y_1|$.	7. Properties of $\mathscr{R}$

The proof of part (i) is left to the exercises.

When we use the expression *properties of $\mathscr{R}$*, as we have in the proof of this theorem, we are using the axioms, definitions, and theorems of Sections 3c and 3d.   See Exercise 2 below.

Exercise Set

1. Prove part (i) of Theorem (4g-1).
2. State the propositions being used in Step 7 of Theorem (4g-1).
3. Find the distance between $(3,2)$ and $(-4,2)$ without Definition (4-l).
*4. If $|3 - 1| + |7 - 3| = |7 - 1|$ is a sentence in which each absolute value difference represents a distance along a grid locus, write the same relationship in terms of inequalities.

4h   The Cartesian Plane

Now that we have found an expression for the distance between two points in a single grid locus, it is very useful to develop a relationship between distances along intersecting grid loci.   Accordingly, the following theorem is of special importance.

Theorem (4h-1):   The square of the distance between two points in intersecting grid loci is equal to the sum of the squares of the distances of each point from the point of intersection.

PROOF

Given: Grid loci $\mathscr{L}_1$ and $\mathscr{L}_2$ intersecting at $A(x,y)$; $B(x,v) \in \mathscr{L}_1$; $C(u,y) \in \mathscr{L}_2$.

To Prove: $(BC)^2 = (AB)^2 + (AC)^2$.

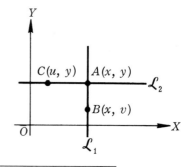

1. The point of intersection of grid loci $\mathscr{L}_1$ and $\mathscr{L}_2$ is $A(x,y)$ and $B(x,v) \in \mathscr{L}_1$, $C(u,y) \in \mathscr{L}_2$.	1. Hypothesis
2. $(AB) = \lvert y - v \rvert$ and $(AC) = \lvert x - u \rvert$.	2. Theorem (4g-1)
3. $(AB)^2 = (y - v)^2$ and $(AC)^2 = (x - u)^2$.	3. Properties of $\mathscr{R}$
4. $(BC) = \sqrt{(x - u)^2 + (v - y)^2}$.	4. Definition (4-1)
5. $(BC)^2 = (x - u)^2 + (y - v)^2$.	5. Same as Step 3
6. $(BC)^2 = (AB)^2 + (AC)^2$.	6. Substitution

Example 1: If $(AB) = 5$ and $(BC) = 7$ along the grid loci in Fig. 4.19, what is the distance from A to C?

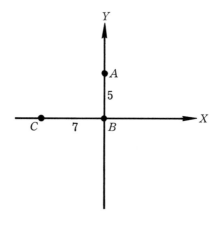

Fig. 4.19

Solution:
$$(AC)^2 = 5^2 + 7^2$$
$$= 74$$
$$(AC) = \sqrt{74}.$$

Now that we have this theorem, we shall call our grid system **rectangular**. Such a rectangular system is often called **Cartesian** in honor of *René Descartes*. The **Cartesian Coordinate System** is the set of grid loci and points having the properties specified in the axioms of Section 4b, ordered number pairs associated with points according to Section 4e, and the distance function of Definition (4-1). The **Cartesian Plane** is the set of all points in the grid loci of the Cartesian coordinate system.

Up to this point in our development of the Cartesian plane, we have only placed one restriction on the one-to-one correspondence between the real numbers and the points in the coordinate axes. That restriction was in having the number zero associated with the point of intersection of the x and y axes. We now establish that this one-to-one correspondence is such that for any point G to the left of any H on $\overleftrightarrow{OX}$, the real numbers g and h, where

$$G \leftrightarrow g \quad \text{and} \quad H \leftrightarrow h,$$

have the property that

(1)
$$g < h.$$

Similarly, for any two points P and Q on $\overleftrightarrow{OY}$, where P is above Q and

$$P \leftrightarrow p \quad \text{and} \quad Q \leftrightarrow q,$$

we have

(2)
$$q < p.$$

The inequalities (1) and (2) give us the order properties of the real numbers in terms of points on a coordinate axis. We have not made careful mathematical definitions of the words *left* and *above*. To do so at this point would involve concepts that are outside the scope of this book. We shall, then, rely on the intuitive meanings of the words.

A **Cartesian Point** is any point in the Cartesian plane.

We immediately see that any Cartesian point is associated with an ordered pair of real numbers and conversely.

The student might well ask whether the Cartesian plane has anything that could be described as a "hole." The Axiom of Completeness (R-17) guarantees that the plane is continuous. That is, we can imagine the plane as an unbroken extension of points in all directions. However, formal development of this idea is well beyond the scope of this book.

We now develop two additional theorems on distance between points in the Cartesian plane.

Theorem (4h-2): $(AB) = 0$ iff $A = B$ for points A and B.

PROOF

Positive: Let $A = (x_1, y_1)$ and $B = (x_2, y_2)$. If $A = B$, then $x_1 = x_2$ and $y_1 = y_2$ by Definition (4-j). Now $(AB) = \sqrt{(x_1 - x_2)^2 + (y_1 - y_2)^2}$ by Definition (4-l). Thus $(AB) = \sqrt{(x_1 - x_1)^2 + (y_1 - y_1)^2}$ by substitution. Hence $(AB) = 0$.

Converse: If $(AB) = 0$ for $A = (x_1, y_1)$ and $B = (x_2, y_2)$, then by Definition (4-l) we have $(AB) = 0 = \sqrt{(x_1 - x_2)^2 + (y_1 - y_2)^2}$ or $0 = (x_1 - x_2)^2 + (y_1 - y_2)^2$. But $(x_1 - x_2)^2 \geq 0$ and $(y_1 - y_2)^2 \geq 0$. For the sum to vanish, each must vanish separately; that is, $(x_1 - x_2)^2 = 0$ and $(y_1 - y_2)^2 = 0$. Therefore $x_1 = x_2$ and $y_1 = y_2$. Hence $A = B$ by the converse of Definition (4-j). Thus the theorem is established.

We will leave the proof of its corollary to the exercises.

Corollary (4h-2a): If $A \neq B$, then $(AB) > 0$ for points A and B.

It is interesting to consider some particular numerical examples of the use of the distance function.

Example 2: Let points A, B, C, and D be given as in Fig. 4.20. Using

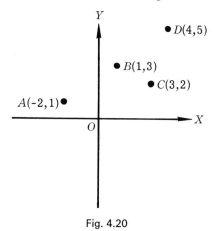

Fig. 4.20

the formula of Definition (4-l), we have $(AB) = \sqrt{13}$, $(AC) = \sqrt{26}$, $(AD) = 2\sqrt{13}$, $(BD) = \sqrt{13}$, and $(CD) = \sqrt{10}$. We find that $(AB) + (BD) = \sqrt{13} + \sqrt{13} = 2\sqrt{13}$. Therefore $(AB) + (BD) = (AD)$. Similarly, $(AC) + (CD) = \sqrt{26} + \sqrt{10} > 2\sqrt{13}$. Thus $(AC) + (CD) > (AD)$.

We have demonstrated in Example 2 that for some Cartesian points A, B, and C, $(AB) + (BC) = (AC)$, and that for some Cartesian points D, E, and F, $(DE) + (EF) > (DF)$. We now ask the question "Are there some Cartesian points *G*, *H*, and *I* for which $(GH) + (HI) < (GI)$?"   This last sentence turns out to be impossible.   The following theorem makes a formal statement of the preceding discussion.   The proof is omitted.

Theorem (4h-3) (*The Triangle Inequality*)*:*   If *A*,*B*,*C* are any Cartesian points, then $(AB) + (BC) \geq (AC)$.

Exercise Set

1. *Prove:* If $B = C$, then $(AB) = (AC)$ for any point *A*.
2. Does Theorem (4h-3) exclude the possibility of $(AB) + (BC) < (AC)$?
3. List the properties of $\mathscr{R}$ used in the proof of Theorem (4h-1).
4. Answer the question "Why" in the proof of Theorem (4h-3).

Find the distance between the following pairs of points by using Theorem (4h-1).

5. $(0, -2)$, $(4,1)$.   6. $(-2,1)$, $(3,13)$.
7. $(2,3)$, $(-1,0)$.   8. $(0,0)$, $(2,2)$.

9. For the three points $A(1, -3)$, $B(2,1)$, and $C(3,4)$, state whether each distance is less than or equal to the sum of the other two.

Find the square of the distance (AC) in each of the following by using Theorem (4h-1) or state why it is impossible.

10. $B = (2, -1)$, $A = (-3, -1)$, $C = (2,2)$.
11. $B = (2, -1)$, $A = (0, -1)$, $C = (3, -1)$.
12. $B = (2, -1)$, $A = (0, -1)$, $C = (2,y)$, $(BC) = 10$.

*13. Prove Corollary (4h-2a).   [*Hint:* State one of the contrapositives of Theorem (4h-2).]

*14. Who was René Descartes and what was his contribution to mathematics?

*15. Carefully outline the development of the logical system that has been created up to this point.

chapter 5

Loci

5a Specification of Loci

We are familiar with the general first-degree inequalities and equations in two variables. That is,

$$px + qy + r = 0$$

and

$$px + qy + r \geq 0$$

are concepts that were established in our algebra course and in Section 3c. In our work with these open sentences, we developed the concept of a replacement and solution set. Recall that the replacement set is the set of ordered pairs of real numbers that can be replaced for the variable without any concern for the truth or falsity of the sentence involved, whereas the solution set is a subset of the replacement set and contains those and only those ordered pairs of real numbers that make the open sentence a true one. Here we shall be primarily concerned with the solution set.

These sentences will be used as *rules* for determining which ordered pairs of real numbers determine a particular locus of points. Basically we are using the concept of subset and the principle established by Theorem (4e-3).

Since the solution set of each sentence determines a locus of points, and these points are in the Cartesian plane, they have geometric meaning. In effect, we have a model of the sentence that determined the locus.

We shall use the word *locate* to mean that we find the points on the Cartesian plane that are in one-to-one correspondence with a set of ordered pairs of real numbers. Thus we would *locate* the solution set of a sentence in the plane.

A **function** is a set of ordered pairs (x,y) such that no two distinct ordered pairs have the same first element. That is, if (x_1,y_1) and (x_2,y_2) are elements of the set and if $x_1 = x_2$, then $y_1 = y_2$. If we write a sentence in the form

$$px + qy + r = 0$$

and then say that **y is a function of x**, we mean that the solution set must be as described above. If we have a solution set that fulfills the definition of a function, then we will often say that the *sentence is a function*. We will also establish the convention that if y is a function of x, then x, the **independent variable**, will be the first element of the ordered pair and y, the **dependent variable**, will be the second element of the ordered pair. If a set of ordered pairs is not a function, then we say it is a **relation**.

Example 1: Locate on the Cartesian plane the locus determined by the set $\{(x,y) \mid x = y\}$.

Solution: The solution set of real numbers for $x = y$ includes $(-1,-1)$, $(1,1)$, $(0,0)$, $(3,3)$, $(-3,-3)$, and so on. A partial geometric model is shown by Fig. 5.1.

Example 2: Locate on the Cartesian plane the locus determined by the set $\{(x,y) \mid x^2 + y + 1 = 0\}$.

Solution: The solution set of real numbers for $x^2 + y + 1 = 0$ includes $(0,-1)$, $(1,-2)$, $(3,-10)$, $(2,-5)$, and so on. A partial geometric model is show by Fig. 5.2.

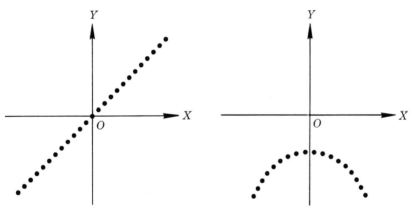

Fig. 5.1   Fig. 5.2

Example 3: Locate on the Cartesian plane the locus determined by the set $\{(x,y) \mid x^2 + y^2 = 1\}$.

Solution: The solution set of real numbers for $x^2 + y^2 = 1$ includes $(1,0)$, $(-1,0)$, $(0,1)$, $(0,-1)$, $(\sqrt{2}/2, \sqrt{2}/2)$, $(-\sqrt{2}/2, -\sqrt{2}/2)$, and so on. A partial geometric model is shown by Fig. 5.3.

Example 4: Locate on the Cartesian plane the locus determined by the set $\{(3,2), (4,-1), (2,2)\}$.

Solution: The solution is the set itself, that is, the points (3,2), (4,−1), and (2,2).   The geometric model is shown by Fig. 5.4.

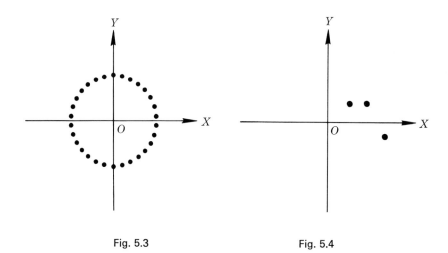

Fig. 5.3   Fig. 5.4

Example 5:   Locate on the Cartesian plane the locus determined by the set $\{(x,y) \mid y > 8\}$.

Solution: The solution set of real numbers for $\{(x,y) \mid y > 8\}$ includes (0,9), (−5,10), (6,20), and so on.   In fact, we see that $y > 8$ is true for all x. Therefore the geometric model is that part of the plane above the horizontal grid locus that intersects $\overleftrightarrow{O\,Y}$ at (0,8).   (See Fig. 5.5.)

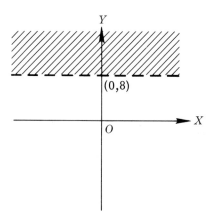

Fig. 5.5

Exercise Set

Locate on the Cartesian plane the following functions.

1. $\{(x,y) \mid y = x + 1\}$.
2. $\{(x,y) \mid y = -x + 1\}$.
3. $\{(x,y) \mid y = 1\}$.
4. $\{(x,y) \mid 3x + y = 1\}$.
5. $\{(x,y) \mid x^2 + 2x + 1 = y\}$.
6. $\{(x,y) \mid 2y + 3x = 0\}$.
7. $\{(x,y) \mid y = 2 - x - x^2\}$.
8. $\{(1,2), (3,-1), (0,1)\}$.

Locate the following relations on the Cartesian plane.

9. $\{(x,y) \mid x^2 + y^2 = 4\}$.
10. $\{(x,y) \mid x^2 + 4y^2 = 4\}$.
11. $\{(x,y) \mid x^2 - y^2 = 4\}$.
12. $\{(x,y) \mid 2x^2 - 3y^2 = 6\}$.
13. $\{(x,y) \mid x = 14\}$.
14. $\{(x,y) \mid x = 3y^2 + 1\}$.
15. $\{(x,y) \mid 3x + 5y > 0\}$.
16. $\{(x,y) \mid x - 7y \le 2\}$.

Which of the following are relations?   Functions?

17. $\{(x,y) \mid y = x\}$.
18. $\{(x,y) \mid x = y^2\}$.
19. $\{(x,y) \mid x^2 + xy = 1\}$.
20. $\{(0,1), (1,0), (0,0), (x,y)\}$.
21. $\{(-1,-1), (1,1), (2,3)\}$.
22. $\{(x,y) \mid x = \sqrt{1 - y^2}\}$.

*23. Locate the geometric model of $\{(x,y) \mid 4x^2 + y^2 = 16\}$.   Is it a function? If not, can the model be represented by a union of functions?   What are they?

24. Is the set $\{(x,y) \mid x = 1\}$ a function?   Why or why not?

*25. What is the replacement set of $y = (3x^2 + x)/x$?   How does its geometric model differ from that model determined by the function $\{(x,y) \mid y = 3x + 1\}$?

*26. Locate the model of the sentence $y + x = y + x$.

*27. Locate the model of the relation $\{(x,y) \mid (x - 1)^2 + (y - 2)^2 = 4\}$.   Is the ordered pair $(1,2)$ in the replacement set of the relation?   In the solution set? What general conclusion does this result lead to in terms of centers of circles?

5b   Intersection of Loci

If we have the sets $A = \{(2,3), (4,5), (6,7)\}$ and $B = \{(1,2), (2,3), (3,4), (5,6)\}$, then $A \cap B = \{(2,3)\}$.   Since each of these sets represents a locus, we then say the **intersection of the loci** is the set $C = \{(2,3)\}$.

Certainly we have loci that intersect at many points or loci that do not intersect at all.   In the latter case, the intersection set would be the *null* set.

Example 1:   Examine the intersection of the sets A and B where $A = \{(x,y) \mid x = y\}$ and $B = \{(1,1), (-2,-2), (4,2), (2,-4)\}$.

Solution: Since $A = \{(x,y) \mid x = y\}$ is a set containing the elements $(-2,-2)$, $(1,1)$, $(2,2)$, $(\sqrt{3},\sqrt{3})$, $\ldots$, (n,n) for $n \in \mathscr{R}$, we have $A \cap B = \{(1,1), (-2,-2)\}$.   A partial geometric model of this intersection is seen in Fig. 5.6.

Example 2: Examine the intersection of the sets A and B where $A = \{(x,y) \mid x^2 - 2x + 1 = y\}$ and $B = \{(x,y) \mid x = 4\}$.

Solution: A contains elements $(0,1)$, $(2,1)$, $(4,9)$,..., and B contains $(4,1)$, $(4,3)$, $(4,9)$,.... We see that *every* element of B has a first coordinate 4. Thus $(4,9)$ is the only element common to both A and B, since A has only *one* element with first coordinate 4. Hence $A \cap B = (4,9)$. See Figure 5.7.

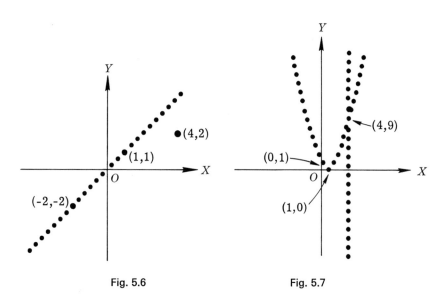

Fig. 5.6   Fig. 5.7

The possibility exists that two loci might have all their points in common; that is, $A \subset B \wedge B \subset A$. This would mean $A = B$. Thus they are the same locus. A second possibility is a locus A is a subset of a locus B. A third possibility is a subset of A might also be a subset of B. (See Exercise 14.)

Definition (5-a): For any two loci defined by the sets A and B, the loci are said to be **distinct** iff $A \not\subset B$ and $B \not\subset A$.

Example 3: Are the sets $A = \{(x,y) \mid x = y, \ x > 0\}$ and $B = \{(x,y) \mid x = y\}$ distinct?

Solution: Some of the elements of A are $(\frac{1}{2},\frac{1}{2})$, $(1,1)$, $(3,3)$, ..., (n,n) for $n > 0$, $n \in \mathcal{R}$. Elements of B include $(-3,-3)$, $(-2,-2)$, $(0,0)$, $(1,1)$, $(2,2)$, ..., (n,n) for all $n \in \mathcal{R}$. We see, then, that $A \cap B = C = \{(\frac{1}{2},\frac{1}{2}), (1,1), (2,2), (3,3), \ldots, (n,n)\}$ for $n > 0$, $n \in \mathcal{R}$. But $C = A$. Therefore $A \subset B$ and hence A and B are not distinct by Definition (5-a).

Definition (5-b): If two loci are not distinct, then they are said to be **coincident**.

Definition (5-b) makes the loci of Example 3 coincident.

Example 4: Are the loci $A = \{(0,1), (1,0), (0,0)\}$ and $B = \{(2,0), (0,2),$ $(2,2)\}$ distinct?

Solution: Since $A \cap B = \emptyset$, then $B \not\subset A$ and $A \not\subset B$. Therefore they are distinct.

Exercise Set

Are the following pairs of loci distinct or coincident? Locate each pair on a Cartesian plane and determine the points of intersection, if any.

1. $A = \{(1,0), (1,1), (2,1)\}$, $B = \{(2,3), (3,4), (2,1)\}$.
2. $A = \{(x,y) \mid x^2 + y^2 - 1 = 0\}$, $B = \{(x,y) \mid y = 0\}$.
3. $A = \{(x,y) \mid x > 0\}$, $B = \{(1,2)\}$.
4. $A = \{(x,y) \mid x + y - 1 = 0\}$, $B = \{(x,y) \mid x = 1 - y\}$.
5. $A = \{(x,y) \mid x^2 = y\}$, $B = \{(x,y) \mid x^2 + 4 = y\}$.
6. $A = \{(x,y) \mid (x^2 - 1)/x = y\}$, $B = \{(x,y) \mid 3x - y - 1 = 0\}$.
7. Locate the models of Example 3.
8. Locate the models of Example 4.
9. Are the grid loci distinct or coincident?

Determine, by locating the loci on Cartesian planes, whether the pairs of loci are distinct or coincident in Exercises 10 through 13.

10. $A = \{(x,y) \mid y = x - 1\}$, $B = \{(x,y) \mid x = y\}$.
*11. $A = \{(x,y) \mid (x - 4)^2 + (y - 2)^2 = 9\}$, $B = \{(4,2)\}$.
*12. $A = \{(x,y) \mid y = x^3\}$, $B = \{(x,y) \mid y = -x\}$.
*13. $A = \{(x,y) \mid x \geq 4\}$, $B = \{(x,y) \mid x = 4\}$.
*14. Give an example of a set C such that $C \subset A$ and $C \subset B$, where A,B, and C are determined by inequalities.

5c Straight Lines

Definition (5-c): The locus $\{(x,y) \mid px + qy + r = 0\}$, where p,q, and r are real number constants and p and q are not both zero, is called a **straight line**.

The model in Fig. 5.1 can now be called a straight line. (See Exercise 9.) We shall adopt still another convention and use the word *line* and the term *straight line* interchangeably. We shall always assume that whenever the sentence $px + qy + r = 0$ is used, the real number constants p and q *are not both zero*.

In $px + qy + r = 0$, if we let $p = 0$, we have

(1)
$$y = \frac{-r}{q}.$$

If we let $q = 0$, we have

(2)
$$x = \frac{-r}{p}.$$

But $-r/q$ and $-r/p$ are both constants and we represent them by letting $b = -r/q$ and $a = -r/p$. We now see that (1) and (2) have become

(3) $\{(x,y) \mid y = b\}$,

(4) $\{(x,y) \mid x = a\}$.

Referring to Theorems (4e-1) and (4e-2), we see that (3) and (4) are grid loci. We summarize as follows.

Theorem (5c-1): If $p = 0$ in the sentence $px + qy + r = 0$, then the locus is a horizontal grid locus; if $q = 0$, the locus is a vertical grid locus.

Definition (5-d): A **vertical line** is the locus $\{(x,y) \mid x = a\}$ for $a \in \mathscr{R}$.

Definition (5-e): A **horizontal line** is the locus $\{(x,y) \mid y = b\}$ for $b \in \mathscr{R}$.

Definition (5-f): An **oblique line** is a line that is neither vertical nor horizontal.

It can be proven in more advanced courses that the solution sets of sentences that can be expressed as polynomials are *continuous*. It is sufficient for our purpose to think of this concept of continuousness as one that requires, for example, a straight line to have *no* "holes" in it. We can now redraw our previous models and make the solid lines as illustrated in Fig. 5.8. (We should be careful, however, to realize that not all sentences will yield a geometric model that is continuous. Some models may have one, two, or more "holes" in them. See Exercise *24. See Fig. 5.9.)

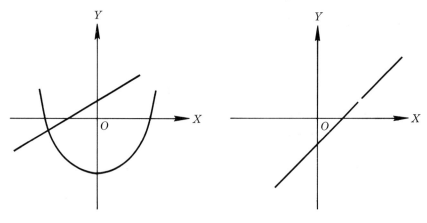

Fig. 5.8   Fig. 5.9

We can now easily show that the grid loci are vertical and horizontal continuous straight lines. This certainly agrees with our intuition!

Theorem (5c-2): Two straight lines are distinct iff they have at most one common point.

PROOF

Positive: Let (a,b) be the only point contained in both loci $\mathscr{L}_1$ and $\mathscr{L}_2$. But $\mathscr{L}_1$ and $\mathscr{L}_2$ have an infinite number of points. Therefore there is at least one noncommon point. By Definition (5-a) $\mathscr{L}_1$ and $\mathscr{L}_2$ are distinct. If there is no common point, then $\mathscr{L}_1 \not\subset \mathscr{L}_2$ and $\mathscr{L}_2 \not\subset \mathscr{L}_1$. Again by Definition (5-a), $\mathscr{L}_1$ and $\mathscr{L}_2$ are distinct. The proof of the converse is omitted.

Consider any two distinct Cartesian points (x_1,y_1) and (x_2,y_2). From the axioms of $\mathscr{R}$, we have

(5) $$y_1 - y_2,\, x_2 - x_1,\, x_1 y_2 - x_2 y_1 \in \mathscr{R}.$$

Using (5) as our constants p,q, and r, we write the straight-line equation

(6) $$(y_1 - y_2)x + (x_2 - x_1)y + (x_1 y_2 - x_2 y_1) = 0.$$

The coefficients of x and y cannot both be zero, for we know that (x_1,y_1) and (x_2,y_2) are distinct points. (See Exercise 12.)

If the points (x_1,y_1) and (x_2,y_2) are in the line, then they must be in the solution set of (6). To determine this we substitute the ordered pairs into (6). Thus we have for (x_1,y_1),

$$(y_1 - y_2)x_1 + (x_2 - x_1)y_1 + (x_1 y_2 - x_2 y_1) = 0 \qquad \text{whence } 0 = 0$$

and for (x_2,y_2),

$$(y_1 - y_2)x_2 + (x_2 - x_1)y_2 + (x_1 y_2 - x_2 y_1) = 0 \qquad \text{whence } 0 = 0.$$

We know then that the two points (x_1,y_1) and (x_2,y_2) are both in the locus $\{(x,y) \mid (y_1 - y_2)x + (x_2 - x_1)y + (x_1 y_2 - x_2 y_1) = 0\}$. The question remains, "Is it the only straight-line locus that contains both of them?" The contrapositive of Theorem (5c-2) assures us that it is. Now using the converse of Definition (5-b), the following theorem is established.

Theorem (5c-3) (*Euclid's First Axiom*): On any two points there is exactly one straight line.

Taken together, Theorems (5c-2) and (5c-3) certainly agree with our intuition as seen in Figs. 5.10 and 5.11.

Since Theorem (5c-3) guarantees a line on any two points A and B, we shall use the notation $\overleftrightarrow{AB}$ to mean the line determined by the points A and B.

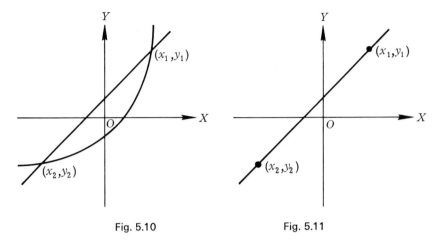

Fig. 5.10   Fig. 5.11

If three or more points are contained in the same straight line, we say they are **collinear**.

At this point in our development we shall begin to solve some linear systems of equations. Generally two simple methods are employed to solve such systems simultaneously. One is elimination by substitution, and the other is elimination by addition and subtraction. In Examples 1 and 2 we demonstrate both methods. Keep in mind that in solving systems simultaneously we are looking for that point which is a member of the solution set of both equations. It may well be, however, that there is no such ordered pair.

Example 1: Find the ordered pair that is in the solution set of both $\{(x,y) \mid 2x - 3y = 5\}$ and $\{(x,y) \mid 2x + y = 1\}$.

Solution: We shall use the method of elimination by substitution. Solving the second equation for y, we obtain

$$y = 1 - 2x.$$

Substituting this for y in the first equation yields

$$2x - 3(1 - 2x) = 5$$
$$2x - 3 + 6x = 5$$
$$-3 + 8x = 5$$
$$8x = 8$$
$$x = 1.$$

Since $y = 1 - 2x$, we find that

$$y = 1 - 2(1)$$
$$y = -1.$$

Therefore the intersection of the solution sets is

$$(1,-1).$$

Example 2: Find A where

$$A = \{(x,y) \mid 2x - 3y = 1\} \cap \{(x,y) \mid 4x + 2y = 18\}.$$

Solution: We shall use the method of elimination by addition or subtraction. First we write the equations in order. That is,

$$2x - 3y = 1$$
$$4x + 2y = 18.$$

We now multiply the first equation by -2 and then add the two together, obtaining

$$-4x + 6y = -2$$
$$4x + 2y = 18$$
$$\overline{}$$
$$8y = 16$$
$$y = 2.$$

Letting $y = 2$ in the second equation, we obtain

$$4x + (2)(2) = 18$$
$$4x = 14$$
$$x = \tfrac{7}{2}.$$

Thus $$A = \{(\tfrac{7}{2},2)\}.$$

Example 3: Find the equation determining the locus $\overleftrightarrow{AB}$ where $A = (2,3)$ and $B = (-3,6)$.

Solution: The points $(2,3)$ and $(-3,6)$ must both satisfy $px + qy + r = 0$. But this gives two equations in three variables, that is, p,q, and r. We know from algebra that we must have as many equations as variables to solve a linear system. Therefore we consider the equation $px + qy + r = 0$ and divide by q.

(7) $$\frac{p}{q}x + y + \frac{r}{q} = 0, \qquad q \neq 0.$$

Replacing x and y by $(2,3)$ and $(-3,6)$ in equation (7), we have equations

(8) $$\frac{p}{q}(2) + 3 + \frac{r}{q} = 0.$$

(9) $$\frac{p}{q}(-3) + 6 + \frac{r}{q} = 0.$$

Subtracting (9) from (8), we have

$$\frac{p}{q}(5) + (-3) = 0$$

(10)
$$\frac{p}{q} = +\frac{3}{5}.$$

Substituting equation (10) into (8) to find r/q, we obtain

(11)
$$\frac{r}{q} = \frac{-21}{5}.$$

Now substituting equations (10) and (11) into (7), we have

$$\frac{3}{5}x + y + \frac{-21}{5} = 0,$$

which was the desired result.

In Example 3 we made the restriction in (7) that $q \neq 0$.   If $q = 0$, then we immediately have a linear system of two equations in two variables.   From Example 3, with $q = 0$, we have

$$px + r = 0,$$

and using (2,3) and (-3,6),

$$2p + r = 0$$

and
$$-3p + r = 0.$$

Solving these equations simultaneously yields $p = 0$ and $r = 0$.   But both p and q cannot equal zero!   Thus our restriction of $q \neq 0$ in (7) of Example 3 is justified.

The following three theorems are obtained by combining facts given in Theorems (5c-2) and (5c-3) and in Definitions (5-d), (5-e), and (5-f).

Theorem (5c-4):   A straight line is horizontal iff it contains two distinct points having the same ordinate.

Theorem (5c-5):   A straight line is vertical iff it contains two distinct points having the same abscissa.

The proofs of these two theorems are left to the exercises.

Theorem (5c-6):   A straight line is oblique iff it contains any two points having abscissas and ordinates respectively different.

PROOF

Positive: We are given straight line $\mathscr{L} \ni (a,b),(c,d)$ such that $a \neq c$ and $b \neq d$. $\mathscr{L}$ is neither vertical nor horizontal by Theorems (5c-4) and (5c-5). Therefore $\mathscr{L}$ is oblique by Definition (5-f).

The proof of the converse is left to the exercises.

Exercise Set

Which of the following are oblique lines, horizontal lines, vertical lines, or none of these?

1. $x + y + 1 = 0$.

2. $x^2 + y^2 - 1 = 0$.

3. $x - 1 = 0$.

4. $2x + 3y = 4$.

5. $x^2 - 2y + 1 = 0$.

6. $x = -y$.

7. $x = \sqrt{y^2}$.

8. $y = 5$.

9. Redraw Figs. 5.1, 5.2, 5.3, and 5.7 using the concept of a continuous locus.

10. Answer the question "Why?" in the proof of the converse of Theorem (5c-2).

11. Give several examples of two loci that are distinct and have no common points.

12. Show that if $(y_2 - y_1)$ and $(x_2 - x_1)$ are not both zero, then (x_1,y_1) and (x_2,y_2) are distinct points.

13. What allows the use of the converse of Definition (5-b) in the proof of Theorem (5c-3)?

Determine the locus $\{(x,y) \mid px + qy + r = 0\}$ containing the following pairs of points. Locate the locus on the plane.

14. $(1,1)$ and $(-1,-1)$.

15. $(2,0)$ and $(3,-4)$.

16. $(-3,-1)$ and $(0,0)$.

17. $(2,-3)$ and $(-2,4)$.

18. $(-2,-1)$ and $(-2,4)$

19. $(-2,4)$ and $(0,4)$.

20. Prove Theorem (5c-4).

21. Prove Theorem (5c-5).

22. Are the points $(2,0)$, $(6,-1)$, and $(-8,6)$ all contained in the same straight line?

23. Is the locus $\{(x,y) \mid y = |x|\}$ a straight line, and if so what kind? Why?

24. Solve the following systems simultaneously using the methods of Examples 1 and 2. Check your result.

(a) $\{(x,y) \mid x = y\} \cap \{(x,y) \mid 2x - y = 1\}$.

(b) $\{(x,y) \mid x + 2y = 1\} \cap \{(x,y) \mid -x + 3y = 4\}$.

(c) $\{(x,y) \mid 2x - 7y = 2\} \cap \{(x,y) \mid 4x - 3y = 4\}$.

(d) $\{(x,y) \mid 6x - 3y = 2\} \cap \{(x,y) \mid -2x + y = 3\}$.

*25. Locate the model for $\{(x,y) \mid 3y = |x + 1|\}$.

*26. Locate the model for $\{(x,y) \mid y = |x|/x\}$.

*27. Prove the converse of Theorem (5c-6). (*Hint:* This is a proof by contradiction.)

*28. Rewrite Theorem (5c-6) making it a stronger statement. Will the converse of your new theorem be true?

*29. Carry out the steps of the simultaneous solution in the proof of the converse of Theorem (5c-2) under the conditions imposed there. Show that $p_1x + q_1y + r_1 = 0$ becomes a constant multiple of $p_2x + q_2y + r_2 = 0$.

5d   Circles

Definition (5-g):   The locus $\{(x,y) \mid (x - h)^2 + (y - k)^2 = a^2\}$, where a,h, and k are real number constants and $a > 0$, is called a **circle**.

Definition (5-h):   In the circle $\{(x,y) \mid (x - h)^2 + (y - k)^2 = a^2\}$, the point (h,k) is called the **center** of the circle.

We shall *always* assume that a,k, and h are in $\mathscr{R}$ and $a > 0$ when we write the equation of a circle.

This definition of a circle, as with lines, selects a particular algebraic sentence as the "rule" that determines the points to be contained in the locus. We shall always assume the properties of continuity for the geometric model of a circle; that is, we will draw the lines in solid!

Example 1:   Locate $\{(x - 2)^2 + (y - 2)^2 = 4\}$ on the Cartesian plane without continuity, then with continuity.

Solution: The geometric models are shown in Fig. 5.12.

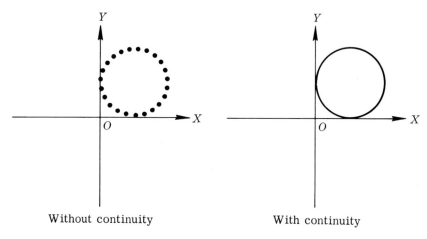

Without continuity   With continuity

Fig. 5.12

We note that the locus of a circle does not include the center. Why? (See Exercise 27, Section 5a.)   It also does not include the "interior" part of the circle; that is, the shaded part of the plane in Fig. 5.13 is not included in the locus of the circle.   For example, the point $(2,2)$ is in the "interior" of the circle of Example 1.   We find that $(2,2)$ is not in the solution set of the equation $(x - 2)^2 + (y - 2)^2 = 4$.   Hence $(2,2)$ is not in the locus of the circle.

The following theorem provides us with the basic *existence* criterion for circles.

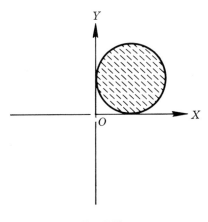

Fig. 5.13

Theorem (5d-1): For any Cartesian point (h,k) and any positive real number a, there is a unique circle $\{(x,y) \mid (x - h)^2 + (y - k)^2 = a^2\}$.

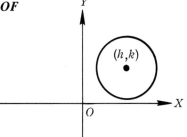

PROOF

Given: A point (h,k) and $a > 0$ such that $a,h,k \in \mathcal{R}$.
To Prove: There is a $\{(x,y) \mid (x - h)^2 + (y - k)^2 = a^2\}$.

1. There is a Cartesian point (h,k) and $a > 0$, $a,h,k \in \mathcal{R}$.	1. Hypothesis
2. There is a Cartesian point (x,y) such that $\sqrt{(x - h)^2 + (y - k)^2} = a.$	2. Theorem (4f-2)
3. $\therefore \{(x,y) \mid (x - h)^2 + (y - k)^2 = a^2\}$ exists.	3. Properties of $\mathcal{R}$
4. $\{(x,y) \mid (x - h)^2 + (y - h)^2 = a^2\}$ is unique.	4. Properties of $\mathcal{R}$

We show the use of Definition (5-h) and Theorem (5d-1) in the following examples.

Example 2: What is the equation of a circle whose center is $(2,3)$ if $a = 5$?

Solution: Since the locus of any circle is defined to be $\{(x,y) \mid (x - h)^2 + (y - k)^2 = a^2\}$, we have then $\{(x,y) \mid (x - 2)^2 + (y - 3)^2 = 25\}$.

Example 3:   In the circle $\{(x,y) \mid (x - 2)^2 + (y - 3)^2 = 25\}$, what is the distance between the center of the circle and the point $(2,-2)$ which is contained in the circle?

Solution: The center is $(2,3)$ by Definition (5-h).   Using Definition (4-1) we have

$$d = \sqrt{(2 - 2)^2 + [3 - (-2)]^2}$$
$$= 5$$

Note that this result is a in the equation of the circle.

The conclusion of Example 3 leads us to the following theorem.

Theorem (5d-2):   On any two distinct Cartesian points, there is a unique circle on either point having the other point as center.

Figure 5.14 illustrates this theorem.   The proof is left to the exercises.

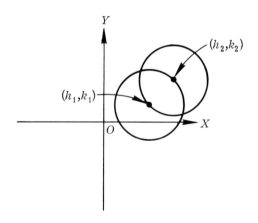

Fig. 5.14

If we consider any two distinct points, as in Fig. 5.15, we find that many "distinct" circles can contain these two points.   The following theorem establishes the number of distinct points that are needed to determine a unique circle.

Theorem (5d-3):   On any three distinct, noncollinear points there is exactly one distinct circle.

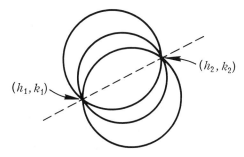

Fig. 5.15

The hypothesis of the theorem gives us three distinct noncollinear points $P(x_1 y_1), Q(x_2, y_2)$, and $R(x_3, y_3)$. We must now prove that a point (h,k) exists and that this point is equidistant from each of the points P, Q, and R. (See Fig. 5.16.) With a considerable display of algebraic virtuosity this

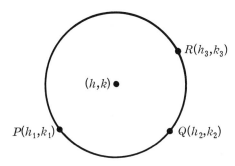

Fig. 5.16

program could be carried out at this point. However, it seems more appropriate to provide a proof later, when we have more geometric facts at our disposal.

Exercise Set

Write the equations of the given circles.

1. Center is (h,k) and $a = 4$.
2. Center is $(2, -3)$ and $a = 1$.
3. Center is $(-2,0)$ and $a^2 = 4$.
4. Center is $(3,3)$ and $a = \sqrt{3}$.
*5. What are the equations of the circles whose centers are $(2,3)$ and $(-1,4)$ and contain the points $(-1,4)$ and $(2,3)$, respectively?
*6. Prove Theorem (5d-2).

5e   Angles

In geometry, as in other branches of mathematics, we often talk about subsets.   Many times the subset will possess important properties that the set does not have.   The locus defined below is one such subset.

Definition (5-i):   A **ray** is the subset of $\{(x,y) \mid px + gy + r = 0\}$ such that $(a,b) \in \{(x,y) \mid px + qy + r = 0\}$ and exactly one of the following holds: (i) $x = a$ and $(y \geq b \lor y \leq b)$; (ii) $x \geq a$; (iii) $x \leq a$.

Definition (5-j):   The point (a,b) in Definition (5-i) is called the **endpoint** of the ray.

After we develop additional properties of straight lines, we shall restate the definition of a ray.

Example 1:   Examine $\{(x,y) \mid y = |x|\}$ for possible rays.

Solution: Locating $\{(x,y) \mid y = |x|\}$ on the Cartesian plane, we see that the locus from $(0,0)$ for $x \geq 0$ fulfills the definition of a ray [part (ii)].   We find that for $x \leq 0$, the locus is also a ray.   See Fig. 5.17.   (In the light of this definition of a ray, check your answer to Exercise 23, Section 5c.)

Example 2:   Locate the ray if $(a,b) = (3,4)$ and part (iii) of the definition is true for $\{(x,y) \mid x - y + 1 = 0\}$.   Locating $\{(x,y) \mid x - y + 1 = 0\}$ in the Cartesian plane, we then find the endpoint $(3,4)$.   We obtain the geometric model in Fig. 5.18 by applying part (iii) of Definition (5-i).

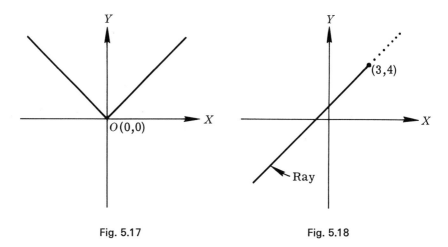

Fig. 5.17   Fig. 5.18

Intuitively, we see that a ray is that part of a straight line that extends without bound in one direction and has as its other end a particular point. Figure 5.19 illustrates some rays.   We shall use the notation $\overrightarrow{AB}$ to indicate

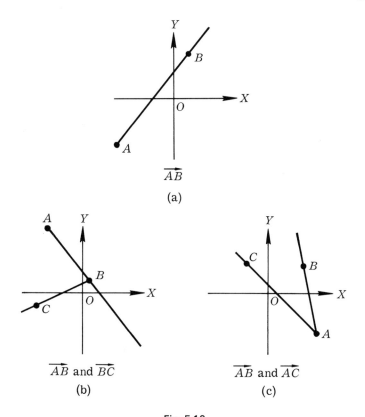

Fig. 5.19

a ray having endpoint A and extending *without bound* through the point B.

Definition (5-k):   For any two rays $\overrightarrow{AB}$ and $\overrightarrow{AC}$, the locus $\overrightarrow{AB} \cup \overrightarrow{AC}$ is called an **angle**.

We can restate this definition without using set notation as follows.

Definition (5-k) (Restatement):   The locus determined by two rays having a common endpoint is called an **angle**.

Figure 5.20 illustrates some rays that determine angles.   We shall often use lower-case Greek letters to name angles.   For example, if we write $\alpha = \beta$, this would read angle α equals angle β.   We also use $\sphericalangle BAC$ as a second kind of notation.   This indicates that the angle ($\sphericalangle$) is formed by the two rays $\overrightarrow{AB}$ and $\overrightarrow{AC}$ with common endpoint A.   All the angles of Fig. 5.20 are indicated by $\sphericalangle BAC$.   Could they also be indicated by $\sphericalangle CAB$?   Why?

Definition (5-l):   The point $\overrightarrow{AB} \cap \overrightarrow{AC} = A$ in an angle is called the **vertex** of the angle.

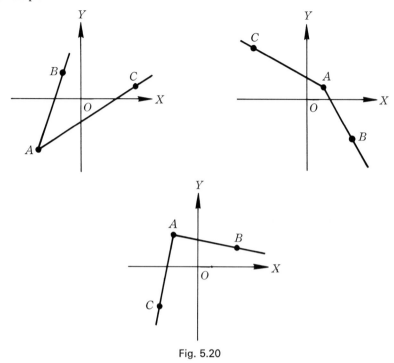

Fig. 5.20

Again, we shall restate this definition without the set notation.

Definition (5-l) (Restatement): The common endpoint of two rays that determine an angle is called the **vertex** of the angle.

We should note here, as in the case of a circle, the locus is only the two rays with their common endpoint. The angle does not include the shaded part of the plane as illustrated in Fig. 5.21.

Definition (5-m): The two rays determining an angle are called the **sides** of the angle.

Definition (5-n): Two angles having a common vertex and one common side in the manner of $\angle ABD$ and $\angle CBD$ in Fig. 5.22, where $\overrightarrow{BC}$ is the common side, are called **adjacent**. (We should realize that this definition is *not at all precise*, depending, as it does, on a drawing. We state it here for convenience of discussion. It will be restated in a precise manner in Section 6d.)

Example 3: List the angles in Fig. 5.23. Indicate any of those angles that are adjacent.

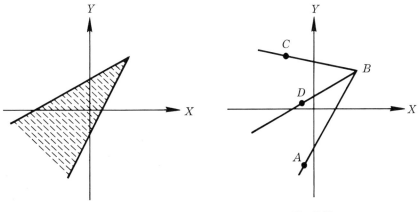

Fig. 5.21   Fig. 5.22

Solution: The angles are (a) $\angle BAC$, (b) $\angle ABC$, (c) $\angle ACB$, (d) $\angle ACG$, (e) $\angle BCD$, (f) $\angle GCD$, (g) $\angle ADF$, (h) $\angle BED$, (i) $\angle BEF$, (j) $\angle FEG$, and (k) $\angle GED$.   The adjacent angles of those listed above are (c) and (d); (c) and (e); (d) and (f); (h) and (i); (i) and (j); (j) and (k); (k) and (h); (e) and (f).

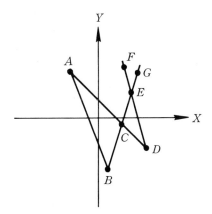

Fig. 5.23

Exercise Set

1. Locate on the Cartesian plane the following angle
$$\{(x,y) \mid x + y + 1 = 0, x \geq -4\} \cup \{(x,y) \mid x = -4, y \geq 3\}$$
whose vertex is $(-4,3)$.

2. In the definition of an angle, express the point A as an intersection.

3. Three distinct lines having a common point determine how many adjacent angles?

4. Three distinct lines each intersecting the other such that there is no common point to all three lines determine how many angles?

5. Will a straight line intersecting one side of an angle intersect the other side also? Why?

6. Give an example of the three conditions for a ray as described by Definition (5-i).

7. Can any point in the plane serve as the vertex of an angle? Discuss.

8. Which models of Fig. 5.19 illustrate the $\sphericalangle ABC$? $\sphericalangle BAC$?

9. Is there another ray in Fig. 5.19(b) besides the two already listed there? Explain.

10. Answer the question "Why?" in the discussion concerning Fig. 5.20.

*11. What is the greatest number of angles that can be determined by straight lines on four distinct points? What is the least number?

*12. Using the definition of an angle, what common characteristic is evident in the angles determined by rays that are subsets of the grid loci?

*13. Can any three distinct points determine a unique angle? Discuss.

5f Graphing

Throughout this chapter we have been locating loci in the Cartesian plane. Such procedures are called **graphing**. The geometric representations are called the **graphs** of the loci.

There are several *techniques* in graphing that we should use in order to proceed efficiently.

After graphing several straight lines (Exercises, Section 5b), we find that every straight line intersects at least one axis. Such points of intersection are called **intercepts**. This term applies not only to straight lines but also to any locus that intersects an axis.

Definition (5-o): An **x intercept** of a locus is that point (or points) where the locus intersects the x axis.

Definition (5-p): An **y intercept** of a locus is that point (or points) where the locus intersects the y axis.

Often the nonzero coordinate of an intercept point is called the **intercept** instead of the point itself. We find these intercepts by locating that ordered number pair in the set of the locus that (1) has y coordinate equal to zero for the x intercept, (2) has x coordinate equal to zero for the y intercept.

Example 1: Find the intercepts of the locus {(2,3), (4,5), (0,1), (6,3), (−2,0)}. Graph the locus.

Solution: The point $(-2,0)$ is the x intercept by property (1) above and $(0,1)$ is the y intercept by (2) above. See Fig. 5.24 for the graph.

Example 2: Find the intercepts of $\{(x,y) \mid x + 2y - 2 = 0\}$. Graph the locus.

Solution: Since we want the coordinate for which $y = 0$, we simultaneously solve the equations

$$x + 2y - 2 = 0$$
$$y = 0.$$

Thus the x intercept is $(2,0)$. We also want the coordinate for which $x = 0$; hence we simultaneously solve the equations

$$x + 2y - 2 = 0$$
$$x = 0.$$

This gives y intercept $(0,1)$. See Fig. 5.25 for the graph.

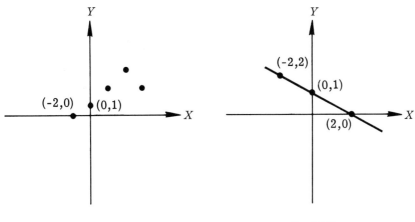

Fig. 5.24   Fig. 5.25

The advantage of using intercepts in graphing is obvious. Since Theorem (5c-3) states that two distinct points determine a unique line, we simply find the intercepts and draw the line. We should, however, always find a third point to check our graph.

Example 3: Graph $\{(x,y) \mid x = 2y\}$.

Solution: Looking for the intercepts of $\{(x,y) \mid x = 2y\}$, we find $x = 0$ when $y = 0$, and conversely. Therefore we have both an x and a y intercept that are *coincident*. Thus the graph contains the origin. We find a second point by choosing any value for x or y and solving for the remaining variable. For example, let $x = 2$. Solving for y, we obtain $y = 1$. Locating $(0,0)$ and $(2,1)$ in the Cartesian plane, we draw a straight line through the two points and obtain the locus $\{(x,y) \mid x = 2y\}$. We check with $(-2,-1)$. See Fig. 5.26.

Example 4: Graph $\{(x,y) \mid x^2 + 1 = y\}$.

Solution: First we look for intercepts. When $y = 0$, we have

$$x^2 + 1 = 0$$
(1)
$$x^2 = -1.$$

No $x \in \mathscr{R}$ will make open sentence (1) a true proposition. We conclude from this the locus does not intersect the x axis. Why? When $x = 0$, we have

$$y = 1.$$

Thus we obtain a y intercept at $(0, 1)$. Since $\{(x,y) \mid x^2 + 1 = y\}$ is not a straight line, we simply *continue* to find elements in its solution set and locate them on the plane. A systematic way to do this is to write a set of ordered pairs having only one coordinate. For example,

$$\{(x,y) \mid x^2 + 1 = y\} = \{(1,?), (2,?), (?, 3), (-1,?), \ldots\}.$$

Now, using these values, solve for the second coordinate. This yields

$$\{(1,?), (2,?), (-2,?), (-1,?), \ldots\} = \{(1,2), (2,5), (-2,5), (-1,2), \ldots\}.$$

We locate these on the graph as in Fig. 5.27. (Note that we have included

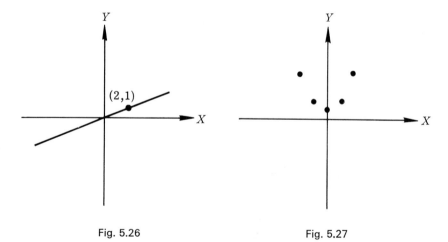

Fig. 5.26   Fig. 5.27

the y intercept.) Using the continuity principle, we know that this locus is continuous. We draw it, estimating what the rest of the graph will look like. (Since the graph is only a geometric model and we use it merely to *represent* certain mathematical ideas, an estimation is certainly sufficient.) Figure 5.28 shows the completed graph. (This locus is called a **parabola**.)

In the definition of a function, we have a locus such that no two distinct ordered pairs have the same first coordinate. For example, $A = \{(2,1),$ $(3,2), (4,1), (6,-2)\}$ is a function.

Now suppose that a vertical line $\{(x,y) \mid x = a\}$ intersects a function $\mathcal{L}$ in two distinct points. Let the points be (a,y_1) and (a,y_2). Now, however, we have two distinct points in $\mathcal{L}$ with the same first elements. Hence $\mathcal{L}$ is not a function. Since the assumption that a vertical line can intersect a function more than once leads to a contradiction, we must conclude that a vertical line can intersect a function once at most.

Theorem (5f-1): If any vertical grid locus intersects a given locus in at most one point, then the given locus is a function.

Example 5: Graph the locus $\{(x,y) \mid x + y = 1\}$. Is the locus a function?

Solution: Locating the intercepts in the plane, we have $(0,1)$ and $(1,0)$. We obtain the model illustrated in Fig. 5.29. Clearly, if we draw any

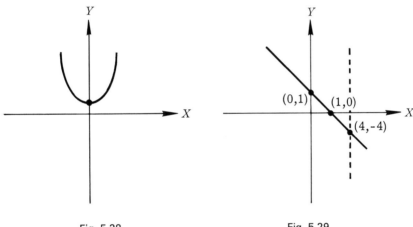

Fig. 5.28   Fig. 5.29

vertical grid locus, say at $(4,0)$, it will intersect the given locus in only one point, that is, $(4,-4)$. Thus we can conclude that all the ordered pairs of $\{(x,y) \mid x + y = 1\}$ will have different first coordinates. Hence the locus is a function.

Example 6: Is the locus of Example 4 a function?

Solution: If we graph any vertical grid locus in Fig. 5.28, we see that it will intersect the given model in only one point. Thus we can conclude that the locus is a function.

Example 7: Graph $\{(x,y) \mid x^2 + 4y^2 = 16\}$.

Solution: Locating the intercepts, we find that they are $(0,2)$, $(0,-2)$,

(4,0), and (−4,0).   Why?   Using a second method of locating more points, we draw a chart as follows.

x	y
−2	
−1	
3	

We then solve for the corresponding y values, obtaining the following table.

x	y
−2	$\sqrt{3}, -\sqrt{3}$
−1	$\sqrt{15/4}, -\sqrt{15/4}$
1	$\sqrt{15/4}, -\sqrt{15/4}$
2	$\sqrt{3}, -\sqrt{3}$

We now locate these eight *ordered pairs* on the graph along with the intercepts. We obtain a model as in Fig. 5.30.   Figure 5.31 shows the model after the principle of continuity has been applied.

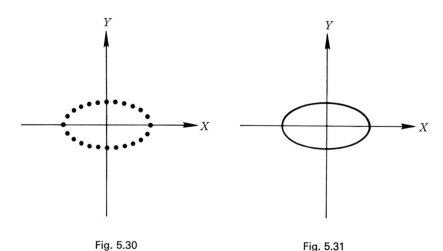

Fig. 5.30   Fig. 5.31

Example 8:   Graph $\{(x,y) \mid (x - 1)^2 + (y - 1)^2 = 17\}$.

Solution: If we are careful, we can graph this locus without too much difficulty.   The first thing we note is that the locus is a circle with center (1,1) and radius $\sqrt{17}$.   Knowing what the locus looks like, we need only find its position on the plane.   This we do with the intercepts.   We obtain (0,5), (0,−3), (5,0), and (−3,0) as intercepts.   Figure 5.32 illustrates the graph.

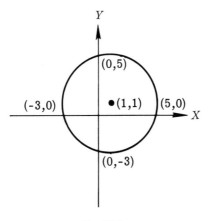

Fig. 5.32

One of the most useful modern applications of mathematics is called *linear programming*. In this field much of the information about the problems considered is stated in the form of inequalities (relations). To locate the geometric model of the locus of such relations, we graph the corresponding function and then determine the region specified by the relation by testing points. Here we are dealing with sets of relations and functions so that the region specified, if any, will be the intersection of the corresponding solution sets.

Example 9: Graph the following set of relations and indicate the region of the plane, if any, which satisfies the complete set.

(a) $\{(x,y) \mid y < 2x + 6\}$

(b) $\left\{(x,y) \mid y \geq \dfrac{x}{2} - \dfrac{2}{3}\right\}$

(c) $\{(x,y) \mid y \geq -x\}$.

Solution: We first graph the loci $\{(x,y) \mid y = 2x + 6\}$, $\{(x,y) \mid y = \frac{1}{2}x - \frac{2}{3}\}$, and $\{(x,y) \mid y = -x\}$. Finding various points for these loci, we have

(a) $y = 2x + 6$

x	y
-3	0
-2	2
0	6

(b) $y = \frac{1}{2}x - \frac{3}{2}$

x	y
0	$-\frac{3}{2}$
1	-1
3	0

(c) $y = -x$

x	y
-2	2
0	0
1	-1

Using these coordinates, we determine that the shaded region of Fig. 5.33 is the one whose coordinates satisfy all three of the given relations.

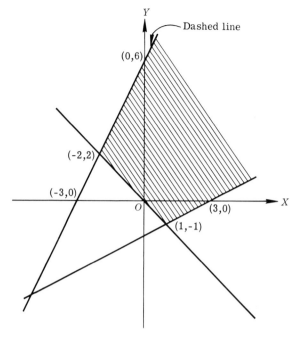

Fig. 5.33

Exercise Set

Locate the intercepts and graph the following loci.

1. $\{(x,y) \mid x + y - 7 = 0\}$.
2. $\{(x,y) \mid x - 7 = 3y\}$.
3. $\{(x,y) \mid \frac{1}{2}x + 2 = 0\}$.
4. $\{(x,y) \mid x^2 + 2x - 6 = y\}$.
5. $\{(x,y) \mid 3x + 4y = 0\}$.
6. $\{(x,y) \mid y = x^2\}$.
7. $\{(x,y) \mid (x - 2)^2 + (y + 1)^2 = 4\}$.
8. $\{(x,y) \mid x^2 + (y + 1)^2 = 1\}$.
9. $\{(x,y) \mid x + y = 0\}$.
10. $\{(x,y) \mid 3x^2 + 4y^2 = 4\}$.

11. What are the intercepts of $y = 0$? $x = 0$?

12. What are the intercepts of $\{(x,y) \mid y = x^2\}$? $\{(x,y) \mid y = (x - 1)^2\}$?   Graph these loci.

13. If the intercept of $\{(x,y) \mid 3x + 3y + r = 0\}$ is $(0,3)$, then what value does r assume?   When the intercept is $(2,0)$?

14. Does $\{(x,y) \mid y = x^2 + 4\}$ intercept the x axis?   Why?

15. Using Theorem (5f-1), determine which of the examples in this section are functions.

16. For some given locus, when will an x intercept and a y intercept be equal?

17. Why is the intersection of the solution sets the simultaneous solution of a set of relations?

In Exercises 18 through 20, determine the region of intersection, if any, of the given sets of loci.

18. $\{(x,y) \mid y \geq 0\}$
$\{(x,y) \mid 0 \leq x\}$
$\{(x,y) \mid 1 - y \leq x + 1\}$.

19. $\{(x,y) \mid y \geq -2x + 6\}$
$\{(x,y) \mid y \geq 2x - 2\}$
$\{(x,y) \mid y \leq \frac{1}{2}x + 1\}$.

20. $\{(x,y) \mid y = x + 2\}$
$\{(x,y) \mid y \geq -\frac{3}{2}x + \frac{5}{2}\}$
$\{(x,y) \mid x \leq 0\}$.

*21. Graph $\{(x,y) \mid x^3 = y\}$.

*22. Graph $\{(x,y) \mid x = |y|\}$.

*23. Graph $\{(x,y) \mid 3x + 2y + 1 > 0\}$. (*Hint:* Graph the equation $3x + 2y + 1 = 0$ and then find out on which side of this line the points satisfy the given inequality.)

*24. Graph $\{(x,y) \mid 4x^2 - 9y^2 = 36\}$.

*25. Graph $\{(x,y) \mid y = 2^x\}$.

*26. Graph the following parts (a) through (i) on *one* graph.

(a) $A = \{(x,y) \mid y + 5 \geq (x + 5)^2\} \cap \{(x,y) \mid y \leq -1\}$ (color in red).

(b) $B = \{(x,y) \mid (x + 2)^2 + (y + 2)^2 \leq 1\}$ (red).

(c) $C = \{(x,y) \mid |x| + |3y| \leq 1\}$ (orange).

(d) $D = \{(x,y) \mid y + 1 \geq -\sqrt{x - y}\} \cap \{(x,y) \mid y \leq -1\}$ (green).

(e) $E = \{(x,y) \mid y + 1 \leq -|x - 4|\} \cap \{(x,y) \mid y < -5\}$ (green).

(f) $F = \{(x,y) \mid |x - 4| + |y - 3| \leq 1\}$ (red).

(g) $G = \{(x,y) \mid 4 \leq |y| \leq 5\}$ (yellow).

(h) $H = \{(x,y) \mid y - 4 \geq (x - 7)\} \cap \{(x,y) \mid y < 4\}$ (red).

(i) $I = \{(x,y) \mid y + 2 \leq -(x + 5)^2\} \cap A$ (deep, heavy red).

chapter 6

Properties of Straight Lines

6a Straight Lines and Numbers

In this chapter we shall make a more detailed study of the properties of the straight-line locus introduced in Chapter 5.

Let us consider any two points (x_1, y_1) and (x_2, y_2) in the locus $\{(x,y) \mid px + qy + r = 0\}$. For these points,

(1) $$px_1 + qy_1 + r = 0$$

and

(2) $$px_2 + qy_2 + r = 0$$

are true. Subtracting equation (2) from (1), we obtain

$$p(x_1 - x_2) = -q(y_1 - y_2).$$

Dividing, we have

(3) $$\frac{y_1 - y_2}{x_1 - x_2} = -\frac{p}{q}, \qquad q \neq 0$$

or

(4) $$\frac{y_2 - y_1}{x_2 - x_1} = -\frac{p}{q}, \qquad q \neq 0.$$

Example 1: What is the constant $-p/q$ for the locus $\{(x,y) \mid 3x + 7y + 1 = 0\}$?

Solution: We find that $p = 3$, $q = 7$, and thus $-p/q = -3/7$.

Example 2: What is the value of $(y_2 - y_1)/(x_2 - x_1)$ if (x_1, y_1) and (x_2, y_2) are contained in the locus $\{(x,y) \mid 3x + 7y + 1 = 0\}$?

Solution: Since $(x_1, y_1), (x_2, y_2) \in \{(x,y) \mid 3x + 7y + 1 = 0\}$, we have

$$3x_1 + 7y_1 + 1 = 0$$
$$3x_2 + 7y_2 + 1 = 0.$$

Subtracting and then rearranging the terms, we obtain

$$3(x_2 - x_1) + 7(y_2 - y_1) = 0$$
$$7(y_2 - y_1) = -3(x_2 - x_1)$$
$$\frac{y_2 - y_1}{x_2 - x_1} = -\frac{3}{7}.$$

Example 3: What is the constant represented by the difference of the ordinates divided by the difference of the abscissas of any two points in the locus $\{(x,y) \mid 3x + 7y + 1 = 0\}$?

Solution: Clearly $(-5,2)$ and $(2,-1)$ are points in the given locus. Thus we have

$$\frac{2 - (-1)}{-5 - 2} = -\frac{3}{7}.$$

In each of these three examples, the same constant, $-3/7$, was obtained. In the following example, we consider a linear locus for which the constant $-p/q$ causes some difficulties.

Example 4: What is the constant $-p/q$ for the locus $\{(x,y) \mid 6x + 4 = 0\}$?

Solution: Since $6x + 4 = 0$ is in the form $px + qy + r = 0$, where $p = 6$, $q = 0$, and $r = 4$, the constant $-p/q = 6/0$. This is meaningless, for division by zero is *not* possible. Thus we conclude that in this case the constant $-p/q$ does not exist.

If in the locus $\{(x,y) \mid px + qy + r = 0\}$, $q = 0$, then we have

$$px + r = 0$$

(5) $$x = -\frac{r}{p}, \qquad p \neq 0.$$

Why can we be sure the statement $p \neq 0$ is a true one in this case? We recognize (5) to be a vertical grid locus. The abscissas of a vertical straight line are constant. That is, if $\mathscr{L}$ is a vertical line and (x_1,y_1) and $(x_2,y_2) \in \mathscr{L}$, then $x_1 = x_2$. Thus for any two points in vertical line $\mathscr{L}$, $x_1 - x_2 = 0$. Keeping these conclusions in mind, we make the following definition about the constant $-p/q$.

Definition (6-a): The slope of a nonvertical straight line is the number $m = -p/q = (y_2 - y_1)/(x_2 - x_1)$, where (x_1,y_1) and (x_2,y_2) are points in the locus $\{(x,y) \mid px + qy + r = 0\}$.

Note that the slope is *not defined* for vertical lines. As shown in Example 4, the vertical case corresponds to the case where $q = 0$. If we write $-p = qm$, we see that Axiom R-11, page 34, does not provide for the existence of a number m in this case. Since there is no number m to associate with a vertical line, *we often say a vertical line has no slope.*

The following theorems are established by using Definition (6-a), our development of equations (1) and (2) above, and the uniqueness property of the result of an algebraic equation. (In this course we shall often be more concerned with the fact that an algebraic manipulation yields a result than with the result itself.) The actual proofs are left to the exercises.

Theorem (6a-1): Any two points in a nonvertical straight line determine a unique slope m.

Theorem (6a-2): Every vertical straight line has no slope.

Theorem (6a-3): Every nonvertical straight line has slope m.

Corollary (6a-3a): The slope of every horizontal line is zero.

Corollary (6a-3b): Every oblique straight line has slope $m \neq 0$.

Recall that Theorem (5c-3) states that two distinct points determine a unique line. We now develop another method for determining a line.

Theorem (6a-4): If P is a point and m is a real number, then there is exactly one straight line on P having slope m.

PROOF

Given: $P(x_1, y_1)$ is a Cartesian point and $m \in \mathcal{R}$.
To Prove: There is exactly one line $\mathcal{L}$ on P having slope m.

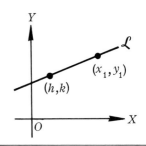

1. $P(x_1, y_1)$ is a Cartesian point and $m \in \mathcal{R}$.	1. Hypothesis
2. Let $h \in \mathcal{R}$ such that $h \neq x_1$.	2. Properties of $\mathcal{R}$
3. $mh, mx_1 \in \mathcal{R}$.	3. Why?
4. There is a $u \in \mathcal{R}$ such that $mx_1 + u = mh$.	4. Solvability under addition in $\mathcal{R}$
5. There is a $k \in \mathcal{R}$ such that $u + y_1 = k$.	5. Why?
6. $u = k - y_1$.	6. Why?
7. $m = \dfrac{k - y_1}{h - x_1}$.	7. Properties of $\mathcal{R}$
8. (h,k) is a Cartesian point.	8. Why?

9. There is exactly one line $\mathscr{L}$ on (h,k) and P.

9. Why?

10. m is the slope of $\mathscr{L}$.

10. Why?

Q.E.D.

Theorem (6a-5):   If P is a point, there is exactly one line on P having no slope.

The proof is left to the exercises.

The number $y_2 - y_1$ in Definition (6-a) is called the **rise** of a line and the number $x_2 - x_1$ is called the **run**.   In Fig. 6.1 these numbers are illustrated.

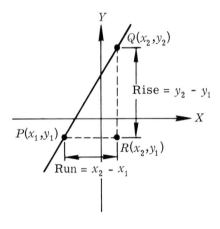

Fig. 6.1

In this figure the real numbers $x_2 - x_1$ and $y_2 - y_1$ each represent a distance along the intersecting grid loci.   The "steeper" the line is relative to the x axis, the larger the number $y_2 - y_1$ will be to $x_2 - x_1$.   That is, the slope provides a measure of the "steepness" of a line.   Figure 6.2 illustrates lines with positive and negative slope.

$x_2 - x_1$ and $y_2 - y_1$ are not distances in the sense of Definition (4-l). Distance according to this definition is a positive number, whereas $x_2 - x_1 > 0$ iff $x_2 > x_1$ and $x_2 - x_1 > 0$ iff $x_1 < x_2$ and similarly for $y_2 - y_1$.   Such distances are called **directed distances** because the signs depend on the order in which we take the coordinates of the points.

Example 5:   Find the slope of the line determined by $(2,-3)$ and $(4,4)$.

Solution: Let $(x_1,y_1) = (2,-3)$ and $(x_2,y_2) = (4,4)$.   Since $m = (y_2 - y_1)/(x_2 - x_1)$, we have $m = [4 - (-3)]/(4 - 2) = 7/2$.   (Note that we must be careful to take the difference of the ordinates in the same order as the difference of abscissas.)

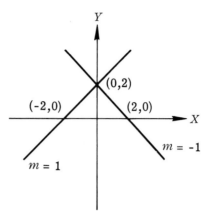

Fig. 6.2

Example 6: Find the slope of the line determined by the points $(2,-3)$ and $(-5,4)$.   Illustrate by an appropriate choice of rise and run.

Solution: Let $(x_1,y_1) = (-5,4)$ and $(x_2,y_2) = (2,-3)$. Since $m = (y_2 - y_1)/(x_2 - x_1)$, we have $m = (-3 - 4)/[2 - (-5)] = -7/7 = -1$. Since run is $(x_2 - x_1)$, we have $2 - (-5) = 7$. Rise is $(y_2 - y_1) = (-3 - 4) = -7$.   (Or we have rise = 7 and run = -7.   Why?)   Depending on which rise (run) we choose, the result is illustrated in Fig. 6.3.   Notice

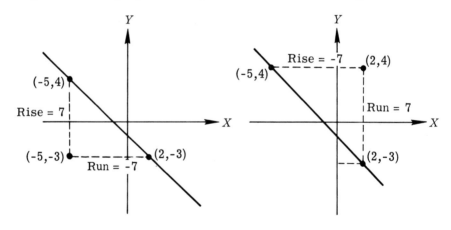

Fig. 6.3

that we take the rise (run) in the same order that we used to find their values.

Exercise Set

1. Carefully explain the restriction $q \neq 0$ in equation (3), page 96.

2. Can $p = 0$ in (5) above?   Explain.

3. Supply the reasons that justify steps labeled "Why?" of Theorem (6a-4) and explain how we know that the divisor in Step 7 does not vanish.

4. Find the slopes of the lines of Fig. 6.4.   Assume that the coordinates of the points shown are integral units.

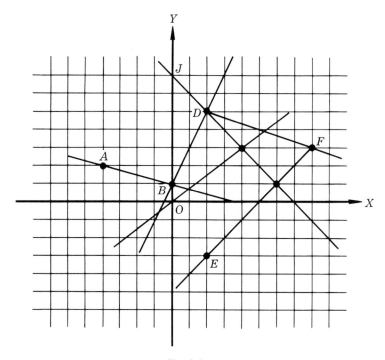

Fig. 6.4

5. If we know a particular slope, does this determine a unique line?   Compare lines OC and EF in Exercise 4.

Find the locus of lines satisfying the given conditions.   Graph the locus.

6. Slope $= m$ and line is on $(0,b)$.

7. Slope $= m$ and line is on (x_1,y_1).

8. Slope $= m$ and oblique line is on $(a,0)$.

Find the slope of the following lines.

9. $\{(x,y) \mid 3x - 4y = 0\}$.

10. $\{(x,y) \mid 4y + 21 = 0\}$.

11. $\{(x,y) \mid 11y - 2 = 3x\}$.

12. $\{(x,y) \mid 4x + 9y = 5\}$.

13. $\{(x,y) \mid 3x - 7 = 0\}$.

14. $\{(x,y) \mid 8y + 3 = 2x\}$.

Given the following points and slope, use a method similar to that of Section 5c to find the locus of a line.

15. $P = (-2,5)$, $m = \frac{3}{7}$.

16. $P = (0,-4)$, $m = \frac{5}{2}$.

Find the slopes of the following lines by assuming that $P_1 = (x_1,y_1)$ and

$P_2 = (x_2, y_2)$ are general points in the lines and deriving the expression for slope as done to obtain equation (2), page 96.

*17. $\{(x,y) \mid x + 3 = 2y\}$.   *18. $\{(x,y) \mid 2x + 3y = 0\}$.

*19. Graph the locus determined by $\{(x,y) \mid 2x + y < 1\}$.

*20. Prove Theorem (6a-2).

*21. Prove Theorem (6a-3).

*22. Prove Corollary (6a-3a).

*23. Prove Corollary (6a-3b).

*24. Prove Theorem (6a-5).

6b   Straight-Line Equations

In Section 5c a straight line was defined to be the locus of points

(1) $$\{(x,y) \mid px + qy + r = 0\}.$$

We shall call

(2) $$px + qy + r = 0$$

the **general equation** of a straight line.   The locus (1) and the equation (2) have exactly the same meaning.   We shall use either form in the rest of the text.

Various forms of equation (2) that have already been established are

Vertical line: $x = a$

(3)   Horizontal line: $y = b$

Oblique line: $px + qy + r = 0$,

$p \neq 0 \vee q \neq 0$.

The following theorem and its corollaries establish further special forms of equation (2).

Theorem (6b-1):   Any nonvertical straight line on a given point (x_1, y_1) has equation $y - y_1 = m(x - x_1)$, where m is the slope of the line.

PROOF

Given: A nonvertical straight line $\mathcal{L}$ on a point (x_1, y_1) with slope m.

To Prove: $\mathcal{L}$ has equation $y - y_1 = m(x - x_1)$.

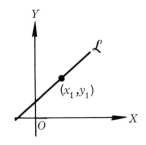

1. $\mathscr{L}$ is a nonvertical line on (x_1, y_1) with slope m.	1. Hypothesis
2. $\mathscr{L} = \{(x,y) \mid px + qy + r = 0\}$.	2. Definition (5-c)
3. $px_1 + qy_1 + r = 0$.	3. Theorem (4e-3)
4. $p(x - x_1) + q(y - y_1) = 0$.	4. Why?
5. $y - y_1 = -\dfrac{p}{q}(x - x_1)$.	5. Why?
6. $m = -\dfrac{p}{q}$.	6. Definition (6-a)
7. $y - y_1 = m(x - x_1)$.	7. Why?
Q.E.D.	

This equation is called the **point-slope form** of the equation of a straight line.

Corollary (6b-1a): Any nonvertical straight line has equation $y = mx + b$, where $(0,b)$ is the y intercept and m is the slope of the line.

PROOF

Given: A nonvertical straight line $\mathscr{L}$ having y intercept $(0,b)$ and slope m.
To Prove: The equation of $\mathscr{L}$ is $y = mx + b$.

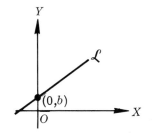

1. $\mathscr{L}$ is a nonvertical line having y intercept $(0,b)$ and slope m.	1. Hypothesis
2. $\mathscr{L}$ is on the point $(0,b)$.	2. Why?
3. An equation of $\mathscr{L}$ is $y - b = m(x - 0)$.	3. Why?
4. $y = mx + b$.	4. Why?
Q.E.D.	

This is called the **slope-intercept form** of the straight-line equation.

Corollary (6b-1b): Any oblique straight line which does not contain the origin has equation $\dfrac{x}{a} + \dfrac{y}{b} = 1$, where $(a,0)$ is the x intercept and $(0,b)$ is the y intercept.

This is called the **intercept form** of the straight-line equation.

Corollary (6b-1c):   Any oblique line has equation $y = m(x - a)$, where $(a,0)$ is the x intercept and m is the slope.

Corollary (6b-1d):   Any point in a nonvertical straight line is determined by an ordered pair $(x, mx + b)$, where m is the slope and $(0,b)$ is the y intercept.

Example 1:   Find the equation of the line on $(-3,2)$ having slope $m = -5$.

Solution: Let $(x_1, y_1) = (-3,2)$.   Then the desired equation is $y - (2) = -5[x - (-3)]$ by Theorem (6b-1).   Simplifying, we have $5x + y + 13 = 0$.

Example 2:   Find the equation of a line having x intercept -3 and y intercept 4.

Solution: Directing our attention to Corollary (6b-1b), we have $\dfrac{x}{-3} + \dfrac{y}{4} = 1$.   Thus $4x - 3y + 12 = 0$ is the required equation.

Example 3:   Find the y intercept and slope determined by the equation $5x + 3y + 2 = 0$.

Solution: We write the equation $5x + 3y + 2 = 0$ in the form $y = mx + b$ and use Corollary (6b-1a).   In this form $y = (-5/3)x - 2/3$.   Therefore $m = -5/3$ and the y intercept is $b = -2/3$.

Example 4:   What is the equation of the line having slope 3 and x intercept 4?

Solution: Using Corollary (6b-1c) we have $m = 3$ and $a = 4$.   Thus $y = 3(x - 4)$.   Simplifying, $3x - y - 12 = 0$.

Exercise Set I

In Exercises 1 through 13, find an equation corresponding to the conditions given.

1. Slope 4 and on $(2, -4)$.
2. Slope -2 and on $(-5,1)$.
3. On points $(3, -4)$ and $(4,2)$.
4. On points $(0,6)$ and $(-7,0)$.
5. Slope $-\frac{5}{2}$ and y intercept -3.
6. On points $(-2,0)$ and $(-2,5)$.
7. Slope 11 and y intercept 0.
8. Slope -3 and x intercept $\frac{2}{5}$.
9. x intercept $\frac{7}{2}$ and y intercept -3.
10. x intercept 3 and on point $(3,13)$.
11. y intercept 2 and on point $(-7,2)$.
12. On points (a,b) and (b,a).

13. On points $(-a,b)$ and (a,b).

14. Find the slope and y intercept of $3y - 5 = 0$ and $2x - 3y - 6 = 0$.

15. Find x intercept and slope of $3y + 4 = 0$.

16. Find both intercepts of $3x + 5y - 15 = 0$.

17. How do we know that $q \neq 0$ in Step 5 of Theorem (6b-1)?   Fill in the missing reasons in Theorem (6b-1) and Corollary (6b-1a).

*18. Complete Corollary (6b-1a).

*19. Prove Corollary (6b-1b).

*20. Prove Corollary (6b-1c).

*21. Prove Corollary (6b-1d).

We now want to consider two straight lines with different slopes.   That is,

(4) $$\mathscr{L}_1: \quad y = m_1x + b_1$$

and

(5) $$\mathscr{L}_2: \quad y = m_2x + b_2$$

such that $m_1 \neq m_2$.   Do their solution sets have an ordered pair in common? Solving (4) and (5) simultaneously, we obtain

(6) $$x = \frac{b_2 - b_1}{m_1 - m_2}$$

and

(7) $$y = \frac{m_1b_2 - m_2b_1}{m_1 - m_2}.$$

Thus we do have a point of intersection when $m_1 \neq m_2$. If $m_1 = m_2$, then (6) and (7) will be undefined.   (Why?)   If we replace $\mathscr{L}_2$ in (5) by a line that has no slope, for example,

(8) $$x = a,$$

then $$y = m_1a + b_1.$$

Again, their solution sets have a point in common.   This discussion establishes the following theorems.

Theorem (6b-2):   (i) If two straight lines have different slopes or (ii) if one has a slope and the other has no slope, then they intersect on exactly one point.

We immediately note that since the point of intersection is unique, the lines are distinct by Theorem (5c-2).   Thus we have the following corollary.

Corollary (6b-2a):   If two straight lines (i) have different slopes or (ii) are such that one has a slope and the other has no slope, then the lines are distinct.

The contrapositive of Theorem (6b-2), part (i) is "If two straight lines do not intersect on exactly one point, then they do not have different slopes."

There are two ways that this lack of intersection on exactly one point could occur. First, there could be no intersection at all, or, second, there could be more than one point of intersection. Using one of the contrapositives of Theorem (5c-2), the condition of more than one point of intersection establishes that the lines are coincident. A similar argument leads to the same conclusion for part (ii) of Theorem (6b-2). Thus we have the following theorem.

Theorem (6b-3):   If two straight lines (i) have the same slope and a common point or (ii) have no slope and a common point, then the lines are coincident.

Various forms of the straight-line equation are readily adapted to graphing.

Example 5:   Graph $\{(x,y) \mid 2x - 3y - 6 = 0\}$.

Solution: We rewrite $2x - 3y - 6 = 0$ in the slope-intercept form $y = mx + b$. That is, $y = \frac{2}{3}x - 2$. Hence we have $m = \frac{2}{3}$ and y intercept $(0, -2)$. From $(0, -2)$ we run $+3$ and rise $+2$. This gives a second point and we can draw the graph. We check our result with a third point, say $(6,2)$. (See Fig. 6.5.)

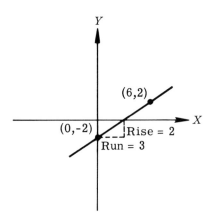

Fig. 6.5

Example 6:   Graph $x/2 + y/3 = 1$.

Solution: Using Corollary (6b-1b), the x intercept is $(2,0)$ and the y intercept is $(0,3)$. The graph is illustrated in Fig. 6.6. A third point, say $(4, -3)$, is used as a check.

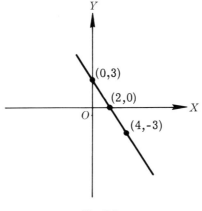

Fig. 6.6

Exercise Set II

1. Graph Exercises 1 through 13 of Exercise Set I, page 104.

2. Restate Theorem (6b-2) and Corollary (6b-2a) as one theorem.

3. Prove Corollary (6b-2b) formally.

4. Graph the locus $\{(x,y) \mid x + y - 25 = 0$ and $x - 2y - 3 = 0\}$.

5. Make careful graphs of the following pairs of equations on one set of axes.
   (a) $x + 3y - 9 = 0$ and $3x - y - 4 = 0$.
   (b) $2x - 3y + 12 = 0$ and $3x + 2y + 2 = 0$.
   (c) $7x - y = 0$ and $x + 7y + 21 = 0$.
   Measure the angles between the lines of each pair with a *protractor*; then find the product of the slopes for each pair.   What does the result seem to indicate?

Graph each pair of equations below and compare the slopes of each.   What does the result seem to indicate?

6. $2x - 3y + 6 = 0$ and $4x - 6y - 5 = 0$.

7. $6x - 3y + 5 = 0$ and $2x - y = 0$.

8. $x = y$ and $x = -y$.

*9. Write the contrapositives of Theorem (5c-2).

6c   Parallel and Perpendicular Lines

Definition (6-b):   Two distinct lines are **parallel** iff their slopes are equal or iff each has no slope.

The following theorem establishes the fact that the horizontal and vertical grid loci are each sets of parallel lines.

Theorem (6c-1):   Every horizontal line is parallel to each other and every vertical line is parallel to each other.

The proof of this theorem follows directly from Definition (6-b), Theorem (6a-2), and Corollary (6a-3a).

Theorem (6c-2):   Straight lines are parallel iff they have no common point.

The proof of this theorem is left to the exercises.

We now see that for lines in 2-space there are the following possibilities: they are coincident, or parallel, or intersecting.   Then if two lines are non-parallel, and noncoincident, they must have different slopes by the argument above.   We state this formally.

Theorem (6c-3):   If two nonparallel straight lines are distinct, then they have different slopes or one has no slope.

The formal proof of this theorem is left to the exercises.

None of the preceding theorems answers the question of the existence of parallel lines.   The following very important existence theorem guarantees that there is a line parallel to any given line.   We use the symbol // to mean "is parallel to."

Theorem (6c-4):   On any point P not in a straight line $\mathscr{L}$ there is exactly one distinct straight line parallel to $\mathscr{L}$.

PROOF

Given: Straight line $\mathscr{L}_1$ and point $P \notin \mathscr{L}_1$.
To Prove: There is eactly one line $\mathscr{L}_2$ on P such that $\mathscr{L}_1 // \mathscr{L}_2$.

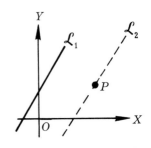

1. $\mathscr{L}_1$ is a straight line and P is a point not in $\mathscr{L}_1$.	1. Hypothesis
2. $\mathscr{L}_1$ has slope m or no slope.	2. Theorem (6a-2) or (6a-3)
3. There is exactly one line $\mathscr{L}_2$ on P having slope m or no slope.	3. Theorem (6a-4) or (6a-5)
4. $\mathscr{L}_1$ and $\mathscr{L}_2$ are distinct.	4. Definition (5-a)
5. $\mathscr{L}_1 // \mathscr{L}_2$.	5. Definition (6-b)

Q.E.D.

Example 1: Find the equation of a line $\mathscr{L}_1$ on $(-2,\frac{1}{3})$ and parallel to the line $\mathscr{L}_2 = \{(x,y) \mid 5x - 6y - 5 = 0\}$.

Solution: Changing the equation of $\mathscr{L}_2$ to the slope-intercept form, we have $y = \frac{5}{6}x - \frac{5}{6}$. Therefore $m = \frac{5}{6}$. Using the point-slope form for $\mathscr{L}_1$, we get $y - \frac{1}{3} = \frac{5}{6}x - (-2)$ or $5x - 6y + 12 = 0$.

Figure 6.7 shows two parallel lines $\mathscr{L}_1$ and $\mathscr{L}_2$ being intersected in P by $\mathscr{L}_3$. Since $\mathscr{L}_3 \cap \mathscr{L}_2 = P$, then will $\mathscr{L}_3 \cap \mathscr{L}_1 = Q$ exist? Theorem (6c-5) establishes this intersection.

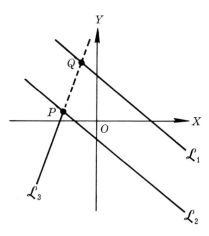

Fig. 6.7

The proofs of the following theorems can be easily made by the use of algebraic techniques. (See Exercises 9 through 12, page 110.)

Theorem (6c-5): If a line intersects one of two parallel lines on exactly one point, then it intersects the other on exactly one point.

Corollary (6c-5a): If a line has a different slope from that of two parallel lines, it intersects each of them on exactly one point.

Corollary (6c-5b): If two parallel lines have slope m and a third line has no slope, then it intersects each of the parallel lines on exactly one point.

Corollary (6c-5c): If two parallel lines have no slope and a third line has slope m, then it intersects each of the parallel lines on exactly one point.

Theorem (6c-6): Two distinct straight lines parallel to a third straight line are parallel to each other.

Exercise Set I

In Exercises 1 through 5, determine which of the given pairs of lines are parallel.

1. $3x + 4y = 5$; $2x - 3y = 4$.
2. $(-2,3)$ and $(1,0)$; $2x + 2y = 14$.
3. $x = 4y + 5$; $2x - 3y = 8$.
4. $m = \frac{2}{3}$ and $(4,5)$; $2x - 3y = 8$.
5. $16x + y + 2 = 0$; $(2,1)$ and $(18,2)$.
6. If $\mathscr{L}_1 \,//\, \mathscr{L}_2$ and $\mathscr{L}_2 \,//\, \mathscr{L}_3$, then is $\mathscr{L}_1 \,//\, \mathscr{L}_3$?
7. If $\mathscr{L}$ is parallel to $3x - 5y + 6 = 0$ and contains the point $(-1,3)$, what is its equation?
8. Show by attempting a solution of the system of equations

$$y = mx + b_1$$
$$y = mx + b_2, \; b_1 \neq b_2$$

   that equations determining parallel lines have no solution.
9. Prove Theorem (6c-1).
10. Prove Theorem (6c-2).
11. Prove Theorem (6c-3).
*12. Prove Theorem (6c-5).
*13. Show, by stating a general argument, that Corollaries (6c-5a), (6c-5b), and (6c-5c) follow directly from Theorem (6c-5).

In the solutions of Exercise 4, Section 6a, and Exercise 5, Section 6b, we find a consistent relationship between the product of the slopes of lines that appear, intuitively, to be "perpendicular." We use the symbol $\perp$ for perpendicular.

Definition (6-c): Two straight lines are **perpendicular** iff the product of their slopes is -1 or one has no slope and the other has slope zero.

Are horizontal and vertical grid loci perpendicular? Recalling Theorem (6a-2) and Corollary (6a-3a), we see that they must be perpendicular. The proof is left to the exercises.

Theorem (6c-7): Each horizontal grid locus is perpendicular to each vertical grid locus and conversely.

The following theorem states the most important fact on the existence of perpendicular lines.

Theorem (6c-8): If $\mathscr{L}$ is a straight line and P is a point, there is exactly one distinct line on P that is perpendicular to $\mathscr{L}$.

PROOF

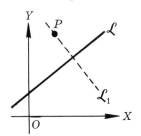

Given: Straight line $\mathscr{L}$ and Cartesian point P.
To Prove: There is exactly one line $\mathscr{L}_1$ on P such that $\mathscr{L}_1 \perp \mathscr{L}$.

Case 1: $\mathscr{L}$ oblique.	
1. $\mathscr{L}$ is an oblique straight line and P is a Cartesian point.	1. Hypothesis
2. $\mathscr{L}$ has slope $m \neq 0$.	2. Theorem (6a-3b)
3. There is an $m' \in \mathscr{R}$ such that $m \cdot m' = -1$.	3. Why?
4. There is exactly one straight line $\mathscr{L}_1$ on P having slope m'.	4. Theorem (6a-4)
5. $\mathscr{L}_1 \perp \mathscr{L}$.	5. Definition (6-d)
Case 2: $\mathscr{L}$ horizontal or vertical.	
1. $\mathscr{L}$ is a grid locus and P is a Cartesian point.	1. Hypothesis
2. There is exactly one horizontal grid locus $\mathscr{L}_1$ on P and exactly one vertical grid locus $\mathscr{L}_2$ on P.	2. Why?
3. $\mathscr{L}_1 \perp \mathscr{L} \vee \mathscr{L}_2 \perp \mathscr{L}$.	3. Why?

Example 2: What is the equation of the line on $(-1,3)$ perpendicular to the line $4x + y + 1 = 0$?

Solution: Theorem (6c-8) guarantees the existence of the required perpendicular line. Writing $4x + y + 1 = 0$ in slope-intercept form, we have $y = -4x - 1$. Therefore $m = -4$. By Definition (6-c), any line perpendicular to it must have slope m' such that $m \cdot m' = -1$. Therefore we have $m'(-4) = -1$ or $m' = \frac{1}{4}$. Now, using the point-slope form for the $\perp$ line, we have $y - 3 = \frac{1}{4}x - (-1)$ or $x - 4y + 13 = 0$, where $(x_1,y_1) = (-1,3)$ and $m' = \frac{1}{4}$.

At this point the reader is asked to renew his acquaintance with Theorem (4h-1).

Since we can easily establish that horizontal and vertical grid loci are perpendicular by using Definition (6-c), we now prove a theorem that restates Theorem (4h-1) in terms of oblique perpendicular lines. As we shall find, this theorem is an extremely important one.

Theorem (6c-9): The square of the distance between two points in

perpendicular, oblique, straight lines is equal to the sum of the squares of
the distance of each point from the point of intersection.

PROOF

Given: Oblique lines $\mathscr{L}_1 \perp \mathscr{L}_2$
on $P(f,g)$ with $Q(h,i) \in \mathscr{L}_1$ and
$R(j,k) \in \mathscr{L}_2$.
To Prove: $(PQ)^2 + (PR)^2 = (QR)^2$.

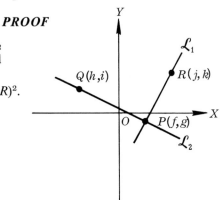

1. Oblique lines $\mathscr{L}_1 \perp \mathscr{L}_2$ at $P(f,g)$, $Q(h,i) \in \mathscr{L}_1$, and $R(j,k) \in \mathscr{L}_2$.	1. Hypothesis
2. Let $\mathscr{L}_1$ have slope m_1 and $\mathscr{L}_2$ have slope m_2.	2. Theorem (6a-3)
3. $m_1 \cdot m_2 = -1$.	3. Why?
4. For $R = P$ or $Q = P$, we have $(PQ)^2 + (PR)^2 = (QR)^2$ immediately.	4. Why?
5. For $R \neq P$ and $Q \neq P$, $h \neq f$ and $j \neq f$.	5. Theorem (5c-6)
6. $\dfrac{i - g}{h - f} \cdot \dfrac{k - g}{j - f} = -1$.	6. Definition (6-a)
7. $(i - g)(k - g) = -(h - f)(j - f)$.	7. Why?
8. $0 = 2fh + 2gi + 2fj + 2gk - 2f^2 - 2g^2 - 2ik - 2hj$.	8. Why?
9. $(PQ) = \sqrt{(h - f)^2 + (i - g)^2}$; $(PR) = \sqrt{(j - f)^2 + (k - g)^2}$; $(QR) = \sqrt{(j - h)^2 + (k - i)^2}$.	9. Why?
10. $(PQ)^2 = h^2 - 2fh + f^2 + i^2 - 2gi + g^2$; $(PR)^2 = j^2 - 2fj + f^2 + k^2 - 2gk + g^2$; $(QR)^2 = j^2 - 2hj + h^2 + k^2 - 2ik + i^2$.	10. Why?

11. $(PQ)^2 + (PR)^2 = j^2 + 2f^2 + 2g^2 + i^2 + h^2 + k^2 - 2fh - 2gi - 2fj - 2gk.$	11. Addition in Step 10
12. $(PQ)^2 + (PR)^2 = j^2 - 2hj + h^2 + k^2 - 2ik - i^2.$	12. Substitution from Step 8 and Step 11
13. $(PQ)^2 + (PR)^2 = (QR)^2.$ Q.E.D.	13. Substitution from Step 10 to Step 12

Some important relationships among intersecting parallel and perpendicular straight lines are given in the following theorems.

Theorem (6c-10): Two straight lines perpendicular to the same straight line on distinct points are parallel.

PROOF

Given: $\mathcal{L}_1 \perp \mathcal{L}_3$ and $\mathcal{L}_2 \perp \mathcal{L}_3$ such that $\mathcal{L}_1 \cap \mathcal{L}_3 \neq \mathcal{L}_2 \cap \mathcal{L}_3$.
To Prove: $\mathcal{L}_1 \parallel \mathcal{L}_2$.

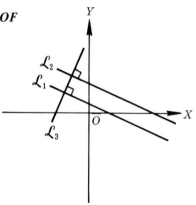

Case 1: $\mathcal{L}_3$ oblique.

1. There are lines $\mathcal{L}_1$, $\mathcal{L}_2$, and $\mathcal{L}_3$ such that $\mathcal{L}_1 \perp \mathcal{L}_3$ and $\mathcal{L}_2 \perp \mathcal{L}_3$ on distinct points.	1. Hypothesis
2. Let slopes of $\mathcal{L}_1, \mathcal{L}_2, \mathcal{L}_3$ be $m_1, m_2, m_3 \neq 0$, respectively.	2. Theorem (6a-3b)
3. $m_1 \cdot m_3 = -1$ and $m_2 \cdot m_3 = -1$.	3. Why?
4. $m_1 \cdot m_3 = m_2 \cdot m_3.$	4. Why?
5. For $m_3 \neq 0$, $m_1 = m_2$.	5. Why?
6. $\mathcal{L}_1 \parallel \mathcal{L}_2.$	6. Why?
7. Case 2: $\mathcal{L}_3$ vertical or horizontal.	7. See Exercise 20, page 116.

Example 3: Straight line $\mathscr{L}_1$ is $\perp$ the line $3x - 7y - 21 = 0$. A line $\mathscr{L}_2$ is $\perp \mathscr{L}_1$ on $(2,3)$. What is the x intercept of $\mathscr{L}_2$?

Solution: We write $3x - 7y - 21 = 0$ in slope-intercept form, getting $y = \frac{3}{7}x - 3$. Thus $m = \frac{3}{7}$. By Theorem (6c-10) the slope of $\mathscr{L}_2$ is $m_2 = \frac{3}{7}$. Using the point-slope form, $m_2 = \frac{3}{7}$, and $(2,3)$, we have $y - 3 = \frac{3}{7}x - 2$. Finding the x intercept, we see that it is $(-5,0)$. As an *alternate method* we could have used Corollary (6b-1c) and written $y = \frac{3}{7}x - a$, where a is the x intercept. Since $(2,3)$ is in the line, this gives $3 = \frac{3}{7}2 - a$ or $a = -5$. (We have worked this example without an illustration. The reader may increase his understanding of the problems involved in finding the solution if he makes a small sketch of the situation.)

Theorem (6c-11): If a straight line is perpendicular to one of two parallel lines, then it is perpendicular to the other also.

PROOF

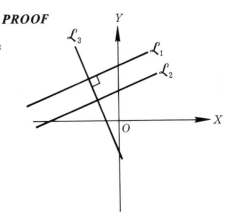

Given: Straight lines $\mathscr{L}_1 /\!/ \mathscr{L}_2$ and $\mathscr{L}_3 \perp \mathscr{L}_1$.
To Prove: $\mathscr{L}_3 \perp \mathscr{L}_2$.

Case 1: $\mathscr{L}_1$ and $\mathscr{L}_2$ have no slope or slope zero.

1. Straight lines $\mathscr{L}_1 /\!/ \mathscr{L}_2$ and $\mathscr{L}_3 \perp \mathscr{L}_1$.	1. Hypothesis
2. $\mathscr{L}_3$ has slope zero or no slope, respectively.	2. Why?
3. $\mathscr{L}_3 \perp \mathscr{L}_2$.	3. Theorem (6c-7)

Case 2: $\mathscr{L}_1$ and $\mathscr{L}_2$ have slopes m_1, m_2.

1. Straight lines $\mathscr{L}_1 /\!/ \mathscr{L}_2$ and $\mathscr{L}_3 \perp \mathscr{L}_1$.	1. Hypothesis
2. $m_1 = m_2$.	2. Why?
3. $m_3 \cdot m_1 = -1$.	3. Why?
4. $m_3 \cdot m_2 = -1$.	4. Why?
5. $\mathscr{L}_3 \perp \mathscr{L}_2$.	5. Definition (6-c)

Theorem (6c-12): If two distinct straight lines are each perpendicular to one of a pair of intersecting straight lines, then they also intersect.

The formal proof is left to the exercises. (Note that there are two cases to consider. Case 1: All lines are oblique. Case 2: One or both given lines are vertical.) Figure 6.8 illustrates the theorem.

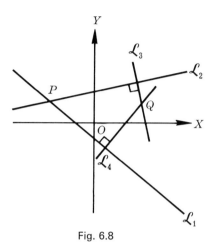

Fig. 6.8

Whenever we say "the distance from a point to a line," we mean the distance along the perpendicular line from the point to the given line.

Theorem (6c-13): Each point in one of two parallel lines is equidistant from the other line.

The proof of this theorem involves only algebraic operations and is left to the exercises. (This theorem is sometimes quoted as "*parallel lines are everywhere equidistant*.")

Exercise Set II

Determine the equations of the lines perpendicular to the given lines and containing the given point.

1. $3x - 5y + 6 = 0$, $(2,0)$.   2. $3x + y = 0$, $(-1,2)$.

3. $x = 5$, $(3,-5)$.   4. $x - y + 1 = 0$, $(0,0)$.

5. $8x + y - 4 = 0$, $(3,2)$.   6. $y = 3$, $(-2,-2)$.

7. What are the equations of lines on $(3,4)$ that are parallel and perpendicular, respectively, to the line $3x - 2y + 1 = 0$?

8. If a line has slope $-\frac{1}{2}$, what is the equation of a line perpendicular to it on $(2,-1)$?

9. If the line $2y - 3x - 1 = 0$ is perpendicular to the line on $(-2,1)$, then what is the equation of a line parallel to the second line that is on $(4,1)$?

10. Supply the missing reasons to justify the corresponding steps in the proof of Theorem (6c-11).

11. Explain why Steps 5 and 6 in the proof of Theorem (6c-11) are impossible if $\mathcal{L}_3$ is horizontal.

12. Write out a formal proof of Theorem (6c-7).

13. Fill in all missing reasons in Theorem (6c-8).

14. Prove Theorem (6c-9) using Corollary (6b-1d).

15. Combine the facts stated in Theorems (4h-1) and (6c-9) into the form of a single statement.

16. Supply the missing reasons in Theorem (6c-9).

17. Verify Theorem (6c-9) by finding the square of the distance between the points (6,6) and $(-4,4)$ on the lines $y - x = 0$ and $y + x = 0$, respectively.

18. Supply the missing reasons in Theorem (6c-10).

19. Explain why the proof given for Case 1 of Theorem (6c-10) would be completely impossible if $\mathcal{L}_3$ were horizontal.

*20. Write out a proof for Case 2 of Theorem (6c-10).

*21. Prove Case 1 and Case 2 of Theorem (6c-12).

*22. Show that if (x,y) is any of the points in the intersection of mutually perpendicular lines on (j,k) and (f,g), then $(y - k)(y - 9) + (x - j)(x - f) = 0$.

*23. Explain why going from Step 5 to Step 6 in the proof of Theorem (6c-11) is justifiable.

*24. Prove Theorem (6c-13).

6d   Betweenness

It is often important to be able to make a specific determination of where a point is located relative to the other points in a line by means other than the use of coordinates.   Consider an angle, as in Fig. 6.9, for example.   It

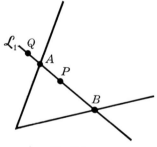

Fig. 6.9

seems obvious from the drawing that P is *interior* to the angle and Q is *exterior* to the angle. But a drawing is not a mathematical device. What do we mean by exterior or interior anyway? The terms have not been defined. We now set ourselves to the task of creating a mathematical concept that will enable us to define such terms.

If we construct a line such as $\mathscr{L}_1$, which contains P and Q and intersects the sides of the angle on A and B, we might say that P is *between* A and B. This seems like a reasonable way to make a distinction provided we have a mathematical criterion for *between*.

Consider the straight line $\mathscr{L}$ in Fig. 6.10. The distances (OA), (OB), and

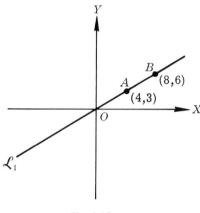

Fig. 6.10

(AB) are respectively 5, 10, and 5. Why? We note that $(OA) + (AB) = (OB)$. This looks like a reasonable relation to use in specifying *between* for points in a line, that is, for *collinear* points.

Definition (6-d): For distinct collinear points P, Q, and R, Q is between P and R (written $\overline{PQR}$) iff $(PQ) + (QR) = (PR)$.

The following theorems deal with the concept of betweenness. These theorems are important properties of *betweenness* and the student should study them carefully. However, the proofs of these theorems require mathematics that is not within the scope of this course. We have included the proof of Theorem (6d-1) in the Appendix to illustrate the general nature of these proofs.

Theorem (6d-1): For any two distinct points in a line $\mathscr{L}$, there is at least one point in $\mathscr{L}$ between the two given points.

Theorem (6d-2): For any two distinct points P and Q in a line $\mathscr{L}$, there is a point R such that $\overline{PQR}$.

Theorem (6d-3):   If $\overline{PQR}$, then $\overline{RQP}$.

Theorem (6d-4):   If three distinct points are in a straight line, then exactly one of them is between the other two.

The various *betweenness* properties make it possible to state some useful definitions.   In addition, we restate Definition (5-n) as promised.

Definition (6-e):   A point A is on **the opposite side of a line** $\mathscr{L}$ from a point B iff for some point $C \in \mathscr{L}$, $\overline{ACB}$.

Definition (6-f):   Points A and B are on the **same side** of a line $\mathscr{L}$ iff $AB \cap \mathscr{L} = \emptyset$.

In considering the following definitions, the reader will want to recall Definition (5-k) very carefully.   Note that rays $\overrightarrow{AB}$ and $\overrightarrow{AC}$ of $\overrightarrow{AB} \cup \overrightarrow{AC}$ could be subsets of the same line.   Such angles have properties not found in other angles and thus must be excluded from the following definitions.

Definition (6-g):   For any angle α whose sides are not subsets of the same line, a point **P is interior** to α iff some line on P intersects the sides of α in distinct points A and B such that $\overline{APB}$.   (See Fig. 6.11.)

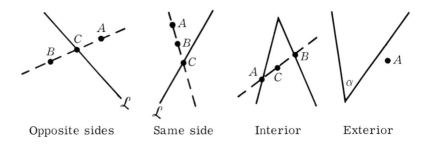

Opposite sides   Same side   Interior   Exterior

Fig. 6.11

Definition (6-h):   For any angle α whose sides are not subsets of the same line, a point **P is exterior** to α iff it is neither in the angle nor interior to the angle.

Definition (5-n) (Restatement):   Two angles are **adjacent** iff they have the same vertex and a pair of coincident sides and the intersection of their interiors is the null set.

For example, $\sphericalangle ABD$ and $\sphericalangle DBC$ are not adjacent in Fig. 6.12.   In Fig. 6.13 they are adjacent.   In Fig. 6.12 P is not interior to $\sphericalangle ABC$.   In Fig. 6.13 P is interior to $\sphericalangle ABC$.

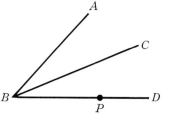

Fig. 6.12

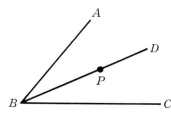

Fig. 6.13

Exercise Set

1. Why was the requirement "distinct" included in Definition (6-e)?

2. Show that if $\overline{ABC}$ and $\overline{BCD}$, then $\overline{ABD}$ and $\overline{ACD}$.

For each of the following sets of three points, determine (a) whether $\overline{PQR}$, (b) the slope of the lines, and (c) the equation of the line. [*Hint:* If $\overline{PQR}$ is not true, then there will be three results to each of parts (b) and (c).]

3. $P(-2,-1)$, $Q(1,3)$, $R(7,11)$.

4. $P(-2,-1)$, $Q(1,4)$, $R(7,11)$.

5. $P(-4,-1)$, $Q(0,2)$, $R(8,5)$.

Find the missing coordinates so that point C is between points A and B.

6. $A(-3,1)$, $B(6,4)$, $C(3,y)$.

7. $A(0,3)$, $B(0,-18)$, $C(x,-4)$.

8. $A(1,1)$, $B(-4,-4)$, $C(x,0)$.

*9. Find the equations of three lines such that a point Q is interior to three of the angles determined by the lines but exterior to nine other angles determined by the lines.

*10. Show that if $P(a,b) \neq Q(c,d)$, then the point $R[(a + c)/2, (b + d)/2]$ is such that $\overline{PRQ}$.

6e Line Segments

In Definition (5-i) we defined a ray as a subset of the set of points determined by the straight-line equation $px + qy + r = 0$. We now define another subset of that straight-line locus.

Definition (6-i): A **line segment** is a subset AB of a line $\overleftrightarrow{AB}$ that contains A,B and all points between A and B.

In Fig. 6.14, if $\mathscr{L}$ is a straight line and $A,B \in \mathscr{L}$, then the line segment $AB = \{A,B\} \cup \{P \mid \overline{APB}\}$.

Definition (6-j):   The points A and B of Definition (6-i) are called the **endpoints** of the line segment.

Definition (5-i) (Restatement):   A **ray** is a subset of a line $\mathscr{L}$ given by $AB \cup \{P \mid P \in \mathscr{L} \text{ and } \overline{ABP}\}$.   (Here A is the endpoint.)

This statement repeats what our original statement said in coordinate terms.   In Fig. 6.15 points $A,B,P \in \mathscr{L}$ are so related that $\overline{ABP}$ is true.

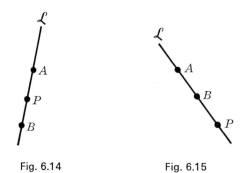

Fig. 6.14   Fig. 6.15

Certainly, then, the union of the subset AB of $\mathscr{L}$ and all such points $P \in \mathscr{L}$ is what we mean by a ray with endpoint A.

At this point in the development of line segments, it is worthwhile to recall a previous theorem.

Theorem (6a-1):   Any two points in a nonvertical straight line determine a unique slope m.

Since we have defined a line segment in terms of two points in a line, and since all our slope theorems depend on Theorem (6a-1), all the slope properties of straight lines *must apply* to line segments as well.

In fact, that two distinct points determine a line segment gives us a chance to associate a particular real number (besides slope) with a line segment. Recall that our distance function is defined in terms of two points in the plane.   We can make our line segments into models of the *straight* sticks or rods of the physical world by associating *length* with the distance between the endpoints.

Definition (6-k):   The **length** of a line segment is the distance between its endpoints.

If line segment AB has length 5, we shall also call 5 the **measure** of AB and write $(AB) = 5$.

According to Definition (4-1) this is an *unscaled* real number length.   By the choice of particular units of measurement and a scale constant telling the number of such units to be associated with each integral unit of unscaled length, we can convert our *length* for use with problems involving particular measurements.

Example 1: What length in feet does the line segment in Fig. 6.16 represent if 3 feet are represented by one unscaled unit?

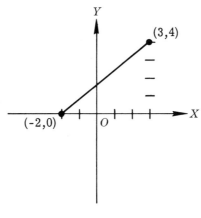

Fig. 6.16

Solution: Since the coordinates of the endpoints are $(3,4)$ and $(-2,0)$, we have $d = \sqrt{(-2-3)^2 + (0-4)^2}$ or $d = \sqrt{41}$. The scaled length in feet is $f = kd = 3\sqrt{41}$.

We now introduce a concept of equivalence that allows us to relate two geometric models in a way that differs from that of equality. We shall, in fact, *never* use *equals* for any other objects besides sets or numbers. The relationship called *congruence* allows us to compare line segments that "look alike" but that are not necessarily coincident.

Definition (6-l): Two **line segments are congruent** ($\cong$) iff their lengths are equal.

Example 2: Are the line segments AB and $OC \cong$ if $A = (-7,-9)$, $B = (-6,-8)$, $C = (0,-\sqrt{2})$ and $O = (0,0)$?

Solution: By Definition (4-1), $(AB) = \sqrt{[-6-(-7)]^2 + [-8-(-9)]^2}$ or $(AB) = \sqrt{2}$; $(OC) = \sqrt{(0,0)^2 + [0-(-2)]^2} = \sqrt{2}$. Therefore $(AB) = (OC)$, and by Definition (6-l) $AB \cong OC$. Note that it makes absolutely no sense to say that AB and OC are equal. *Line segments are not numbers!* Number equality simply does not apply. They are indeed sets, but clearly in this example $AB \cap OC = \emptyset$; so they certainly are not equal sets.

We have defined congruence in terms of a real number.   Each definition of congruence that we make actually will depend on a real number relationship.   Since Axiom E-3 states that the real numbers are transitive, then the concept of congruence must also be transitive.

In Example 2 we saw that two different line segments had equal lengths. Suppose, however, that we were given only one line segment AB such that $(AB) = 4$.   Are there any other line segments in the plane with length 4 and endpoints different from A and B?   Clearly, we would say yes.   This concept of having another line segment in some different position from AB, yet having the important properties of AB, is called *positional equivalence*.

Since we want the proofs of our theorems to be general in nature, we have not previously been able to take advantage of some of the characteristics of our coordinate system.   Primarily, the concept of positional equivalence will allow us to choose coordinates and positions on the Cartesian plane that will result in a good deal of algebraic simplification.   It can be shown, although we will not do it here, that whatever theorem we prove using positional equivalence to gain a simplified proof is also true in *any other* position in the plane.   The proof of Theorem (6e-4) uses this concept. (See Exercise 9.)   The following theorem states this principle for line segments.

Theorem (6e-1):   For any line segment and for any point in any line, there is a line segment in the given line that has the given point as one of its endpoints and is congruent to the given line segment.

The proof of this theorem can be found in the Appendix.

The following corollary to a theorem not given here is stated without proof.   The discussion and theorems leading to its proof can be found in the Appendix under the title of *Axial Projections.**

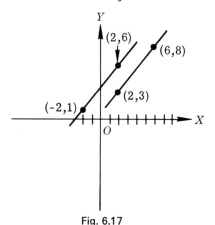

Fig. 6.17

* The theorem numbers are listed in such a way that this section can be included in the material at this point.

Corollary (6e-2a):   If congruent line segments have equal slopes or no slopes, then the differences of their abscissas (ordinates) taken in their same order are equal.

Figure 6.17 illustrates this corollary.

Another useful concept when working with line segments is that of *midpoint*. The meaning that we attach to this term is what our intuition tells us it should be. Certainly the number $(AB)/2$ is a unique real number for any (AB). Therefore we may talk about the point that produces such a division.

Definition (6-n):   The point P in the line segment AB that determines two congruent segments AP and PB is called the **midpoint** of AB.

The actual coordinates of the midpoint of a line segment are established in the following theorem.   The proof of the converse is left for the exercises.

Theorem (6e-3):   The coordinates of the point P in the line segment AB determined by $A(a,b)$ and $B(c,f)$ are $x = (a + c)/2$ and $y = (b + f)/2$ iff P is the midpoint of AB.

PROOF

Given: (Positive): $P(x,y)$ the midpoint of AB where $A = (a,b)$ and $B = (c,f)$.
To Prove: $P(x,y) = [(a + c)/2, (b + f)/2]$.

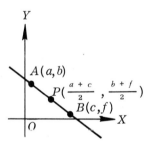

1. $P(x,y)$ is the midpoint of AB, where $A = (a,b)$ and $B = (c,f)$.	1. Hypothesis
2. $AP \cong PB$.	2. Why?
3. $m_{AP} = m_{PB}$ or each has no slope.	3. Theorem (6a-1) or (6a-2)
4. $x - a = c - x$ and $y - b = f - y$.	4. Corollary (6e-2a)
5. $x = \dfrac{a + c}{2}, y = \dfrac{b + f}{2}.$	5. Properties of $\mathcal{R}$

If a line segment AB has midpoint C, certainly there is a line that intersects AB on C. Thus the following definition is appropriate.

Definition (6-o):   A line that intersects a line segment on its midpoint is called a **bisector** of the line segment.

If the bisector is also perpendicular to the line segment, then we shall call it the **perpendicular bisector** of the line segment.

Example 3:   What is the midpoint of the line segment whose endpoints are (3,6) and (−7,6)?

Solution: By Theorem (6e-3) the midpoint formula is

$$x = \frac{3 + (-7)}{2}, \qquad y = \frac{6 + 6}{2}.$$

Thus the coordinates of the point are (−2,6).

Example 4:   Is the line $y = 3$ a bisector of the line segment whose endpoints are (−2,6) and (6,0)?   Is it a perpendicular bisector?

Solution: By Theorem (6e-3) the midpoint formula is

$$x = \frac{-2 + 6}{2}, \qquad y = \frac{6 + 0}{2}.$$

Thus the midpoint is (2,3).   Testing this point in the equation $y = 3$, we have

$$3 = 3.$$

Thus the line lies on the point and is a bisector of the line segment.   Since the slope of $y = 3$ is $m = 0$ and the slope of the line segments is $(6 - 0)/(-2 - 6) = \frac{3}{4}$, we see that $y = 3$ is *not* a perpendicular bisector.

The following theorem establishes a particular type of bisector of a line segment.   The proof is carried out for the line segment that is in the most advantageous position in the coordinate plane.   The principle of positional equivalence then assures us that other line segments would have the same property.

Theorem (6e-4):   A locus of points is equidistant from two given points iff it is the perpendicular bisector of the line segment determined by the two points.

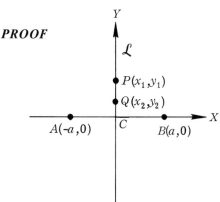

PROOF

Given (Converse):
Points $A(-a,0)$ and $B(a,0)$ determining line segment AB and locus $\mathcal{L}$ containing points $P(x_1,y_1)$, $Q(x_2,y_2)$, each equidistant from A and B.

To Prove: $\mathcal{L}$ is the perpendicular bisector of AB.

1. The endpoints $A(-a,0)$ and $B(a,0)$ of line segment AB are equidistant from points $P(x_1,y_1)$ and $R(x_2,y_2)$ in a locus $\mathscr{L}$.	1. Hypothesis
2. $\sqrt{(-a-x_1)^2-y_1^2} = \sqrt{(a-x_1)^2+y_1^2}$; also $\sqrt{(-a-x_2)^2+y_2^2} = \sqrt{(a-x_2)^2+y_2^2}$.	2. Definition (4-k)
3. $x_1 = 0$; also $x_2 = 0$.	3. Properties of R from Step 2
4. $\mathscr{L}$ is the vertical straight line $\{(x,y) \mid x = 0\}$.	4. Why?
5. AB is the horizontal straight line $\{(x,y) \mid y = 0\}$.	5. Why?
6. $\therefore \mathscr{L} \perp AB$.	6. Why?
7. $\mathscr{L}$ intersects AB at $C = (0,0)$.	7. Why?
8. $\dfrac{-a+a}{2} = 0$ and $\dfrac{0+0}{2} = 0$.	8. Why?
9. C is the midpoint of AB.	9. Why?
10. $AC \cong BC$.	10. Why?
11. $\therefore \mathscr{L}$ is the $\perp$ bisector of AB.	11. Why?

The proof of the positive form is left to the exercises.

Exercise Set

Locate the midpoints of the line segments whose endpoints are given in Exercises 1 through 6.

1. $(-1,7)$, $(3,-2)$.

2. $(6,9)$, $(-4,1)$.

3. $(0,0)$, $(6,-2)$.

4. $(8,-7)$, $(-1,2)$.

5. $(-1,-1)$, $(2,2)$.

6. $(-2,2)$, $(2,-2)$.

7. Determine the equations of the perpendicular bisectors of the line segments of Exercises 1 through 6.

8. What kind of locus is the set $\overleftrightarrow{PQ} \cap \overleftrightarrow{PQ}$ for any $\overleftrightarrow{PQ}$?

9. Reprove Theorem (6e-3) using positional equivalence in that points A and B are placed on the coordinate axes.

10. The midpoint of the line segment PQ is $(-4,4)$. If $P = (-8,5)$, find the coordinates of Q.

11. The equation of a line is $3x - 5y + 7 = 0$. If PQ is a line segment in the given line and if the abscissa of P is 2 and the ordinate of Q is -9, find the midpoint of PQ.

12. Consider the points $A(0,0)$, $B(4,0)$, $C(2,2)$. Find the slopes and midpoints of AB, AC, BC. Then find the slopes, if any, of the line segments joining the midpoints. What conclusion might you draw?

*13. Prove the converse of Theorem (6e-3).

*14. Complete the proof of the converse of Theorem (6e-4).

*15. Prove the positive of Theorem (6e-4).

*16. Using the theorems and definitions of axial projections that are in the Appendix, prove Corollary (6e-2a).

6f   Figures Determined by Line Segments

Many of the loci that are most important in geometry are made up of line segments joined together in some particular way. We shall often term a locus composed of several distinct loci a **figure**. When each of the intersections of several line segments contains only the endpoints of exactly two line segments and when each endpoint is an element of a nonempty intersection, we have a figure called a **polygon**. We also refer to this situation as determining a **closed figure**. (In Section 11a we make a formal definition of a polygon.)

In the three figures of Fig. 6.18 only (b) represents a polygon. The most

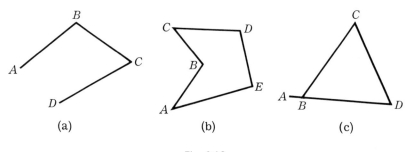

(a)   (b)   (c)

Fig. 6.18

important polygon for our use is the triangle. As the prefix *tri* indicates, a triangle is a polygon determined by exactly three line segments.

Definition (6-p):   A **triangle** is a set of any three noncollinear points and the line segments determined by each pair of these points.

Definition (6-q):   Each of the line segments of Definition (6-p) is called a **side** of the triangle.

Definition (6-r):   Each of the points of Definition (6-p) is called a **vertex** of the triangle.

Remembering that each side is only a subset of a straight line or ray, each nonvertical side must have a slope.   Obviously, each side has a length.   In addition, each pair of sides determines an angle with the vertex of the triangle becoming the vertex of the angle.   In Fig. 6.19, a triangle ABC is determined

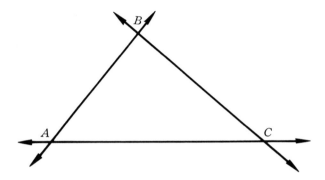

Fig. 6.19

by line segments AB, BC, and AC.   (A triangle will be named by its vertices. We use the notation triangle ABC or $\triangle ABC$.)   These line segments are contained in the lines $\overleftrightarrow{AB}$, $\overleftrightarrow{BC}$, and $\overleftrightarrow{AC}$.   Note the angles that are formed. The angles $\sphericalangle ABC$, $\sphericalangle BCA$, and $\sphericalangle CAB$ have a special name.

Definition (6-s):   An **interior angle** of a triangle is that angle determined by two sides and a vertex of the triangle such that points in the third side of the triangle are interior to the angle.

Definition (6-t):   An angle whose vertex is a vertex of a triangle and that is adjacent to an interior angle of the triangle is called an **exterior angle** of the triangle.

Exercise Set

1. Explain why (a) and (c) of Fig. 6.18 do not represent polygons.
2. Find the midpoints and slopes of the sides of a triangle whose vertices are (2,6), (2,7), and (7,2).
3. Find each axial length projection of each side in the triangle of Exercise 2.
4. In Fig. 6.20, list the interior and exterior angles determined by triangle PQR.

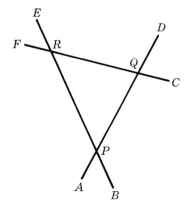

Fig. 6.20

*5. In Exercise 2, find the length of the line segments joining the midpoints and compare these with the lengths of the sides of the triangle.   Can you reach any conclusion concerning these line segments?

6. Does Definition (6-f) implicitly require the points to be distinct?   Explain.

chapter 7

Circles

7a Circles and Straight Lines

In Chapter 5 we defined the locus $\{(x,y) \mid (x - h)^2 + (y + k)^2 = a^2\}$, where a,h,k are real constants and $a > 0$, as a circle. [See Definition (5-g).] Graphically, if we locate these (x,y) on the Cartesian plane, we obtain what is intuitively thought of as a circle. We also defined (h,k) as the center of the circle. We now make additional definitions concerning circles.

Definition (7-a): A line segment having one endpoint the center of a circle and the other endpoint an element of the circle is a **radius** of the circle.

In Chapter 5 we learned that, for the circle $(x - h)^2 + (y - k)^2 = a^2$, a is the distance between the center of the circle and any point in the circle. In Chapter 6 we defined the length of a line segment to be the distance between its endpoints. Hence "a" is now the length of the radius of any circle $(x - h)^2 + (y - k)^2 = a^2$.

Definition (7-b): A line that intersects a circle at two distinct points is a **secant**.

Definition (7-c): A line that intersects a circle at exactly one point is a **tangent**.

Definition (7-d): A line segment that has both of its endpoints in a circle is a **chord**.

Definition (7-e): A chord containing the center of a circle is a **diameter**.

In Fig. 7.1 we have a circle with center P, diameter AB, secant $\mathscr{L}_1$, tangent $\mathscr{L}_2$, and chord BC.

With these definitions as the foundation, we shall prove some relations among circles, circles and lines, and radii and chords, using basically algebraic techniques.

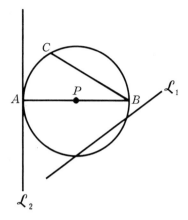

Fig. 7.1

These techniques are reviewed in the next three examples.

Example 1: Find

$$A = \{(x,y) \mid (x - 1)^2 + (y - 1)^2 = 4\}$$
$$\cap \{(x,y) \mid (x - 2)^2 + (y - 1)^2 = 5\}.$$

Solution: We use the method of substitution. Solving the first equation for $(y - 1)^2$, we have

$$(y - 1)^2 = 4 - (x - 1)^2.$$

Substituting this into the second equation for $(y - 1)^2$, we obtain

$$(x - 2)^2 + 4 - (x - 1)^2 = 8.$$

Simplifying leads to the compact sentence

$$-2x = -2$$
$$x = 1.$$

Letting $x = 1$ in the first equation, we have

$$(y - 1)^2 = 4 - (1 - 1)^2$$
$$= 4.$$

At this point we can expand $(y - 1)^2$ and use the quadratic formula or factor, or we can take the square root of both members. Doing the latter, we obtain

$$|y - 1| = 2$$
$$y - 1 = \pm 2$$
$$y = -1$$
$$y = 3.$$

Thus the set A becomes $\{(1, -1), (1,3)\}$.

Example 2: Find

$$A = \{(x,y) \mid (x - 1)^2 + (y - 2)^2 = 8\} \cap \{(x,y) \mid x + y - 3 = 0\}.$$

Solution: We will use the method of substitution. Solving the second equation for x, we obtain

$$x = 3 - y.$$

Substituting this value for x in the first equation yields

$$(3 - y - 1)^2 + (y - 2)^2 = 8$$
$$(2 - y)^2 + (y - 2)^2 = 8.$$

Simplifying reduces this to the form

$$2y^2 - 8y = 0$$
$$y^2 - 4y = 0.$$

We can now either factor or use the quadratic formula. Since it factors easily, we use that method and obtain

$$y(y - 4) = 0$$
$$y = 0$$
$$y = 4.$$

Since these solutions are different, we take each one and substitute it into the first equation. That is,

$$x + (0) - 3 = 0 \quad \text{or} \quad x + (4) - 3 = 0$$
$$x = 3 \qquad\qquad\qquad x = -1.$$

Thus the set $A = \{(3,0), (-1,4)\}$.

Example 3: Solve the quadratic equation $4x^2 + 3x - 1 = 0$.

Solution: We recall from our algebra that the quadratic formula is given by

$$x = \frac{-b \pm \sqrt{b^2 - 4ac}}{2a},$$

where $ax^2 + bx + c = 0$. Furthermore, we remember that $b^2 - 4ac$ is called the **discriminant**, for it determines what type of solution we obtain. Since the trichotomy law (R-13) holds for $b^2 - 4ac$, we have one and only one of the following:

(1) $$b^2 - 4ac > 0;$$

(2) $$b^2 - 4ac < 0;$$

(3) $$b^2 - 4ac = 0.$$

If either (1) or (3) is true, then the quadratic equation will have a real number solution.   If (1) holds, then there will be two distinct solutions.   If (3) holds, then there will be one solution of multiplicity two.   (The multiplicity of two comes from the concept that we want every quadratic equation to have *two* solutions.)   If (2) is true, then there will be *no* real solutions, for we will have the square root of a negative number.   We now solve our equation using the quadratic formula.

$$x = \frac{-(3) \pm \sqrt{9 - 4(4)(-1)}}{2(4)}$$

$$= \frac{-3 \pm \sqrt{9 + 16}}{8}.$$

Since $b^2 - 4ac = 9 + 16$, which is greater than zero, the discriminant tells us that we should get two real distinct solutions.

$$x = \frac{-3 \pm \sqrt{25}}{8},$$

which simplifies to

$$x = -\frac{1}{4}$$

$$= +1.$$

In many of our applications we are only concerned as to whether we have a solution or not.   We need only check the discriminant to determine this. If we keep this concept in mind, it will save us considerable work later on.

Consider a circle

(4) $$(x - h)^2 + (y - k)^2 = a^2$$

and grid loci

(5) $$x = h$$

(6) $$y = k.$$

Solving (4) and (6) simultaneously, we have

(7) $$(x - h)^2 + (k - k)^2 = a^2$$

$$(x - h)^2 = a^2$$

(8) $$x = h + a \quad \text{or} \quad h - a.$$

Solving (4) and (5) simultaneously, we easily have

(9) $$y = k + a \quad \text{or} \quad k - a.$$

From (6) and (8) we have points of intersection $(h + a, k)$ and $(h - a, k)$. Furthermore, from (5) and (9), we have points of intersection $(h, k + a)$ and $(h, k - a)$.

Figure 7.2 illustrates the results of this development.   This leads directly to the following theorem.

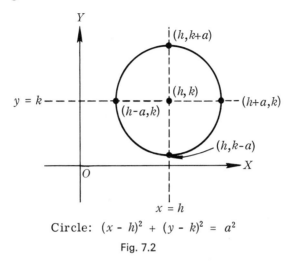

Circle: $(x - h)^2 + (y - k)^2 = a^2$

Fig. 7.2

Theorem (7a-1):   Any circle with center (h,k) intersects grid loci $y = k$ and $x = h$ at points $(h + a, k)$, $(h - a, k)$ and $(h, k + a)$, $(h, k - a)$, respectively.

The proof of the next theorem resembles the proof of Theorem (7a-1) and is left to the exercises.   Figure 7.2 illustrates the theorem.   Note that the theorem states that the line does intersect the circle.

Theorem (7a-2):   If a straight line $px + qy + r = 0$ intersects a circle $(x - h)^2 + (y - k)^2 = a^2$, then there are points (x_1,y_1) and (x_2,y_2) that satisfy both equations.

In Fig. 7.3 we see that if (x_1,y_1) and (x_2,y_2) are distinct, then the line is a secant.   In Fig. 7.4, however, $(x_1,y_1) = (x_2,y_2)$.   Thus the line, by Definition (7-c), is a tangent.

In Example 3 we discussed the discriminant of a quadratic equation. We now put these ideas to work!

The fact that we represent a straight line $\mathscr{L}$ as intersecting a circle on two points, as in Figs. 7.3 or 7.4, does not give us the right to assume that the intersection actually exists.   We must provide some proof.   Remembering that the points (x_1,y_1) and (x_2,y_2) exist only if the intersection is given, we are now concerned that there is such an intersection.

Consider a circle determined by

(10) $$(x - h)^2 + (y - k)^2 = d^2$$

and any line

(11) $$px + qy + r = 0.$$

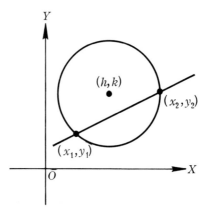

Fig. 7.3

Solving (10) and (11) simultaneously, we have

(12) $(q^2 + p^2)x^2 + (2kpq + 2pr - 2hq^2)x$
$$+ (h^2q^2 + r^2 + 2kqr + k^2q^2 - d^2q^2) = 0, \qquad q \neq 0.$$

Letting the coefficient of x^2 be a, the coefficient of x be b, and the constant term c, we may rewrite (12) as

$$ax^2 + bx + c = 0.$$

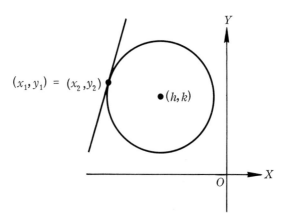

Fig. 7.4

This is a quadratic equation that requires two solutions.   If the discriminant $b^2 - 4ac = 0$, we have one real root of multiplicity two; that is, $(x_1, y_1) = (x_2, y_2)$ and the line is a tangent.   If $b^2 - 4ac > 0$, we have two real distinct roots; that is, $(x_1, y_1) \neq (x_2, y_2)$ and the line is a secant.   If $b^2 - 4ac < 0$, we have no real solutions.   This discussion leads to the following theorem.

Theorem (7a-3): A straight line intersects a circle on at most two points.

In the foregoing argument we required that $q \neq 0$. We leave the case for $q = 0$ to the exercises. Another theorem that is easily shown to be true by algebraic methods is

Theorem (7a-4): Any straight line on the center of a circle intersects the circle at exactly two distinct points.

Exercise Set

If the following equations are the result of solving a straight-line equation simultaneously with the equation of a circle, determine whether the straight line is a secant, a tangent, or does not intersect at all.

1. $3x^2 + 4x + 5 = 0$.
2. $y^2 - y + 1 = 0$.
3. $13x^2 + x - 1 = 0$.
4. $y^2 - 3y - 1 = 0$.
5. $y^2 + 2y + 1 = 0$.
6. $4x^2 - 8x - 4 = 0$.

What is the length of the radius and coordinates of the center of the following circles.

7. $x^2 + y^2 = 1$.
8. $(x - 1)^2 + y^2 = 4$.
9. $(x - 2)^2 + (y + 1)^2 = 9$.
10. $x^2 + 2x + 1 + y^2 - 2 = 0$.
11. $y^2 = 16 - x^2$.
12. $(x - 3)^2 + (y - 4)^2 - 8 = 0$.

13. Prove Theorem (7a-2).

14. Prove Theorem (7a-4).

15. Prove that a diameter of a circle includes two radii of the circle.

16. Complete Theorem (7a-3) for the case $q = 0$.

*17. Is there any relationship between the slope of a line, which contains a radius of a circle, and a tangent to the circle at the endpoint of the radius?

*18. How many radii are determined by a given circle?

*19. Show that there is no circle on points $(2,2)$, $(0,1)$, and $(-4, -1)$ by showing that it is impossible to solve for the required real numbers h,k, and a.

Which of the following straight lines intersect the given circle? If they do intersect the circle, identify them as to type.

*20. $x = y; x^2 + y^2 = 4$.

*21. $x - y = 1; x^2 + 2x + y^2 = 3$.

*22. $x - 4 = y; x^2 = 1 - y^2$.

*23. $\frac{1}{2}x - y = 4; (x - 4)^2 + (y + 2)^2 = 9$.

7b Chords, Diameters, and Angles

In Fig. 7.5, we remember from the definitions of Section 7a that if O is the center of a circle, then AB is a secant, CD is a diameter, OE is a radius, and

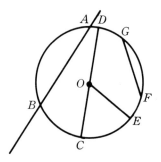

Fig. 7.5

FG is a chord.   Yet it also appears from the figure that OC and OD are radii.   Since our graph does not provide us with anything but a model, we prove the following statement.   (Note that this is another existence theorem.)

Theorem (7b-1):   There is a radius containing the center of the circle and any point in the circle.

PROOF

Given any point P in a circle, we know by Theorem (5c-3) there is a straight line on P and on the center O of the circle.   Since $a \neq 0$ in Definition (5-g), then P and O are distinct; hence PO is a line segment by Definition (6-i) and is the required radius by Definition (7-a).

Looking at Fig. 7.5 again, we now know that OC and OD are radii.   But COD is also a diameter.   Can we conclude that the measure of a diameter is twice the measure of a radius in a given circle?   Yes, we can.   Why?

Example 1:   If the circle $(x - 2)^2 + (y - 1)^2 = 1$ has diameter AB such that $A = (2,2)$ and $B = (0,2)$, find the length of the radius and the length of AB.   Compare the results.

Solution: The length of the radius is $\sqrt{1} = 1$.   The length of AB is

$$(AB) = \sqrt{(2 - 0)^2 + (2 - 2)^2}$$
$$= \sqrt{4}$$
$$= 2.$$

We see that (AB) is twice the length of the radius.

We conclude, then, that for any circle *the measure of the diameter is twice the measure of the radius.*

The next theorem uses the fact that a circle is a locus of points and that a radius is a line segment.   The proof is left to the exercises.

Theorem (7b-2):   A circle with its center at the intersection of n straight lines determines $2n$ radii of the given circle.

We introduce still another existence theorem.   It is easily established, for it depends only on the existence of the real numbers.   It can also be proved by using Theorem (5d-1).

Theorem (7b-3):   Given any Cartesian point and any line segment, there is a circle having that point as center and having a radius of length equal to the length of the given line segment.

Example 2:   Find a circle with center $P(2,-1)$ and having a radius PQ of length equal to that of AB, where $(AB) = 4$.

Solution: The locus of a circle is given by

$$(x - h)^2 + (y - k)^2 = a^2,$$

where (h,k) is the center and a is the length of the radius.   Hence $(h,k) = (2,-1)$ and $a = 4$.   Thus we have

$$(x - 2)^2 + (y + 1)^2 = 16$$

as the required circle.

The formal proof of Theorem (7b-3) is, again, left to the exercises.

If there are two points, say $A(a,b)$ and $B(c,d)$, such that A and B are in a circle $(x - h)^2 + (y - k)^2 = r^2$, then we have

(1) $$(a - h)^2 + (b - k)^2 = r^2$$

(2) $$(c - h)^2 + (d - k)^2 = r^2.$$

Setting (1) and (2) equal to each other, we obtain

(3) $$(a - h)^2 + (b - k)^2 = (c - h)^2 + (d - k)^2.$$

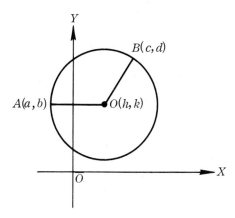

Fig. 7.6

Referring to Fig. 7.6, we use Definition (4-1) and have

(4) $$(OA)^2 = (a - h)^2 + (b - k)^2$$

(5) $$(OB)^2 = (c - h)^2 + d - k)^2.$$

Step (3) allows us to write (4) and (5) as

(6) $$(OA)^2 = (OB)^2$$

(7) $$(OA) = (OB).$$

Using Definition (6-1) with Step (7), we have

(8) $$OA \cong OB$$

We restate this argument as the following proposition.

Theorem (7b-4):   All radii of the same circle are congruent.

We now look for relationships between chords and radii.   We first carefully graph a circle, say

(9) $$(x - 2)^2 + (y - 2)^2 = 8,$$

as in Fig. 7.7.

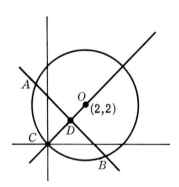

Fig. 7.7

We then graph two mutually perpendicular lines, say

(10) $$\mathcal{L}_1: \quad x + y = 2$$

(11) $$\mathcal{L}_2: \quad x - y = 0,$$

such that both intersect the circle and that (11) is on the center of the circle. Using the points indicated, we find the coordinates of points A, D, and B by finding the points of intersection of the given loci.   (The actual algebraic steps are left to the exercises.)   We then find (AD) and (DB) and conclude that

(12) $$(AD) = (DB)$$

and thus we have

(13) $$AD \cong DB.$$

The result (13) leads us to the following theorem. We provide a formal proof using our previous definitions and theorems. [Note that the proof is different from the methods we used to obtain (1).]

We shall adopt the notation (A,AB) as meaning "circle with center A and radius AB."

Theorem (7b-5): A radius of a circle bisects a chord iff it is perpendicular to the chord.

PROOF

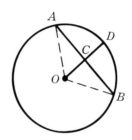

Given (Positive): (O,OD) with chord AB such that $AB \perp OD$.
To Prove: OD bisects AB.

1. There is a (O,OD) with chord AB such that $AB \perp OD$ at C.	1. Hypothesis
2. There are radii OA and OB.	2. Why?
3. $OA \cong OB$.	3. Why?
4. $(OA) = (OB)$.	4. Definition (6-1)
5. $(OA)^2 = (OC)^2 + (AC)^2$ and $(OB)^2 = (OC)^2 + (BC)^2$.	5. Theorem (6c-9)
6. $(OC)^2 + (AC)^2 = (OC)^2 + (BC)^2$.	6. Why?
7. $(AC)^2 = (BC)^2$.	7. Properties of $\mathscr{R}$
8. $(AC) = (BC)$.	8. Why?
9. $AC \cong BC$.	9. Why?
10. OD bisects AB.	10. Definition (6-o)

The converse case is left to the exercises.

In Chapter 5 a definition of angles was discussed. This definition is clearly satisfied if we use the center of a circle as the vertex and the radii as subsets of the sides.

Definition (7-f): Any angle whose sides each include a radius of a circle and whose vertex is the center of the circle is called a **central angle.**

Figure 7.8 illustrates this definition. Figure 7.9 illustrates the following one. Note in both cases that the sides of the angles intersect the circle.

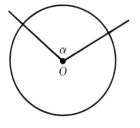
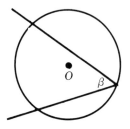

Fig. 7.8   Fig. 7.9

Definition (7-g):   An angle whose sides each include a chord of a circle and whose vertex is in the circle is called an **inscribed angle**.

These are reasonable definitions, for we know chords and radii exist for any given circle.

We shall now prove Theorem (5d-3) as promised in Section 5d.   The proof is a direct application of previous theorems and definitions.   The student should rewrite the proof in a more formal style.   (See Exercise 16.)   We first restate the theorem.

Theorem (5d-3):   On any three distinct, noncollinear points there is exactly one distinct circle.

PROOF

Using Fig. 7.10 for reference, we are given that points P, Q, and R are

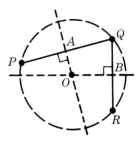

Fig. 7.10

distinct and noncollinear.   Since they are noncollinear, the pairs (P, R, Q could be in any order) P, Q and Q, R determine distinct lines.   Let A and B be the midpoints of PQ and QR, respectively.   Theorem (6c-8) guarantees a line on $A \perp$ to PQ and a line on $B \perp$ to QR.   By theorem (6c-12), they intersect, at some point O.   By Theorem (4h-1) or Theorem (6c-9), we have

$$(AO)^2 + (PA)^2 = (PO)^2,$$
$$(QA)^2 + (AO)^2 = (QO)^2,$$
$$(QB)^2 + (OB)^2 = (QO)^2,$$

and
$$(RB)^2 + (OB)^2 = (RO)^2.$$

Since A and B are midpoints, we have

$$(PA) = (QA),$$

and $$(QB) = (RB).$$

Using these equalities, we simplify and obtain

$$(PO) = (QO) = (RO).$$

Thus by Theorem (5d-1) a unique circle is determined.   Q.E.D.

Exercise Set

Determine which of the following discussions is true and which is false.   Explain why in each case.

1. If in Fig. 7.11, O is the center of the circle, then $OA \cong OB$.

2. In Fig. 7.11, AB is a radius.

3. In Fig. 7.12, if $OE \perp DF$ and $OB \perp AC$, then $AB \cong DE$ and $BC \cong EF$.

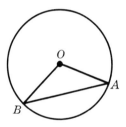

Fig. 7.11

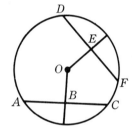

Fig. 7.12

4. In Fig. 7.12, if $OE \perp DF$ and $OB \perp AC$, and $DF \cong AC$, then $DE \cong BC$, and $EF \cong AB$.

5. In Fig. 7.12, if $AB \cong BC$, then $OB \perp AC$.

6. In Fig. 7.13, if O is the center of the circle, then $\sphericalangle COA$, $\sphericalangle COB$, and $\sphericalangle AOB$ are central angles.

7. In Fig. 7.13, $\sphericalangle ACO$ is an inscribed angle.

8. In Fig. 7.14, $\overline{ABF}$ is a secant.

9. In Fig. 7.14, if O is the center of the circle and $\overline{ABF}$ is a tangent at B, then $\sphericalangle ABD$, $\sphericalangle DBF$, and $\sphericalangle CBF$ are inscribed angles.

10. Prove Theorem (7b-2).

11. Prove the converse statement of Theorem (7b-5) and fill in the missing reasons of the positive case.   [*Hint:* Look at Theorem (6e-4).]

*12. Prove Theorem (7b-3).

*13. For the circle $(x - 3)^2 + (y + 1)^2 = 16$, what is the equation of the perpendicular bisector of the chord determined by the line $x - y = 1$?

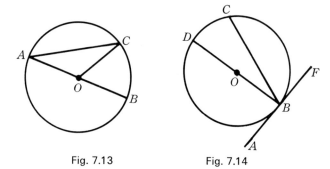

Fig. 7.13   Fig. 7.14

*14. Complete the algebra that establishes equation (12).

*15. What is the equation of the perpendicular bisector of the chord whose endpoints are $(0,2)$ and $(-2,0)$?

*16. Rewrite the proof of Theorem (5d-3) in formal style.

7c   Congruent Circles

We are now at the point where we can develop equivalence relations for circles.   As with line segments, we shall use the concept of congruence.

Definition (7-h):   Circles with **congruent** radii are congruent.

Since radii are line segments, we are thus ensured of their existence.   In Chapter 6 we proved the existence of congruent line segments.   Therefore our definition seems reasonable.

Example 1:   A circle $(x - 1)^2 + (y + 2)^2 = 3$ is congruent to a circle with center $(3,4)$.   What is the equation of the second circle?

Solution: Since $(x - h)^2 + (y - k)^2 = a^2$ is the equation of any circle with center (h,k) and length of radius a, it immediately follows from Definition (7-h) that the length of the radius of the second circle is also $\sqrt{3}$.   Hence the required equation is $(x - 3)^2 + (y - 4)^2 = 3$.

Example 2:   Are the two circles $x^2 + (y - 4)^2 = 16$ and $(x + 4)^2 + (y - 2)^2 = 16$ congruent?

Solution: The length of the radii of both circles is 4.   Therefore the radii are congruent.   Thus the circles are congruent.

Exercise Set

Which of the following sets of circles are congruent?   What, if anything, would make them congruent?

1. $x^2 + y^2 = a^2$, $x^2 + y^2 = 1$.

2. $(x - 4)^2 + (y - 4)^2 = 2$, $\{(x,y) \mid x^2 + y^2 - 2 = 0\}$.

3. Circle with radius 3, circle with center $(c,2)$ and containing point $(2,c)$.

4. Circle with radius 1, circle with diameter 2.

5. $(x + 1)^2 + (y - 1)^2 = 2$, $(x - 1)^2 + (y + 1)^2 = 2^2$.

*6. $x^2 + 4x + y^2 - 5 = 0$, $x^2 + 6x + y^2 - 4y + 4 = 0$.

*7. If the points $(2,2)$, $(0,0)$, and $(1, \sqrt{3})$ determine a circle, what is the equation of a congruent circle whose center is $(3, -2)$?

*8. Find the equations of two circles congruent to $(x + 4)^2 + (y + 1)^2 = 25$ and containing the points $(2,4)$ and $(4, -2)$.

*9. Are two circles, one having diameter $\sqrt{2}$ and the other radius $1/\sqrt{2}$, congruent?

7d   Positional Equivalence of Circles

In Chapter 6, we established positional equivalence for line segments. We now establish the same principle for circles.

Theorem (7d-1):   For any circle and any point in the plane, there is a circle that has the given point as center and is congruent to the given circle.

PROOF

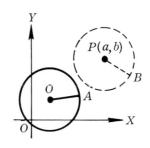

Given: A circle (O,OA) and a point $P(a,b)$.
To Prove: A circle (P,PB) exists such that $(P,PB) \cong (O,OA)$.

1. There is a (O,OA) and a point $P(a,b)$.	1. Hypothesis
2. (OA) is a real number.	2. Definition (4-1)
3. There is a circle at $P(a,b)$ such that (OA) is the distance of any point in it from the center $P(a,b)$.	3. Theorem (5d-1)
4. P and any point in the circle, say B, determines a radius PB.	4. Theorem (7b-1)
5. $(PB) = (OA)$.	5. Why?
6. $PB \cong OA$.	6. Why?
7. $(P,PB) \cong (O,OA)$.	7. Why?

This theorem will now allow the algebra of circles to be simplified. For example, we can now use $x^2 + y^2 = a^2$ in place of $(x - h)^2 + (y - k)^2 = a^2$ by letting the center (h,k) be the origin $(0,0)$.

In the following sections, we make full use of this simplification technique. The reader should be alert and recognize when it has been used in the solution of a particular problem.

Exercise Set

Are the following pairs of circles positionally equivalent? Congruent?

1. $x^2 + y^2 = a^2$ and $(x - a)^2 + (y - b)^2 = a^2 + 9$.

2. $x^2 + y^2 + 2a - 9 = 0$ and $(x - a)^2 + (y - b)^2 = a^2 + 9$.

3. $x^2 + y^2 = a^2$ and $(x - a)^2 + (y - 9)^2 = a^2$.

4. $3x^2 + 2y^2 = x - y^2 + 1$ and $(x - 1)^2 + (y + 1)^2 = 1$.

5. Exercises 1 through 6 of Section 7c.

6. Fill in the missing reasons in the proof of Theorem (7d-1).

7. Discuss the difference between congruence of circles and positional equivalence of circles.

*8. For Exercises 7 through 12 of Section 7a, which circles are positionally equivalent?

7e Intersecting Circles

We shall immediately use the positional equivalence of circles in the following theorem.

Theorem (7e-1): If the center of one circle belongs to the locus of a second circle, then the circles will intersect on at most two points.

PROOF

We see, as in Fig. 7.15, that there are three possibilities to consider. Since we have not restricted the diameter of either circle, we shall prove it for a general case and then restate the theorem with restrictions on the diameters.

Using Theorem (7d-1), we consider circles

(1) $$x^2 + y^2 = a^2, \qquad a \neq 0,$$

and

(2) $$x^2 + (y - a)^2 = b^2, \qquad b \neq 0.$$

The situation in (1) and (2) is illustrated in Fig. 7.16. Now (1) becomes

$$x^2 = a^2 - y^2,$$

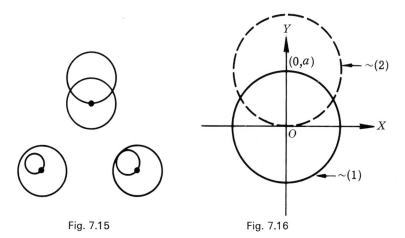

Fig. 7.15   Fig. 7.16

and substituting this into (2) we have

$$a^2 - y^2 + y^2 - 2ay + a^2 = b^2.$$

This simplifies to the expression,

(3) $$y = \frac{b^2 - 2a^2}{-2a}.$$

Then using (3) to find x in (1), we have

(4) $$x = \pm \frac{b}{2a}\sqrt{4a^2 - b^2}.$$

To get real numbers for x from (4), we must have

$$4a^2 - b^2 \geq 0$$
$$4a^2 \geq b^2.$$

Since $a > 0$ and $b > 0$, we can take the square root and obtain

(5) $$2a \geq b.$$

Using (3) and (4), our points of intersection are

$$\left(\frac{b}{2a}\sqrt{4a^2 - b^2}, \frac{2a^2 - b^2}{2a}\right)$$

and

$$\left(-\frac{b}{2a}\sqrt{4a^2 - b^2}, \frac{2a^2 - b^2}{2a}\right)$$

and $$2a \geq b. \quad \text{Q.E.D.}$$

We see from Fig. 7.17 that if $2a > b$, then the length of the diameter of the intersected circle is greater than the length of the radius of the intersecting circle, thus determining two points of intersection.

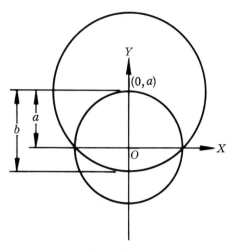

Fig. 7.17

If $2a = b$, as in Fig. 7.18, then the diameter of the intersected circle equals the radius of the intersecting circle.   Then from (4) above, we have $x = 0,0$ (a multiplicity of two).   Since the circles intersect in only one point, we say that they are internally tangent at that point.   If $2a < b$, as in Fig. 7.19,

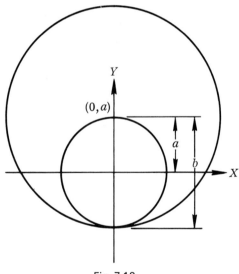

Fig. 7.18

then the two circles do not intersect in the plane, for we do not obtain real numbers for the points of intersection.   These conclusions are not stated in Theorem (7e-1); hence we establish a corollary to that theorem.

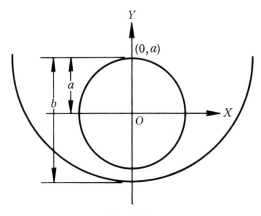

Fig. 7.19

Corollary (7e-1a):   For circles (O,OA) and $(O',O'B')$ such that $B \in (O,OA)$, $(O',O'B)$ will intersect (O,OA) on (i) two points if $2(OA) > (O'B)$; or on (ii) one point (multiplicity of two) if $2(OA) = (O'B)$.   There will be no intersection if $2(OA) < (O'B)$.

These theorems only pertain to situations where the center of one circle is contained in another circle.   In other cases only investigation by solving the system simultaneously will determine whether the circles intersect.   We can, however, make an estimation of their possibilities for intersection by graphing them.

Example 1:   Do the circles $x^2 + (y + 4)^2 = 16$ and $x^2 + y^2 = 4$ intersect?

Solution (Estimation):   Graphing the loci, we get the models in Fig. 7.20. They appear to intersect.

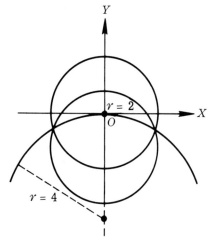

Fig. 7.20

Solution (Algebraic):   Solving $x^2 + y^2 = 4$ for x^2, we have $x^2 = 4 - y^2$. Substituting this into $x^2 + (y + 4)^2 = 16$, we obtain $4 - y^2 + y^2 + 8y + 16 = 16$.   Thus $y = -\frac{1}{2}$.   Solving for x, we get $x = \sqrt{15/2}$ and $-\sqrt{15/2}$. We have, then, points of intersection $(\sqrt{15/2}, -\frac{1}{2})$ and $(-\sqrt{15/2}, -\frac{1}{2})$.   The circles do intersect.

Example 2:   Do the circles $(x - 1)^2 + (y - 2)^2 = 9$ and $(x - 1)^2 + (y - 2)^2 = 4$ intersect?

Solution (Estimation):   Graphing the loci, we get the models in Fig. 7.21. They appear not to intersect.

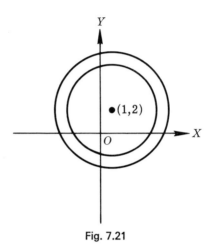

Fig. 7.21

Solution (Algebraic):   Since the left-hand side of each equation is the same, we have the result that $9 = 4$.   This is a contradiction because $9 \neq 4$. Thus the circles do not intersect.

In Example 2 we note that the circles have the same center; that is, $(h,k) = (+1, +2)$.   Such circles have a special name.

Definition (7-i)   Circles having the same centers are called **concentric circles.**

Definition (7-j):   The straight line containing the centers of two non-concentric circles is called the **line of centers.**

In Fig. 7.22, $\overleftrightarrow{AB}$ is the line of centers.   Since the centers of the circles are known, we can easily find the equation of the line of centers for two intersecting circles.

Example 3:   What is the equation of the line of centers for the circles $(x - 4)^2 + (y - 1)^2 = 4$ and $(x + 1)^2 + (y - 5)^2 = 6$?

Solution: Since the centers of the two circles are $(4,1)$ and $(-1,5)$, for the slope of AB, $m = -\frac{4}{5}$. Using the point-slope formula, we get $4x + 5y - 21 = 0$.

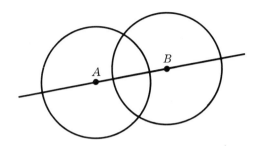

Fig. 7.22

Exercise Set

1. Explain why the restriction of nonconcentric circles is made in Definition (7-j).

For each set of circles below, determine whether
  (a) the center of one is contained in the other.
  (b) they intersect.
  (c) they have a line of centers, and if they do, its equation.

2. $(x - 4)^2 + (y - 4)^2 = 4$ and $(x - 4)^2 + y^2 = 9$.

3. $(x - 4)^2 + (y - 4)^2 = 4$ and $(x - 4)^2 + (y - 2)^2 = 16$.

4. $(x - 4)^2 + (y - 4)^2 = 4$ and $(x - 4)^2 + (y - 4)^2 = 8$.

5. $(x - 4)^2 + (y - 4)^2 = 16$ and $(x - 2)^2 + (y - 2)^2 = 1$.

6. $(x - 4)^2 + (y - 4)^2 = 1$ and $(x - 3)^2 + (y - 4)^2 = \frac{1}{2}$.

7. $(x - 4)^2 + (y - 4)^2 = a^2$ and $(x + 1)^2 + (y + 1)^2 = b^2$.

8. What is the slope of the line of centers of the two nonconcentric circles $(x - h_1)^2 + (y - k_1)^2 = a_1{}^2$ and $(x - h_2)^2 + (y - k_2)^2 = a_2{}^2$?

9. Show that the circles $x^2 + y^2 = 4$ and $(x - 4)^2 + y^2 = 4$ are tangent.

*10. Construct a formal style proof of Theorem (7e-1).

**11. Show that $x^2 + y^2 = 4$, $(x - 4)^2 + y^2 = 4$, and $(x - 2)^2 + (y - \frac{24}{5})^2 = (\frac{16}{5})^2$ are all mutually tangent.

7f Circles and Tangents

In Section 7a, Definition (7-c) defined a tangent to a circle.

Example 1: Show that the line $x + y - 2 = 0$ is tangent to a circle whose equation is $x^2 + y^2 = 2$.

Solution: Solving $x + y - 2 = 0$ for x, we have

(1) $$x = 2 - y,$$

and squaring yields

(2) $$x^2 = 4 - 4y + y^2.$$

Substituting (2) into $x^2 + y^2 = 2$, we have

(3) $$4 - 4y + y^2 + y^2 = 2,$$

or $$y^2 - 2y + 1 = 0.$$

(4) $$y = 1,1.$$

Using the values of (4) in (1), we get the points (1,1) and (1,1). These are coincident points. Thus by Definition (7-d) the line $x + y - 2 = 0$ is tangent to the circle $x^2 + y^2 = 2$.

If we explore Example 1 further and find the equation of the line containing the center of the circle (0,0) and the point of tangency (1,1), we obtain $y = x$. The slope of this line is $m_1 = 1$.   The slope of the tangent line is $m_2 = -1$. The product of these two slopes is $m_1 \cdot m_2 = 1 \cdot (-1)$.   Thus by Definition (6-c) the lines are perpendicular.   We now formalize this into a proposition.

Theorem (7f-1):   A line tangent to a circle is perpendicular to the radius at the point of tangency.

The proof involves the solving of a simultaneous system of equations. It can be found in the Appendix.

The converse of Theorem (7f-1) is also true.   Because of its continual use, we have stated it as a separate theorem.   A simple indirect proof will establish the proposition.   It is left as an exercise.

Theorem (7f-2):   A line perpendicular to a radius of a circle at the point of intersection of the radius and the circle is tangent to the circle at that point.

Figure 7.23 illustrates these two theorems.   We shall use the symbol

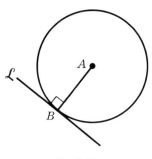

Fig. 7.23

⊥ with our models to indicate that the two lines are perpendicular.

Exercise Set

Determine whether the following lines are tangent to the given circles.

1. $x^2 + y^2 - 1 = 0$ and $x = 1$.

2. $(x - 4)^2 + (y - 4)^2 = 16$ and $x = 0, y = 0$.

3. $(x - 4)^2 + y^2 = 16$ and $x = 0, y = 0$.

4. $(x - 1)^2 + (y - 1)^2 = 1$ and $x = 0, y = 0$.

5. $(x - 1)^2 + y^2 = 1$ and $x = 1, y = 1$.

6. $(x - 2)^2 + (y + 3)^2 = 4$ and $x = -1, y = -1$.

Determine the equation of the tangent line for the given endpoint and slope of the radius.

7. $m = 3, (2, -1)$.   8. $m = 0, (-1, 6)$.

9. $m = 4, (0,0)$.   10. No slope, $(-2, 3)$.

11. No slope, $(0,0)$.   12. $m = -1, (1,1)$.

Determine the slope of the radius of a circle that is tangent to the given line at the given point.

13. $3x - 4y + 5 = 0, (-3, -1)$.   14. $x = 7, (7, 0)$.

15. $x + y = 2, (6, -4)$.   16. $7y + 5 = 0, (0, -\frac{5}{2})$.

17. $2x - y + 1 = 0$.   18. $x = y, (0,0)$.

*19. *Prove:*   The square of the length of a tangent segment AB is equal to the difference of the squares of the lengths of the radius and the line segment whose endpoints are the center of the circle and the endpoint of the tangent segment.

*20. Prove Theorem (7f-2).

*21. Find the length of the tangent segment from $(-1, 2)$ to the circle $(x - 5)^2 + (y - 5)^2 = 60$.

7g   Arc Lengths of Circles

In Section 7b we defined central angles of circles.   From our definition of chords, each central angle of a circle certainly determines a chord.   Chord AB of Fig. 7.24 is determined by central angle ACB.

Definition (7-k):   An **arc of a circle** is that subset of the circle that contains the points of intersection of a central angle and the circle and all those points of the circle interior to the angle $\lor$ the points of intersection of the angle and the circle and all those points of the circle exterior to the angle.

When a central angle intersects a circle, we shall call the points of intersection, together with all points in the circle interior to the angle, the **minor**

arc, and the points of intersection, together with all the points in the circle exterior to the angle, the **major arc**.

We shall establish a convention and refer only to minor arcs when using the term *arc* unless specifically stated to the contrary.

Definition (7-1):   Either arc determined by a diameter of a circle is called a **semicircle**.

Let us consider a central angle α of some circle that determines a chord AB. (See Fig. 7.25.)   Now let us divide the chord AB into $(n + 1)$ segments, n

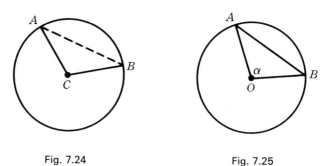

Fig. 7.24   Fig. 7.25

a natural number.   Figure 7.26 shows our chord AB with $n + 1$ segments determined by n points between A and B.

Containing each of these new points $a_1, a_2, a_3, a_4, \ldots, a_n$ there is a radius that determines a new central angle, which in turn determines a new chord. Figure 7.27 shows this new pattern.   If we now repeat this process for the

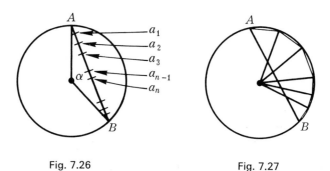

Fig. 7.26   Fig. 7.27

$n + 1$ new chords, intuitively we see that the chords begin to approximate the arc of the circle.

We continue this process of creating more and more central angles that determine smaller and smaller chords.   Since each chord is a line segment, thus having a real number length, we may add up these lengths.

Therefore, if we let the *number* of central angles increase without end, in the manner described, the sum of the lengths of the chords thus determined *approximates* the "length" of the arc more and more closely.

The preceding argument has been made for chords and central angles of circles. Since we are essentially talking about a "limit," the rigorous details have been left for more advanced courses. It is adequate for our use to realize that we can associate a real number with each arc in such a way that the number can be used as a measure of the "length" of the arc.

Furthermore, if we examine two particular arcs determined by chords of adjacent angles (see Fig. 7.28), we see that the sum of the lengths of the individual arcs is equal to the length of the arc determined by the angle formed by the remote sides of the adjacent angles That is, $(\overset{\frown}{AC})$ (Read: measure of arc AC) plus $(\overset{\frown}{CB})$ equals the measure of arc AB. See Fig. 7.28 again.

This can easily be verified intuitively, for by the process described above we can find the lengths of $\overset{\frown}{AC}$ and $\overset{\frown}{CB}$. To find the length of $\overset{\frown}{AB}$, we again use our summing process, but we find (see Fig. 7.29) that we are duplicating

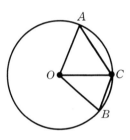

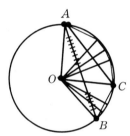

Fig. 7.28   Fig. 7.29

the chords that were used to find the lengths of $\overset{\frown}{AC}$ and $\overset{\frown}{BC}$. We summarize this discussion in the following theorem. A formal proof is left to the study of calculus.

Theorem (7g-1):   For any two adjacent arcs $\overset{\frown}{AB}$ and $\overset{\frown}{BC}$, there are real numbers $(\overset{\frown}{AB})$, $(\overset{\frown}{BC})$, and $(\overset{\frown}{AC})$, called the arc lengths of $\overset{\frown}{AB}$ and $\overset{\frown}{BC}$ and $\overset{\frown}{AC}$, such that $(\overset{\frown}{AB}) + (\overset{\frown}{BC}) = (\overset{\frown}{AC})$.

As this theorem implies, the length of an arc is simply a real number and has no necessary connection with particular units of measurement. As with lengths of line segments, we can scale the arc length by multiplying it by some suitable constant.

Definition (7-m):   The **scaled arc length** is $s = k \cdot u$, where k is a suitable constant and u is the unscaled arc length.

Example 1:   What is the scale factor k if $u = \pi$ when $s = 5$ inches?

Solution: We have 5 inches $= k\pi$. Therefore $k = 5/\pi$ inches per integral unit.

If we examine Theorem (7g-1), we see that the number called arc length could be positive, negative, or zero. In this book we shall make *no* use of negative numbers as arc length. As usual, however, it would be useful to be able to make use of zero.

By Definition (7-1) each arc, except a semicircle, is determined by a central angle. A central angle is determined in turn by radii. Consider Fig. 7.30. By Definition (5-k) radii OA and OB determine a *collapsed* angle. Hence no arc is determined in this case. It should seem reasonable to associate 0 with this coincident radius case. Even though there is no actual arc, we shall call 0 the arc length associated with the point $A = B$ in a circle determined by radii OA and OB.

How do we determine the particular number to associate with other arcs? Imagine that the coincident radii OA and OB in Fig. 7.30 determine $\overset{\frown}{AB}$, which includes the entire circle. This time OA and OB do not determine a collapsed angle. Consider, however, the union $\overset{\frown}{AB} \cup \overset{\frown}{BC} \cup \overset{\frown}{CA}$ as in Fig. 7.31. This union includes the entire circle, and since Theorem (7g-1)

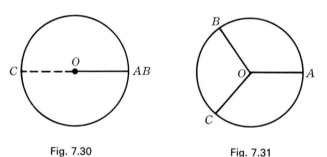

Fig. 7.30 Fig. 7.31

guarantees that we can add lengths of such adjacent arcs, there must be an "arc length" to associate with the circle. We only need find what it is. Certainly it is not zero as in the case where OA and OB determined no arc at all.

The unscaled arc length of a complete circle can be found by methods of calculus. The following theorem states what we need.

Theorem (7g-2): The unscaled arc length of a complete circle (O, OA) is $2\pi(OA)$, where π (pi) is a real irrational number, $\pi = 3.14159\ldots$.

We note that the unscaled arc length of a complete circle depends only on the length of the radius, the number π being a constant. We call the arc length of a circle the **circumference** of the circle.

Exercise Set

What is the unscaled arc length of the complete circle given by the following?

1. Diameter 4.   2. Radius 3.

3. Radius $\sqrt{2}$.   4. Diameter $2\sqrt{2}$.

5. $\{(x,y) \mid x^2 + y^2 = 8\}$.   6. $\{(x,y) \mid (x + 1)^2 + y^2 = 4\}$.

For each of the following, determine (a) the scaled arc length s, or (b) the unscaled arc length u, or (c) the constant k.

7. $s = 1000$ mils, $k = 13$ mils per integral unit; find u.

8. $s = 300$ degrees, $u = 5\pi/3$; find k.

9. $u = 4\pi/3$, $k = 180/\pi$ degrees per integral unit; find s.

10. $s = 84$ valchos, $u = 22$; find k.

*11. Is the statement "Congruent arcs determine congruent chords" true? Why?

7h Circular Functions

Consider a circle (O,OA) such that A is on the x axis. (See Fig. 7.32.) If A has coordinates $(a,0)$ and O has coordinates $(0,0)$, then the locus of (O,OA) is

(1) $\{(x,y) \mid x^2 + y^2 = a^2\}$.

Now if $P(x,y)$ is any point in (1), we can form various ratios of the coordinates of P with the length of radius a of (O,OA). We give these ratios

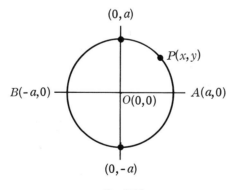

Fig. 7.32

arbitrary names in order to distinguish one from another. (We recall from algebra that a ratio is the comparison of one object to another by division. In this case, we are comparing real numbers.)

Definition (7-n): For any $P(x,y) \in (O,OA)$, where $OA \subset \overrightarrow{OX}$ and $(OA) = a$,

$$\textbf{sine } (\widehat{AP}) = \frac{y}{a} \qquad\qquad \textbf{tangent } (\widehat{AP}) = \frac{y}{x}, \ x \neq 0$$

$$\textbf{cosine } (\widehat{AP}) = \frac{x}{a} \qquad\qquad \textbf{secant } (\widehat{AP}) = \frac{a}{x}, \ x \neq 0$$

$$\textbf{cosecant } (\widehat{AP}) = \frac{a}{y}, \ y \neq 0. \qquad \textbf{cotangent } (\widehat{AP}) = \frac{x}{y}, \ y \neq 0.$$

From (1) *we also have* $x^2 + y^2 = a^2$. What are these new quantities we have defined? Since each defining ratio is the quotient of two real numbers, all six are also real numbers.

To illustrate this fact, consider the circle $\{(x,y) \mid x^2 + y^2 = 4\}$, as in Fig. 7.33. For this circle $a = 2$.

Example 1: Find the sine $(\widehat{AP_2})$, tangent $(\widehat{AP_2})$, and cosine $(\widehat{AP_2})$. (See Fig. 7.33.)

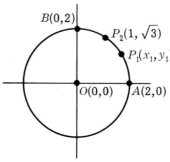

Fig. 7.33

Solution: sine $(\widehat{AP_2}) = \dfrac{y_2}{a} = \dfrac{\sqrt{3}}{2}$

$\qquad\qquad$ cosine $(\widehat{AP_2}) = \dfrac{x_2}{a} = \dfrac{1}{2}$

$\qquad\qquad$ tangent $(\widehat{AP_2}) = \dfrac{y_2}{x_2} = \dfrac{\sqrt{3}}{1} = \sqrt{3}.$

Example 2: Find the cosine $(\widehat{AB})$ and sine $(\widehat{AB})$ in Fig. 7.33.

Solution: cosine $(\widehat{AB}) = \dfrac{x_B}{a} = \dfrac{0}{2} = 0.$

$\qquad\qquad$ sine $(\widehat{AB}) = \dfrac{y_B}{a} = \dfrac{2}{2} = 1.$

Example 3: Find sine $(\widehat{AP_1})$ if $x_1 = y_1$ in Fig. 7.33.

Solution: sine $(\widehat{AP_1}) = y_1/a = y_1/2$. In order to calculate sine $(\widehat{AP_1})$, we obviously need to find a particular value for y_1. What else do we know?

By Definition (4-n) the point P_1 must be a point in the circle. Hence its coordinates must satisfy the equation of the given circle; that is, $P_1 = (x_1, y_1) \in \{(x, y) \mid x^2 + y^2 = 4\}$. Thus $x_1{}^2 + y_1{}^2 = 4$. Remembering that $x_1 = y_1$ was given, we substitute to obtain $y_1{}^2 + y_1{}^2 = 4$ or $y_1 = \sqrt{2}$. Therefore sine $(\widehat{AP_1}) = \sqrt{2}/2$.

Since these new quotients are numbers, we use algebra to establish some facts about them.

Theorem (7h-1): (a) sine $(\widehat{AP})$/cosine $(\widehat{AP}) = $ tangent $(\widehat{AP})$; (b) cosine $(\widehat{AP})$/sine $(\widehat{AP}) = $ cotangent $(\widehat{AP})$. (These are called *ratio identities*.)

Theorem (7h-2): (a) sine $(\widehat{AP}) \cdot$ cosecant $(\widehat{AP}) = 1$; (b) cosine $(\widehat{AP}) \cdot$ secant $(\widehat{AP}) = 1$; (c) tangent $(\widehat{AP}) \cdot$ cotangent $(\widehat{AP}) = 1$. (These are called *reciprocal identities*.)

Theorem (7h-3): (a) sine^2 $(\widehat{AP}) + $ cosine^2 $(\widehat{AP}) = 1$; (b) tangent^2 $(\widehat{AP}) + 1 = $ secant^2 $(\widehat{AP})$; (c) $1 + $ cotangent^2 $(\widehat{AP}) = $ cosecant^2 $(\widehat{AP})$. (These are called *squared or quadratic identities*.)

The proofs of these theorems are a direct application of Definition (7-n) and of the equation of the circle $x^2 + y^2 = a^2$. The proof of Theorem (7h-3), part (a), is worked out below as an example. The remaining proofs are left to the exercises.

Proof of Theorem (7h-3), part (a): Since by definition, sine $(\widehat{AP}) = y/a$ and cosine $(\widehat{AP}) = x/a$, then we have sine^2 $(\widehat{AP}) = y^2/a^2$ and cosine^2 $(\widehat{AP}) = x^2/a^2$. But $x^2 + y^2 = a^2$ or, since $a > 0$, $x^2/a^2 + y^2/a^2 = 1$. Hence we have sine^2 $(\widehat{AP}) + $ cosine^2 $(\widehat{AP}) = 1$ and part (a) is established.

Exercise Set

1. Why are no restrictions stated when $a = (OA)$ appears in a denominator in Definition (7-n)?

2. Prove Theorem (7h-1).

3. Prove Theorem (7h-2).

4. Prove the remaining parts of Theorem (7h-3).

5. Find all six ratios of Definition (7-n) for the circle $x^2 + y^2 = 3$ and the point $(\sqrt{3}/2, \tfrac{3}{2})$.

6. Using Fig. 7.33, find cosine $(\widehat{AP_1})$ and tangent $(\widehat{AP_1})$ if $x_1 = y_1$.

7. Using Fig. 7.33, find all six ratios of Definition (7-n) if $x_1 = 2y_1$.

8. Calculate all six ratios of Definition (7-n) for the circle $\{(x_1, y_1) \mid x^2 + y^2 = 9\}$ if $x_1 = y_1$. Compare these values with those obtained in Exercise 6.

In the following exercises, find the remaining five ratios where the given ratio is true by Definition (7-n).   Assume that $x > 0$ and $y > 0$.

9. Tangent $(AP_1) = \frac{4}{3}$.

10. Tangent $(AP_2) = 1$.

11. Sine $(AP_3) = \frac{1}{4}$.

12. Cosecant $(AP_4) = 2$.

13. Cosine $(AP_5) = \frac{1}{4}$.

14. Secant $(AP_6) = 4$.

*15. Calculate all six ratios of Definition (7-n) for the point $P \in [\{(x,y) \mid x^2 + y^2 = 25\} \cap \{(x,y) \mid x = 2y\}]$.   Compare these results with those from Exercise 7.

*16. Do the comparisons suggested in Exercises 8 and 9 suggest a reasonable conjecture about the relationship of the values of the circular ratios to the lengths of radii of various circles?

chapter 8

Properties of Angles

8a   Congruence of Angles

In Chapter 5 we defined an angle to be the set of real number pairs in two rays having a common endpoint.   Let α be an angle defined by set A.   Let β be an angle defined by set B.   If set A is equal to set B, may we conclude that $\alpha = \beta$?   Yes, as long as we are talking about the *set* α and the *set* β. Remember, we use the equality relation *only* between numbers or sets.   We *do not* use the equality relation between geometric figures.

To have a relation between angles that have some common characteristics besides strict equality, we call upon our concept of congruence once again.

Definition (8-a):   Two angles are **congruent** iff they are central angles of the same or congruent circles and determine congruent chords.

This definition of congruent angles may seem to leave us with an added burden of first establishing congruent circles.   However, the vertex of any angle can always be used as the center of some circle.   Thus the existence of the congruent circles is almost immediate by Theorem (7d-1).

A useful result of the definition of congruent angles is in determining the relation of the angles formed by the grid loci.

Theorem (8a-1):   Adjacent angles determined by grid loci are congruent.

PROOF

Given: Grid loci $\mathscr{L}_1$ and $\mathscr{L}_2$ intersecting at O where α and β are adjacent angles on the same side of $\mathscr{L}_1$.
To Prove: $\alpha \cong \beta$.

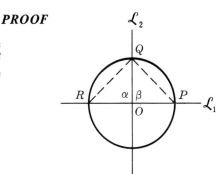

1. There are grid loci $\mathscr{L}_1$ and $\mathscr{L}_2$ intersecting at O with α and β adjacent angles on the same side of $\mathscr{L}_1$.	1. Hypothesis
2. Circle O intersects $\mathscr{L}_1$ and $\mathscr{L}_2$ at $P,R \in \mathscr{L}_1$ and $Q \in \mathscr{L}_2$.	2. Theorem (7a-4)
3. $(RO)^2 + (OQ)^2 = (RQ)^2$ and $(PO)^2 + (OQ)^2 = (PQ)^2$.	3. Theorem (4h-1)
4. $RO \cong PO$.	4. Theorem (7b-4)
5. $(RO) = (PO)$.	5. Why?
6. $(PO)^2 + (OQ)^2 = (RQ)^2$.	6. Why?
7. $(RQ)^2 = (PQ)^2$.	7. Why?
8. $(RQ) = (PQ)$.	8. Why?
9. $RQ \cong PQ$.	9. Why?
10. $\alpha \cong \beta$.	10. Definition (8-a)
Q.E.D.	

We note that since this theorem was done in general, we have proven that $\alpha \cong \beta \cong \delta \cong \gamma$.   Why?   (See Fig. 8.1.)

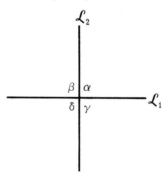

Fig. 8.1

We know that vertical grid loci have no slope and that horizontal grid loci have slope zero.   By Theorem (6c-7) we then have that any two intersecting grid loci are mutually perpendicular.   Therefore, to specialize our description of the angles formed by intersecting grid loci, the following definition becomes appropriate.

Definition (8-b):   The adjacent angles determined by perpendicular lines at their point of intersection are called **right angles**.

We note immediately that this definition includes more than just intersecting grid loci.   Since we know that the right angles formed by the intersecting grid loci are congruent, is it also true that the right angles formed by other perpendicular loci are congruent? The following theorem answers this question.

Theorem (8a-2): Adjacent angles determined by straight lines $\mathscr{L}_1$ and $\mathscr{L}_2$ with slopes m_1 and m_2, such that $m_1 \cdot m_2 = -1$, are congruent.

The proof of this theorem is left to the exercises.

We now have two sets of right angles. The sets are those right angles formed by grid loci and those right angles formed by lines that are not grid loci. Are these right angles congruent? That is, are the right angles themselves congruent?

Theorem (8a-3): An angle determined by two lines, one having no slope and the other slope zero, and an angle determined by two lines that have the product of their slopes minus one, are congruent.

PROOF

Given: Intersecting grid loci $\mathscr{L}_1$ and $\mathscr{L}_2$ and lines $\mathscr{L}_3$ and $\mathscr{L}_4$ with slopes m_3 and m_4 such that $m_3 \cdot m_4 = -1$.

To Prove: $\alpha \cong \beta$.

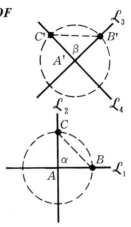

1. Grid loci $\mathscr{L}_1$ and $\mathscr{L}_2$ intersect at point A, and lines $\mathscr{L}_3$ and $\mathscr{L}_4$ intersect at A' such that $m_3 \cdot m_4 = -1$.	1. Hypothesis
2. Let $B \in \mathscr{L}_1$.	2. Theorem (4e-3)
3. There are circles with centers A and A' having radii of length (AB).	3. Theorem (7b-3)
4. (A, AB) intersects $\mathscr{L}_2$ on C; the circle with center at A' and radius of length (AB) intersects $\mathscr{L}_3$ at B' and $\mathscr{L}_4$ at C'.	4. Theorem (7a-4)
5. $AB \cong A'B'$.	5. Definition (6-1)
6. $AC \cong AB$; $A'C' \cong A'B'$.	6. Theorem (7b-4)

7. $AC \cong A'C'$.	7. Why?
8. $(AC)^2 + (AB)^2 = (CB)^2$.	8. Theorem (4h-1)
9. $(A'C')^2 + (A'B')^2 = (C'B')^2$.	9. Why?
10. $(CB) = (C'B')$.	10. Properties of $\mathscr{R}$
11. Chords CB and $C'B'$ exist.	11. Theorem (5c-3)
12. $CB \cong C'B'$.	12. Why?
13. $\alpha \cong \beta$.	13. Why?

These theorems have shown that adjacent angles formed by *any* perpendicular lines are congruent. By Definition (8-b) we have agreed to call such angles right angles. The following theorem is thus an immediate consequence of the previous three theorems.

Theorem (8a-4):   All right angles are congruent.

Exercise Set

Which of the sets of lines determine right angles in Exercises 1 through 7?

1. $3x - 4y + 5 = 0$, $x - 2y + 1 = 0$.
2. $x = 5$, $x + y = 1$.
3. $x = 0$, $y = 6$.
4. $2x - 11y = 4$, $11y - 2x + 5 = 0$.
5. Line with slope $m = 2$, $2x + 4y = 0$.
6. $x + y = 1$, $x - y = 1$.
7. $x + 2y + 4 = 0$, $3x = 4 - 6y$.
8. Fill in the missing reasons for Theorem (8a-3).
9. Prove Theorem (8a-4).
*10. Prove Theorem (8a-2) using Theorem (6c-9).
**11. Prove Theorem (8a-1) without the use of Theorem (4h-1).
**12. Prove Theorem (8a-2) without using Theorem (6c-9).

8b   Positional Equivalence of Angles

In Chapters 6 and 7 we developed theorems concerning positional equivalence of circles and line segments. We now prove a theorem that establishes the positional equivalence of angles.

Theorem (8b-1):   For any angle α and for any point P in some line $\mathscr{L}$, there is an angle α' congruent to α having point P as its vertex and having line $\mathscr{L}$ as one of its sides.

PROOF

Given: Angle α with Q as its vertex; a point P in line $\mathscr{L}$.
To Prove: Angle $\alpha' \cong \alpha$ exists having one side in $\mathscr{L}$ and vertex on P.

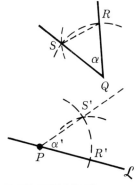

1. There is a point P in a line $\mathscr{L}$ and an angle α with vertex Q.	1. Hypothesis
2. Let $R \neq Q$ be a point in α.	2. Theorem (4e-3)
3. At Q there is a (Q,QR).	3. Theorem (7b-3)
4. α intersects (Q,QR) at S.	4. Theorem (7a-4)
5. R and S determine a chord RS.	5. Theorem (5c-3)
6. There is a line segment in $\mathscr{L}$ congruent to QR having P as an endpoint. (Call the other endpoint R'.)	6. Theorem (6e-1)
7. At P there is a (P,PR') such that $(P,PR') \cong (Q,QR)$.	7. Theorem (7d-1)
8. At R', circle (R,RS) intersects (P,PR') at S'.	8. Theorem (7e-1)
9. R' and S' determine a line segment.	9. Why?
10. $R'S' \cong RS$.	10. Why?
11. There is a ray PS' determining α'.	11. Why?
12. $\alpha' \cong \alpha$.	12. Definition (8-a)
Q.E.D.	

Exercise Set

1. State Theorem (8b-1) in your own words.

2. Complete the missing reasons in Theorems (8b-1).

*3. Following the steps of Theorems (8b-1), prove the theorem where $P(2,1)$, $Q(4,7)$, $R(8,4)$, $S(6,8)$, and $R'(5,1)$.

8c   Measure of Angles

In Chapter 7 we added arc length arithmetically for the arcs of the same or congruent circles.   If we are to use arc length to help us establish properties of angles, we must provide ourselves with some additional terminology and the concept of congruence of arcs.

Suppose we have a central angle α intersecting a given circle on points A and B.   (See Fig. 8.2.)   Three subsets of the circle are obtained: the inter-

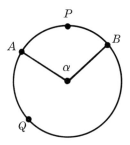

Fig. 8.2

section set of the circle and α; the points in the circle and interior to α; and the points in the circle and exterior to α.

The discussion in Section 7g indicates that the following definition is reasonable.

Definition (8-c):   Arcs in the same or congruent circles are congruent iff they are subtended by congruent chords.

We now go again to the calculus for a theorem that will help us establish some important arcs and angles.

Theorem (8c-1):   The measures of two arcs in the same or congruent circles are equal iff the arcs are congruent.

Definition (8-d):   The measure of an angle α is the number ks_α, where s_α is the length of the minor arc determined by α in a circle whose center is the vertex of α and k is a positive constant for that circle or any circle congruent to it.

Theorem (8c-2):   The measures of two angles are equal iff the angles are congruent.

PROOF

Given (Positive):   Angles α and β such that $\alpha \cong \beta$.
To Prove: $(\alpha) = (\beta)$.

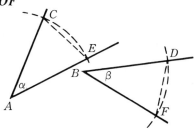

1. α and β are congruent angles.	1. Hypothesis
2. Let C be a point in α.	2. Theorem (4e-3)
3. There is a point D in β such that $AC \cong BD$.	3. Theorem (6e-1)
4. Circles (A,AC) and (B,BD) exist.	4. Theorem (7b-3)
5. $(A,AC) \cong (B,BD)$.	5. Definition (7-h)
6. α intersects (A,AC) on point E; also, β intersects (B,BD) on point F.	6. Theorem (7a-4)
7. Chords CE and DF are determined.	7. Theorem (5c-3)
8. $CE \cong DF$.	8. Definition (8-a)
9. $\overarc{CE} \cong \overarc{DF}$.	9. Definition (8-c)
10. $(\overarc{CE}) = (\overarc{DF})$.	10. Theorem (8c-1)
11. $(\alpha) = k \cdot (\overarc{CE})$; also, $(\beta) = k \cdot (\overarc{DF})$.	11. Definition (8-d)
12. $(\alpha) = (\beta)$.	12. Properties of $\mathscr{R}$

The proof of the converse is left to the exercises.

Since the measure of an angle has been defined in terms of arc length, the following proposition is easily shown to be true.

Theorem (8c-3):   The sum of the measures of two adjacent angles equals the measure of the angle determined by the remote sides of the given adjacent angles.

Using the theorem on positional equivalence of angles, we have a corollary that allows us to add the measures of any two angles.

Corollary (8c-3a):   The sum of the measures of any two angles is equal to the measure of the angle determined by the remote sides of adjacent angles that are congruent respectively to the given angles.

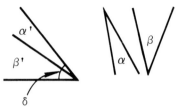

Fig. 8.3

For an example of this theorem, see Fig. 8.3.

The following theorems utilize the idea of measure of a right angle. It is strictly an arbitrary choice, but a convenient one.

Theorem (8c-4): The measure of the angle formed on one side of a line at a point in the line is equal to the sum of the measure of two right angles.

Corollary (8c-4a): The sum of the measures of the angles about a point is equal to the sum of the measures of four right angles.

Corollary (8c-4b): The sum of the measures of the angles formed on one side of two intersecting lines is equal to the sum of the measures of two right angles.

Corollary (8c-4c): The adjacent angles determined by intersecting lines are congruent iff the lines are perpendicular.

The proofs of these are simple applications of previous theorems and definitions. We leave them to the exercises. Figure 8.4 illustrates these theorems.

Definition (8-e): Two angles are **supplementary** iff the sum of their measures is equal to the sum of the measures of two right angles.

Definition (8-f): Two angles are **complementary** iff the sum of their measures is equal to the measure of a right angle.

As our measure for angles, we have been using multiples of the measure of a right angle. Any number can be chosen to represent the measure of a right angle. Some examples of possible choices for the measure of a right angle are as follows.

Example 1: *Degree measure.* If we choose the number 90 as the measure of a right angle, we say that we are using degree measure. We shall write $90°$ to mean 90 degrees of measure. The angle of 1 degree of measure can be represented by 60 minutes of measure (written $60'$). Each angle of 1 minute of measure can be represented by 60 seconds of measure (written $60''$). Using this system, the measure of the angle of Theorem (8c-4) is $180°$ and

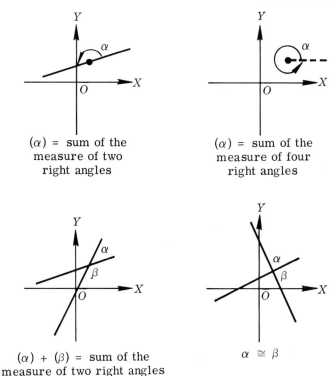

(α) = sum of the
measure of two
right angles

(α) = sum of the
measure of four
right angles

(α) + (β) = sum of the
measure of two right angles

$\alpha \cong \beta$

Fig. 8.4

of the angle of Corollary (8c-4a) is 360°. Since Definition (8-d) establishes the measure of a central angle as equal to the measure of its intercept arc, the measure of the length of arc is also in degrees.

In Section 7g, Definition (7-m) said the scaled arc length is $u = ks$, where k is a constant and s is the unscaled arc length. Theorem (7g-2) states that the unscaled arc length of the complete circle is 2π times the length of the radius. Since the scaled arc length of a complete circle must be 360° (Why?), the constant k must be $360/2\pi r$, where r is always the length of the radius of the particular circle. Thus we can conclude that we have divided up the circumference of a circle into 360 equal parts, each of which we would call "a degree of arc."

Example 2: *Radian measure.* This time we shall choose the number $\pi/2$ as the measure of a right angle. We shall refer to this as the radian measure of an angle. The measure of the angle of Corollary (8c-4a) is 2π radians. Why? Repeating the argument of Example 1, we find that $2\pi = k(2\pi r)$ or $k = 1/r$, where r is the length of the radius of a particular circle. Note that the measure of the angle of Theorem (8c-4) is π radians.

In radian measure, if the radius is 1, then the length of arc is equal to the measure of the angle.

To change from degree measure to radian measure involves a simple proportion. If $(\alpha) = 45°$, then the measure of α in radians can be found by the proportion:

(1)
$$\frac{45}{360} = \frac{x}{2\pi}.$$

(Here we are assuming that for degree measure k is $360/2\pi r$ and for radian measure $k = 1/r$ for the given length r. We shall always make these assumptions when dealing with radian or degree measure.) The result of (1) is clearly $\pi/4$.

Definition (8-g): An angle whose measure is less than the measure of a right angle is called an **acute angle**.

Definition (8-h): An angle whose measure is greater than the measure of a right angle, but less than the measure of two right angles, is called an **obtuse angle**.

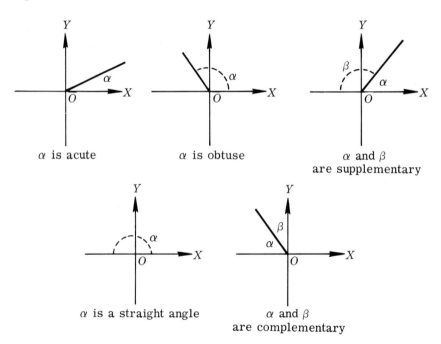

α is acute α is obtuse α and β are supplementary

α is a straight angle α and β are complementary

Fig. 8.5

Definition (8-i): An angle whose measure is equal to the measure of two right angles is called a **straight angle**.

Exercise Set

1. Restate the theorems and definitions of this section where applicable in terms of (a) degree measure and (b) radian measure.

2. If we choose the measure of a right angle to be 1000 mils, what will be the value of k?

Find the degree measure of the following angles whose radian measure is given.

3. 2π.

4. $\pi/3$.

5. $\pi/6$.

6. π.

7. $7\pi/4$.

8. $4\pi/3$.

9. $2\pi/3$.

10. $3\pi/2$.

11. $6\pi/5$.

Find the radian measure of the following angles whose degree measure is given.

12. $45°$.

13. $60°$.

14. $30°$.

15. $120°$.

16. $270°$.

17. $15°$.

18. $135°$.

19. $37°$.

20. $225°$.

21. When is a major arc a minor arc?

If the right angle γ is such that $(\gamma) = 90$, then classify each of the angles in Exercises 22 through 29.

22. $(\alpha) = 39$.

23. $(\beta) = 145$.

24. $(\delta) = 180$.

25. $(\epsilon) = \frac{1}{2}$.

26. $(\alpha') = 90$.

27. $(\beta') = 1$.

28. $(\delta') + (\lambda) = 90$.

29. $(\epsilon') + (\mu) = 180$.

Supply the missing word or reason to make each of the following a true statement.

30. If $\alpha \cong \beta$, then $(\alpha) = $ ___ .

31. If γ is a right angle and $(\beta) = \frac{1}{2} (\gamma)$, then $(\beta) = 45$ if ___ .

32. If $(\gamma) = 90$, then $2(\gamma)$ is the measure of a straight angle if ___ .

33. If $(\alpha) = 30$, then $3(\alpha)$ is the measure of a right angle if ___ .

34. Is a diameter a straight angle?   What type of arc does it determine?

35. Prove the converse of Theorem (8c-2).

36. If γ is a right angle in Fig. 8.6, identify α or α and β in each case.

*37. Prove Theorem (8c-3).

*38. Prove Corollary (8c-3a).

*39. Prove Theorem (8c-4).

*40. Prove Corollary (8c-4a).

*41. Prove Corollary (8c-4b).

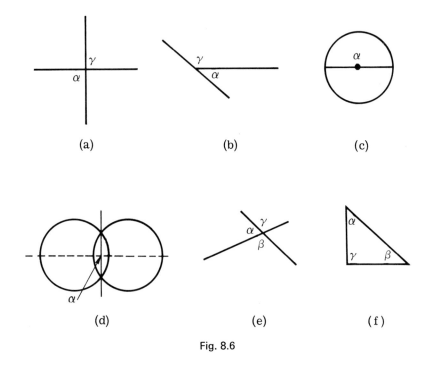

Fig. 8.6

8d   Congruence of Angles (Continued)

We have proved that angles formed by perpendicular lines are congruent. But are there any other methods for determining congruence of angles?

Every angle is determined by lines and (or) line segments. In turn, all lines have certain definite properties. In particular, they have, except in the case of a vertical line, the property of slope. This means that every angle has particular slopes, or no slope, associated with its sides.

Before carrying this idea further, we shall agree that corresponding sides of angles are those that are left-to-left and right-to-right when looking "into" the angle from the vertex. This statement of corresponding sides of angles could be defined analytically, but the complexities would reach beyond the scope of our purpose here.

Example 1:   In Fig. 8.7, *AB* corresponds to *FE*; *BC* corresponds to *ED*.

Since these corresponding sides of angles might have equal slopes, the possibility exists that this might be one method of determining congruent angles. In looking at right angles whose sides are neither vertical nor horizontal, we see that the corresponding sides have equal slope only if the respective sides are parallel. (See Fig. 8.8.) This means that the proposition

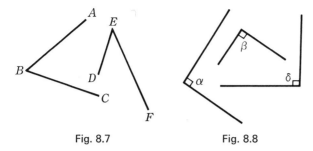

Fig. 8.7   Fig. 8.8

"If two angles are congruent, then their corresponding sides have equal slope" is false.   But what about the converse of this statement?   That is, "If the corresponding sides have equal slopes, then the angles are congruent." Let us consider a specific example.

Example 2:   Consider two congruent circles (A,AB) and (C,CD) on the x axis such that $A = (0,0)$, $B = (1,0)$, $C = (4,0)$ and $D = (5,0)$.   (See Fig. 8.9.)   In addition, let α be an angle with side AB and β be an angle with side

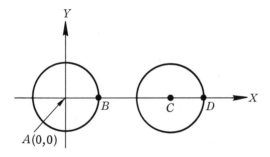

Fig. 8.9

CD.   Clearly, if the vertex of α is A and the vertex of β is C, then the corresponding sides AB and CD have equal slope.   Now, as in Fig. 8.10, let side

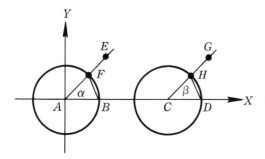

Fig. 8.10

AE of α intersect (A,AB) at F and have slope 1. Also, let side CG of β intersect (C,CD) at H and have slope 1. Finding the coordinates of F and H (see Exercise 2), we get $F = (\sqrt{2}/2, \sqrt{2}/2)$ and $H = (\sqrt{2}/2 + 4, \sqrt{2})$. Using the distance formula to find FB and HD, we have $(FB) = \sqrt{2 - \sqrt{2}}$, and $(HD) = \sqrt{2 - \sqrt{2}}$. Therefore we know that $FB \cong HD$, and by Definition (8-a) we have $\alpha \cong \beta$. Thus the converse statement holds in this one specific example. Can we prove it in general?

Theorem (8d-1): If the corresponding sides of two angles have equal slopes, then the angles are congruent.

PROOF

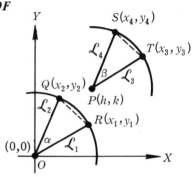

[Note that Theorem (8b-1) is used with α.]

Given: Line $\mathcal{L}_1$ and $\mathcal{L}_2$ forming α with vertex at $(0,0)$ and $\mathcal{L}_3$ and $\mathcal{L}_4$ forming β with vertex (h,k) such that $m_1 = m_3$ and $m_2 = m_4$.
To Prove: $\alpha \cong \beta$.

1. $\mathcal{L}_1$ and $\mathcal{L}_2$ determine α at $O(0,0)$ and $\mathcal{L}_3$ and $\mathcal{L}_4$ determine β at $P(h,k)$ such that $m_1 = m_3, m_2 = m_4$.

1. Hypothesis

2. There are circles
$$O = \{(x,y) \mid x^2 + y^2 = a^2\}$$
and
$$P = \{(x,y) \mid (x - h)^2 + (y - k)^2 = a^2\}.$$

2. Theorem (5d-1)

3. Circles O and P intersect the sides of α and β at the indicated points.

3. Theorem (7a-4)

4. S and T are a distance a from P; also, Q and R are a distance a from O.

4. Definition (5-g)

5. $OR \cong OQ \cong PT \cong PS$.

5. Definition (6-l)

6. $x_3 - h = x_1 - 0 = x_1$;
$x_4 - h = x_2 - 0 = x_2$;
$y_3 - k = y_1 - 0 = y_1$;
$y_4 - k = y_2 - 0 = y_2$.

6. Corollary (6e-2a)

7. $x_4 - x_3 = x_2 - x_1;$ $y_4 - y_3 = y_2 - y_1.$	7. Why?
8. $(QR) =$ $\sqrt{(x_1 - x_2)^2 + (y_1 - y_2)^2},$ $(ST) =$ $\sqrt{(x_3 - x_4)^2 + (y_3 - y_4)^2}.$	8. Why?
9. $(QR) = (ST).$	9. Why?
10. Q and R and S and T determine line segments QR and ST, respectively.	10. Why?
11. $QR \cong ST.$	11. Why?
12. $\alpha \cong \beta.$	12. Why?

Theorem (8d-1) deals only with those lines that have slope. Theorem (8d-2) below concerns the case where one pair of the corresponding sides has no slope. The proof remains virtually the same; only changes in the coordinates are necessary. The actual proof is left to the exercises.

Theorem (8d-2): If one pair of corresponding sides of two angles has no slope and the other pair of corresponding sides has equal slope, then the angles are congruent.

Now we might ask the question "Are angles for which both pairs of corresponding sides have no slope congruent?" These sides are clearly coincident by Corollary (6b-2b). If we make the following definition, then the congruence of these angles is ensured.

Definition (8-j): Coincident rays determine **angle measure zero.**

Exercise Set

1. Prove Theorem (8d-2).

2. In Example 2, show algebraically how the coordinates of H and F were found.

3. Fill in the missing reasons in the proof of Theorem (8d-1).

4. *Prove:* If the corresponding sides of two angles have no slope, then the angles are congruent.

5. What is the measure of the angle $\overrightarrow{AB} \cap \overrightarrow{AB}$?

6. Find the slopes of the missing sides in order to claim by Theorem (8d-1) that the angles are congruent in Fig. 8.11.
   (a) $m_1 = -1,\ m_2 = 7,\ m_3 = \ ?,\ m_4 = \ ?$
   (b) $m_1 = +2,\ m_2 = -2,\ m_3 = \ ?,\ m_4 = \ ?$
   (c) $m_1 = m_2 = 0,\ m_3 = \frac{1}{2},\ m_4 = \ ?$

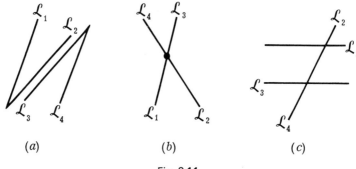

Fig. 8.11

8e   Angle Congruence and Straight Lines

Several important theorems and corollaries should be included in our development of congruent angles.

First we define angles determined by the intersection of two lines.

Definition (8-k): Nonadjacent angles determined by two intersecting straight lines such that the point of intersection is their common vertex are **vertical angles**.

Theorem (8e-1): Vertical angles are congruent.

We shall prove the theorem for the case where both lines have slope. The case for which one line is vertical is left to the exercises.

PROOF

Given: Lines $\mathscr{L}_1$ and $\mathscr{L}_2$ intersecting at P, forming angles α and β, where α and β are vertical angles.

To Prove: $\alpha \cong \beta$.

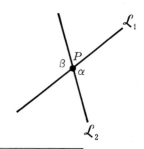

1. There are lines $\mathscr{L}_1$ and $\mathscr{L}_2$ intersecting at P that determine vertical angles α and β having vertex P.	1. Hypothesis
2. The right sides of α and β have slopes m_1 and m_2, respectively. The left sides of α and β have slopes m_3 and m_4, respectively.	2. Theorem (6a-3)

3. $m_1 = m_2$; $m_3 = m_4$.	3. Theorem (6a-1)
4. $\alpha \cong \beta$.	4. Theorem (8d-1)
Q.E.D.	

Definition (8-l): A **transversal** is a straight line that intersects any two other straight lines on two distinct points.

We note that at least three distinct lines are involved when we talk about transversals.

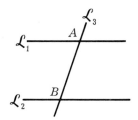

Fig. 8.12

Consider Fig. 8.12. If the lines $\mathscr{L}_1$ and $\mathscr{L}_2$ are intersected by the transversal $\mathscr{L}_3$ at points $A \in \mathscr{L}_1$ and $B \in \mathscr{L}_2$, then those points that are in $\mathscr{L}_3$ and on the A side of $\mathscr{L}_2$ and on the B side of $\mathscr{L}_1$ are said to be points on the transversal *inside* the straight lines $\mathscr{L}_1$ and $\mathscr{L}_2$. All other points in $\mathscr{L}_3$ (points of intersection excluded) are said to be *outside* the straight lines $\mathscr{L}_1$ and $\mathscr{L}_2$.

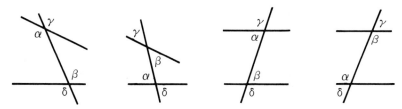

Fig. 8.13

In each of the illustrations of Fig. 8.13, the angles α and β are called *alternate interior angles* and γ and δ are called *alternate exterior angles*. In each of the illustrations of Fig. 8.14, we call α and β *corresponding angles*.

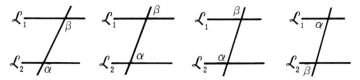

Fig. 8.14

We now make concise definitions about these pairs of angles.   The reader should draw the figures described in the following definitions.

Definition (8-m):   For points A in $\mathscr{L}_1$ and B in line $\mathscr{L}_2$, where A and B are on opposite sides of the transversal $\mathscr{L}_3$ intersecting $\mathscr{L}_1$ and $\mathscr{L}_2$ at points C and D, respectively, $\sphericalangle ACD$ and $\sphericalangle BDC$ are **alternate interior angles.**

Definition (8-n):   If $\mathscr{L}_1$ and $\mathscr{L}_2$ are intersected by a transversal $\mathscr{L}_3$ such that α and β are alternate interior angles and if γ and α, δ and β are vertical angles, then γ and δ are **alternate exterior angles.**

Definition (8-o):   The angles α and δ, γ and β of Definition (8-n) are called **corresponding angles.**

We see that these definitions only have meaning for pairs of angles.

Using these definitions and the important Theorem (8d-1), we now prove a proposition that will be extremely useful to us.

Theorem (8e-2):   If parallel lines are cut by a transversal, the alternate interior angles determined are congruent.

PROOF

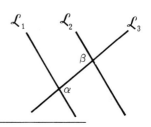

Given: $\mathscr{L}_1 \parallel \mathscr{L}_2$ with transversal $\mathscr{L}_3$ determining alternate interior angles α and β.
To Prove: $\alpha \cong \beta$.

Case 1: $\mathscr{L}_1$ and $\mathscr{L}_2$ have slope.	
1. There are parallel lines $\mathscr{L}_1$ and $\mathscr{L}_2$ with transversal $\mathscr{L}_3$ determining alternate interior angles α and β.	1. Hypothesis
2. The right sides of α and β have slopes m_1 and m_2, respectively. The left sides of α and β have slopes m_3 and m_4, respectively.	2. Theorem (6a-3)
3. $m_1 = m_2$.	3. Definition (6-b)
4. $m_3 = m_4$.	4. Corollary (6b-2a)
5. $\alpha \cong \beta$.	5. Theorem (8d-1)
Case 2: $\mathscr{L}_1$ and $\mathscr{L}_2$ vertical.	
1. There are parallel lines $\mathscr{L}_1$ and $\mathscr{L}_2$ with transversal $\mathscr{L}_3$ determining alternate interior angles α and β.	1. Hypothesis

2. The right sides of α and β have no slope.	2. Theorem (6a-2)
3. The left sides of α and β have slopes m_3 and m_4, respectively.	3. Why?
4. $m_3 = m_4$.	4. Why?
5. $\alpha \cong \beta$.	5. Why?

Case 3: $\mathscr{L}_3$ vertical.

1. There are parallel lines $\mathscr{L}_1$ and $\mathscr{L}_2$ with transversal $\mathscr{L}_3$ determining alternate interior angles α and β.	1. Hypothesis
2. The right sides of α and β have slopes m_1 and m_2, respectively.	2. Why?
3. The left sides of α and β have no slope.	3. Why?
4. $m_1 = m_2$.	4. Why?
5. $\alpha \cong \beta$.	5. Why?

Q.E.D.

Some immediate results of this theorem are stated as corollaries.

Corollary (8e-2a): If parallel lines are cut by a transversal, the alternate exterior angles determined are congruent.

Corollary (8e-2b): If parallel lines are cut by a transversal, the interior angles on the same side of the transversal are supplementary.

Corollary (8e-2c): If parallel lines are cut by a transversal, then the corresponding angles determined are congruent.

The following corollary is included for its historical importance. It was used by Euclid (300 B.C.) as an axiom for geometry. If we use Fig. 8.15 as a guide, the theorem states that if $(\alpha) + (\beta) < 2(\gamma)$, where γ is a right angle (i.e., $180°$ or π radians), then $\mathscr{L}_1$ will intersect $\mathscr{L}_2$ on that side of $\mathscr{L}_3$

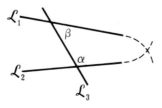

Fig. 8.15

with α and β. The proof of the theorem is an interesting use of "proof by contradiction." It may be found in the Appendix.

Corollary (8e-2d): If two lines are cut by a transversal in such a way that the sum of the measures of the two interior angles on the same side of the transversal is less than the measure of two right angles, then the lines will intersect on the same side of the transversal as the two interior angles.

We now prove the converse of Theorem (8e-2).

Theorem (8e-3): If two lines are cut by a transversal so that the alternate interior angles determined are congruent, then the two lines are parallel.

PROOF

Given: Lines $\mathcal{L}_1$ and $\mathcal{L}_2$ with transversal $\mathcal{L}_3$ intersecting $\mathcal{L}_1$ at A and $\mathcal{L}_2$ at B and determining alternate interior angles α and β such that $\alpha \cong \beta$.
To Prove: $\mathcal{L}_1 \mathbin{/\!/} \mathcal{L}_2$.

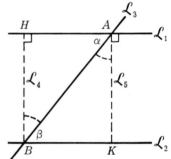

1. There are lines $\mathcal{L}_1$ and $\mathcal{L}_2$ with transversal $\mathcal{L}_3$ intersecting $\mathcal{L}_1$ at A and $\mathcal{L}_2$ at B and determining alternate interior angles α and β such that $\alpha \cong \beta$.	1. Hypothesis
2. There is a line $\mathcal{L}_4$ containing B such that $\mathcal{L}_4 \perp \mathcal{L}_1$; there is a line $\mathcal{L}_5$ containing A such that $\mathcal{L}_5 \perp \mathcal{L}_1$. (Call the points of intersection H and K, respectively.)	2. Theorem (6c-8)
3. $\mathcal{L}_4 \mathbin{/\!/} \mathcal{L}_5$.	3. Theorem (6c-10)
4. $\measuredangle KAB \cong \measuredangle HBA$.	4. Theorem (8e-2)
5. $(\alpha) = (\beta)$ and $(\measuredangle KAB) = (\measuredangle HBA)$.	5. Theorem (8c-2)
6. $\measuredangle KAH$ and $\measuredangle BHA$ are right angles.	6. Definition (8-b)
7. $(\alpha) + (\measuredangle KAB) = (\measuredangle KAH)$ and $(\beta) + (\measuredangle HBA) = (\measuredangle HBK)$.	7. Corollary (8c-3a)

8. $(\alpha) + (\sphericalangle KAB) = (\beta) + (\sphericalangle HBA)$.	8. Properties of $\mathscr{R}$
9. $(\sphericalangle HBK) = (\sphericalangle KAH)$.	9. Why?
10. $\sphericalangle HBK \cong \sphericalangle KAH$.	10. Why?
11. $\mathscr{L}_4 \perp \mathscr{L}_2$.	11. Definition (8-b)
12. $\mathscr{L}_1 // \mathscr{L}_2$.	12. Why?

The proofs of the following corollaries are again left to the exercises.

Corollary (8e-3a): If two lines are cut by a transversal so that the alternate exterior angles determined are congruent, then the two lines are parallel.

Corollary (8e-3b): If two lines are cut by a transversal so that the corresponding angles determined are congruent, then the two lines are parallel.

Corollary (8e-3c): If two lines are cut by a transversal so that the sum of the measures of the interior angles on the same side of the transversal equals the measure of two right angles, then the two lines are parallel.

Exercise Set

1. In Fig. 8.16, if $\mathscr{L}_1 // \mathscr{L}_2$ and $\mathscr{L}_3 // \mathscr{L}_4$, prove $\alpha \cong \beta$.
2. In Fig. 8.17, if $\alpha \cong \beta$ and $\mathscr{L}_1 // \mathscr{L}_2$, prove that $\delta \cong \gamma$. (Use two different methods.)

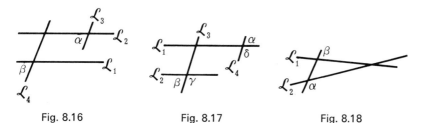

Fig. 8.16   Fig. 8.17   Fig. 8.18

3. Explain how Corollary (6b-2a) actually justifies Step 4 of Theorem (8e-2).
4. Complete the proof of Theorem (8e-2).
5. Explain which properties of $\mathscr{R}$ are used and complete the proof of Theorem (8e-3).
6. In Fig. 8.18, if $(\alpha) + (\beta) = 2(\gamma)$ for γ a right angle, prove that $\mathscr{L}_1 \cap \mathscr{L}_2 = \emptyset$. (*Hint:* Assume the contrary.)
7. Prove Theorem (8e-1) for the cases
   (a) where one line has no slope.
   (b) where both lines have the same slope.
   (c) where both lines have no slope.
8. Prove Corollary (8e-2a).

9. Prove Corollary (8e-2b).

10. Prove Corollary (8e-2c).

11. Prove Corollary (8e-3a).

12. Prove Corollary (8e-3b).

13. Prove Corollary (8e-3c).

*14. If two angles are congruent to a third angle, then they are congruent to each other. Prove this proposition.

8f   Angle Congruence and Triangles

Theorem (8f-1):   The sum of the measures of the interior angles determined by a triangle is equal to the sum of the measures of two right angles.

PROOF

Given: Triangle ($\triangle$) ABC.
To Prove: $(\sphericalangle ABC) + (\sphericalangle BCA)$
$+ (\sphericalangle CAB) = 2(\gamma)$ for some right angle γ.

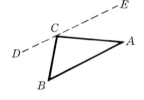

1. There is a $\triangle ABC$ and some right angle γ.	1. Hypothesis
2. There is a line $\overleftrightarrow{DCE}$ such that $\overleftrightarrow{DCE} \parallel AB$.	2. Theorem (6c-4)
3. $\sphericalangle DCB \cong \sphericalangle CBA$ and $\sphericalangle ECA \cong \sphericalangle CAB$.	3. Theorem (8e-2)
4. $(\sphericalangle DCB) = (\sphericalangle CBA)$ and $(\sphericalangle ECA) = (\sphericalangle CAB)$.	4. Theorem (8c-2)
5. $(\sphericalangle DCB) + (\sphericalangle BCA) + (\sphericalangle ACE) = 2(\gamma)$.	5. Theorem (8c-4)
6. $(\sphericalangle ABC) + (\sphericalangle BCA) + (\sphericalangle CAB) = 2(\gamma)$.	6. Why?

Another theorem of considerable value follows.   The reasons have been omitted; they should be filled in by the reader.   (See Exercise 11.)

Theorem (8f-2):   The measure of an exterior angle of a triangle is equal to the sum of the measures of the two remote interior angles.

PROOF

Given: $\triangle ABC$ with $AB \subset \overrightarrow{AD}$
and exterior angle δ.
To Prove: $(\delta) = (\alpha) + (\beta)$.

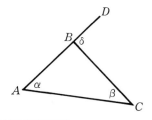

1. $\triangle ABC$ with $AB \subset \overrightarrow{AD}$, exterior angle δ, remote interior angles α and β, and some right angle γ.	1. Hypothesis
2. $(\delta) + (\sphericalangle CBA) = 2(\gamma)$.	2. Why?
3. $(\alpha) + (\beta) + (\sphericalangle CBA) = 2(\gamma)$.	3. Why?
4. $(\delta) - (\alpha) - (\beta) = 0$.	4. Why?
5. $(\alpha) + (\beta) = (\delta)$.	5. Why?
Q.E.D.	

Theorem (8f-3): If two angles of one triangle are correspondingly congruent to two angles of another triangle, the third pair of angles is also congruent.

The proof of this theorem is a direct application of Theorem (8f-1) and of the properties of $\mathscr{R}$. We leave it as an exercise.

We shall discuss additional properties of triangles in Chapter 9. The following theorem, although not directly concerned with triangles, is a direct consequence of Theorem (8f-3).

Theorem (8f-4): If two angles have their corresponding sides respectively perpendicular, then they are congruent.

PROOF

Given: Angle α with sides $\mathscr{L}_1$
and $\mathscr{M}_1$ and angle β with sides $\mathscr{L}_2$
and $\mathscr{M}_2$ such that $\mathscr{L}_1 \perp \mathscr{L}_2$ and
$\mathscr{M}_1 \perp \mathscr{M}_2$.
To Prove: $\alpha \cong \beta$.

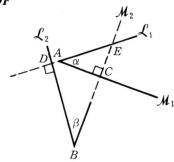

Case 1: Assume $m_{\mathscr{L}_1} \neq m_{\mathscr{M}_2}$.

1. There are angles α and β having their respective sides $\perp$.	1. Hypothesis
2. $\mathscr{L}_1 \cap \mathscr{L}_2 = D$ and $\mathscr{M}_1 \cap \mathscr{M}_2 = C$.	2. Definition (6-c)
3. $\mathscr{L}_1 \cap \mathscr{M}_2 = E$.	3. Theorem (6b-2)
4. $\triangle ACE$ and BDE are determined by $\mathscr{L}_1, \mathscr{L}_2, \mathscr{M}_1$, and $\mathscr{M}_2$.	4. Why?
5. $\sphericalangle BDE, \sphericalangle ACE$ are right angles.	5. Why?
6. $\sphericalangle BDE \cong \sphericalangle ACE$.	6. Why?
7. $\sphericalangle AEC \cong \sphericalangle BED$.	7. Why?
8. $\alpha \cong \beta$.	8. Theorem (8f-3)

Case 2: Assume $m_{\mathscr{L}_1} = m_{\mathscr{M}_2}$.

1. There are angles α and β having their respective sides $\perp$.	1. Hypothesis
2. $\mathscr{L}_1 \cap \mathscr{L}_2 = D$ and $\mathscr{M}_1 \cap \mathscr{M}_2 = C$.	2. Definition (6-c)
3. $\mathscr{L}_1 \parallel \mathscr{M}_2$.	3. Why?
4. $\mathscr{M}_2 \perp \mathscr{L}_2$ and $\mathscr{L}_1 \perp \mathscr{M}_1$.	4. Theorem (6c-11)
5. α, β are right angles.	5. Why?
6. $\alpha \cong \beta$.	6. Why?

Case 3: One of the sides has no slope. Left to the exercises.

The reader may feel that the proof of Theorem (8f-4) leans rather heavily on the illustration. Certainly the picture would not have to be drawn as it is. Figures 8.19 and 8.20 illustrate two other possibilities.

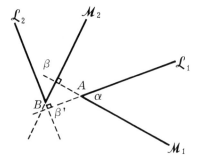

Fig. 8.19

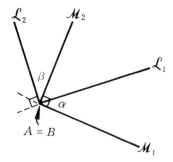

Fig. 8.20

A modification of the proof given will take care of the case illustrated in Fig. 8.19. A proof for the case in Fig. 8.20 is much easier. (See Exercises 13 and 14.)

Exercise Set

Use Figure 8.21 and determine the measure of the following angles.

1. $(\alpha) = 30°$, $(\theta) = 40°$, find (ϕ).
2. $(\phi) = 45°$, $(\theta) = 60°$, find (ϵ).
3. $(\alpha) = 60°$, $(\delta) = 4(\theta)$, find (ϕ).
4. $(\delta) = (\theta) = 60°$, find (λ).
5. $(\epsilon) = \dfrac{2\pi}{3}$, $(\eta) = \dfrac{5\pi}{6}$, find (ϕ).

In Fig. 8.21, if $(\gamma) = r$ for some right angle γ, then find the required measure.

6. $(\mu) = a$, $(\theta) = b$, then $(\delta) = $?
7. $(\eta) = a$, $(\delta) = b$, then $(\phi) = $?
8. $(\epsilon) = a$, $(\theta) = b$, then $(\mu) = $?
9. $(\delta) = (\theta) = a$, then $(\mu) = $?
10. In Fig. 8.22, $DF \parallel AB$. Show that the angles of $\triangle CDF$ are congruent respectively to the angles of $\triangle ABC$.

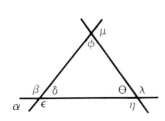

Fig. 8.21

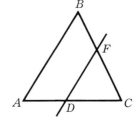

Fig. 8.22

11. Complete the reasons in the proof of Theorem (8f-2).
12. Complete the proof of Theorem (8f-4).
13. Prove Theorem (8f-4) for the case shown in Fig. 8.20. [*Hint:* See Corollary (8c-4c).]
*14. Do the proof of Theorem (8f-4) for the situation shown in Fig. 8.19.
*15. Prove Theorem (8f-3).

8g Angle Congruence and Circles

Many interesting and useful cases of angle congruence arise from relationships among radii, chords, and tangents of circles.

Theorem (8g-1):   If a radius of a circle is perpendicular to a chord, then the central angles determined by the given radius and the radii on the end-points of the chord are congruent.

Figure 8.23 illustrates this theorem.   We are given a circle (O, OC) and chord AB such that $OC \perp AB$. OA and OB are radii of (O, OC).   Theorem (7b-5) says that $AH \cong HB$, which, by Definition (6-l), means $(AH) = (HB)$.

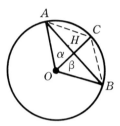

Fig. 8.23

Theorem (5c-3) establishes chords AC and CB.   Using Theorem (4h-1) or Theorem (6c-9), we have $(AH)^2 + (CH)^2 = (AC)^2$ and $(HB)^2 + (CH)^2 = (CB)^2$.   Subtracting these two and employing the foregoing identity, we have $(AC)^2 = (CB)^2$ or $(AC) = (CB)$.   Then, by Definition (8-a), we obtain $\alpha \cong \beta$, which was the desired result.   Thus the theorem is established.

We also see in Fig. 8.23 that $\sphericalangle OHA \cong \sphericalangle OHB$, for both are right angles determined by the perpendicular lines OC and AB.   Since Theorem (8g-1) says that $\alpha \cong \beta$, then by Theorem (8f-3) we have that $\sphericalangle OAB \cong \sphericalangle OBA$. We state this as a proposition and leave the formal proof for the exercises.

Theorem (8g-2):   Radii on the endpoints of a chord determine congruent angles with the chord.

Another theorem that uses algebraic techniques in the construction of the proof is the following.

Theorem (8g-3):   If an angle has its vertex in a circle and its sides on the endpoints of a diameter, then it is a right angle.

See Exercise 19.   Figure 8.24 illustrates Theorem (8g-3).   That is, AB is a diameter and $\sphericalangle ACB$ is a right angle.   This gives another relationship

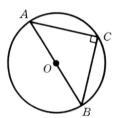

Fig. 8.24

that determines right angles. Theorem (8a-4) guarantees that all these right angles are congruent regardless of the method used to construct them.

Theorem (8g-3) provides us with a fact about a very particular inscribed angle. We need to relate general inscribed angles to central angles to make the concept useful.

Theorem (8g-4): The measure of an inscribed angle is equal to one-half the measure of its intercepted arc.

PROOF

(We note that there are three possibilities for the position of the inscribed angle. Accordingly, a three-part proof is needed.)

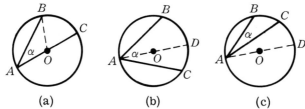

(a)	(b)	(c)

Given: (O,OA) with inscribed angle α determining arc BC.

To Prove: $(\alpha) = \frac{1}{2}(\overset{\frown}{BC})$.

---

1. Inscribed angle α determines $\overset{\frown}{BC}$ in (O,OA). [Part 1: $O \in AC$. See diagram (a).]	1. Hypothesis
2. There is a radius OB.	2. Theorem (7b-1)
3. $(\sphericalangle COB) = (\overset{\frown}{BC})$.	3. Definition (8-d)
4. $(\sphericalangle COB) = (\alpha) + (\sphericalangle ABO)$.	4. Theorem (8f-2)
5. $(\overset{\frown}{BC}) = (\alpha) + (\sphericalangle ABO)$.	5. Why?
6. $\alpha \cong \sphericalangle ABO$.	6. Theorem (8g-2)
7. $(\alpha) = (\sphericalangle ABO)$.	7. Theorem (8c-2)
8. $(\alpha) = \frac{1}{2}(\overset{\frown}{BC})$. [Part 2: O interior to α. See diagram (b).]	8. Why?
9. There is a diameter $\overline{AOD}$.	9. Why?
10. $(\sphericalangle BAD) = \frac{1}{2}(\overset{\frown}{BD})$ and $(\sphericalangle DAC) = \frac{1}{2}(\overset{\frown}{DC})$.	10. Step 8 above

11. $(\sphericalangle BAD) + (\sphericalangle DAC) =$ $\frac{1}{2}[(\widehat{BD}) + (\widehat{DC})]$.	11. Addition in Step 10
12. $(\alpha) = (\sphericalangle BAD) + (\sphericalangle DAC)$.	12. Theorem (8c-3)
13. $(\alpha) = \frac{1}{2}(\widehat{BC})$.	13. Theorem (7g-1)
[Part 3: O exterior to α. See diagram (c).]	
14. $(\sphericalangle BAD) - (\sphericalangle DAC) =$ $\frac{1}{2}[(\widehat{BD}) - (\widehat{DC})]$.	14. Subtraction in Step 10
15. $(\alpha) + (\sphericalangle DAC) = (\sphericalangle BAD)$.	15. Why?
16. $(\alpha) = \frac{1}{2}(\widehat{BC})$.	16. Theorem (7g-1)

Corollary (8g-4a):   The measure of an inscribed angle is equal to one-half the measure of a central angle when both angles determine the same or congruent chords in the same or congruent circles.

The proof is left to the exercises.

The following proposition gives us a congruence relation between inscribed angles.

Theorem (8g-5):   Inscribed angles that intercept the same or congruent chords in the same or congruent circles are congruent.

This theorem and the following one can be proved by straightforward application of Theorems (8c-2) and (8g-4).   (See Exercises 12 and 13.)

Theorem (8g-6):   Congruent inscribed angles in the same or congruent circles intercept the same or congruent chords.

If we now use Theorems (8f-2), (8g-4), (8g-5), and Corollary (8g-4a) in a careful manner, the following propositions can be easily proven.   (See Exercise 14.)

Theorem (8g-7):   In a circle the measure of an angle determined by a chord and a tangent that intersects the chord is equal to one-half the measure of its intercepted arc.   (See Fig. 8.25.)

Theorem (8g-8):   The measure of an angle determined by two tangents to a circle is equal to one-half the difference of the measures of the intercepted arcs.   (See Fig. 8.26.)

Theorem (8g-9):   The measure of an angle determined by two secants exterior to a circle is equal to one-half the difference of the measures of its intercepted arcs.   (See Fig. 8.27.)

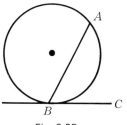

Fig. 8.25

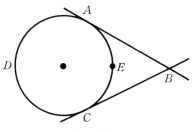

Fig. 8.26

Theorem (8g-10):   The measure of an angle formed by two intersecting chords of a circle is equal to one-half the sum of the measure of its intercepted arcs.   (See Fig. 8.28.)

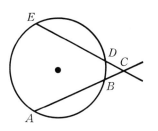

Fig. 8.27

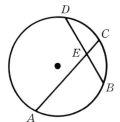

Fig. 8.28

Exercise Set

1. In Fig. 8.29, if O is the center of the circle, show that $\alpha \cong \eta$.
2. In Fig. 8.30, if $AB \perp CD$ in circle O, show that $\alpha \cong \beta$.

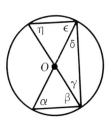

Fig. 8.29

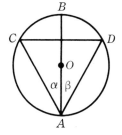

Fig. 8.30

3. In Fig. 8.31, what is the sum of the measures of α and β if AB is the diameter?

In Fig. 8.32, if $AB \cong CD$ are chords and AC and BD are diameters in Exercises 4 through 6, show that:

4. $(\alpha) + (\beta) = (\delta) + (\gamma)$.

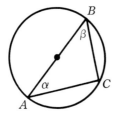

Fig. 8.31

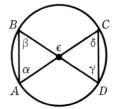

Fig. 8.32

5. $\alpha \cong \gamma$ and $\beta \cong \delta$.

6. $BC \cong AD$.

7. Write a formal proof of Theorem (8g-1).

8. Prove Theorem (8g-2).

9. Prove Theorem (8g-3) as a corollary to (8g-4).

10. Complete the proof of Theorem (8g-4).

11. Prove Corollary (8g-4a).

12. Prove Theorem (8g-5).

13. Prove Theorem (8g-6).

14. Prove Theorem (8g-7).

15. Prove Theorem (8g-8).

16. Prove Theorem (8g-9).

17. Prove Theorem (8g-10).

18. In Fig. 8.33, determine the measure of $\angle BCD$ in terms of the measure of the arcs AC and BC.

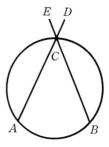

Fig. 8.33

19. What is the measure of an angle exterior to a circle determined by a secant and a tangent to the circle?

*20. Prove Theorem (8g-3).

8h   Angle Bisectors

Definition (8-p):   An **angle bisector** is a ray interior to an angle whose endpoint is the vertex of the angle and that determines congruent angles with the sides of the given angle.

In Fig. 8.34, AD is an angle bisector of $\angle BAC$ such that $\angle BAD \cong \angle DAC$.   It appears that we may "sketch" an angle bisector; yet this does not guarantee that the bisector exists.   Thus the following existence theorem is appropriate.

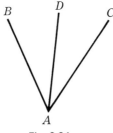

Fig. 8.34

Theorem (8h-1):   For any angle there is an angle bisector.

PROOF

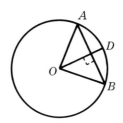

Given: $\angle AOB$.
To Prove: OD is an angle bisector of $\angle AOB$.

1. There is an angle AOB.	1. Hypothesis
2. There is a circle (O, OB).	2. Theorem (5d-1)
3. There is a chord AB.	3. Why?
4. OA is a radius.	4. Why?
5. Let $OD \perp AB$.	5. Theorem (6c-8)
6. $\angle AOD \cong \angle DOB$.	6. Theorem (8g-1)
7. OD is an angle bisector of $\angle AOB$.	7. Definition (8-p)

Q.E.D.

Theorem (8h-2):   For any angle, there is at most one angle bisector.

PROOF

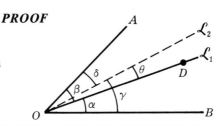

Given: $\angle AOB$.
To Prove: Angle bisector OD is unique.

1. There is an angle AOB.	1. Hypothesis
2. There is an angle bisector $\mathscr{L}_1$ of $\angle AOB$.	2. Theorem (8h-1)

3. Assume there is a second angle bisector $\mathscr{L}_2$.	3. Theorem (8h-1)
4. $\mathscr{L}_1$ determines $\cong$ angles α and β with sides OA and OB; $\mathscr{L}_2$ determines $\cong$ angles γ and δ with OA and OB, respectively.	4. Definition (8-p)
5. $\mathscr{L}_1$ and $\mathscr{L}_2$ determine an angle θ.	5. Definition (5-k)
6. $(\theta) \neq 0$.	6. Definition (8-d)
7. $(\alpha) = (\beta)$ and $(\delta) = (\gamma)$.	7. Why?
8. $(\alpha) + (\theta) + (\delta) = (\sphericalangle AOB)$ or, if $\mathscr{L}_2$ is on the other side of $\mathscr{L}_1$, $(\gamma) + (\theta) + (\beta) = (\sphericalangle AOB)$. (We shall consider the former case.)	8. Why?
9. $(\alpha) + (\beta) = (\sphericalangle AOB)$ and $(\gamma) + (\delta) = (\sphericalangle AOB)$.	9. Why?
10. $(\theta) + (\delta) - (\beta) = 0$ and $(\theta) + (\alpha) - (\gamma) = 0$.	10. Properties of $\mathscr{R}$
11. $2(\theta) + (\alpha) - (\beta) + (\delta) - (\gamma) = 0$.	11. Why?
12. $2(\theta) + (\alpha) - (\alpha) + (\delta) - (\delta) = 0$.	12. Why?
13. $(\theta) = 0$. Contradiction of Step 6.	13. Why?
14. The contradiction of the second case of Step 8 is left to the exercises.	14. See Exercise 3
15. There is only one bisector of $\sphericalangle AOB$.	15. Principle of contradiction

Theorem (8h-3):   Every point in the angle bisector of an angle is equidistant from the two sides of the angle.

Recall that when we are talking about the distance from a point to a line, we mean the *perpendicular distance*.   The proof is again left to the exercises.

Exercise Set

1. Show that if $\sphericalangle AOC \cong \sphericalangle COB$, then $AD \cong DB$ in Fig. 8.35.
2. Complete the reasons in the proof of Theorem (8h-1).

3. Complete the reasons in the proof of Theorem (8h-2), and do Step 14 completely.

*4. Prove Theorem (8h-3).

*5. In Fig. 8.36, if lines AOB, COD, and EOF intersect at O such that OD is the angle bisector of $\sphericalangle AOF$, then show that OC is an angle bisector of $\sphericalangle EOB$.

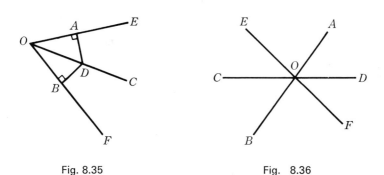

Fig. 8.35   Fig. 8.36

8i   Angles and Circular Functions

The reader will recall that in Section 7h we defined some special numbers called sine (u), and so on, where u is the length of an arc of a circle. These special numbers were called *circular functions* (cf). However, no argument was made to show that the use of the term "function" is justified.

Let us find a few values of sine (u) for the particular circle $\{(x,y) \mid x^2 + y^2 = 4\}$. As shown in Fig. 8.37, certain ordered pairs are easily obtained.

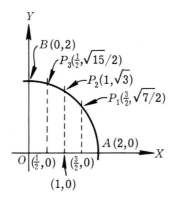

Fig. 8.37

Using Definition (7-n),

for $u_1 = \widehat{AP}_1,$ $\text{sine } (u_1) = \dfrac{y_1}{a} = \dfrac{\sqrt{7}}{4} \approx 0.66;$

for $u_2 = \widehat{AP}_2,$ $\text{sine } (u_2) = \dfrac{y_2}{a} = \dfrac{\sqrt{3}}{2} \approx 0.87;$

for $u_3 = \widehat{AP}_3,$ $\text{sine } (u_3) = \dfrac{y_3}{a} = \dfrac{\sqrt{15}/2}{2} \approx 0.97;$

for $u_4 = \widehat{AB},$ $\text{sine } (u_4) = \dfrac{y_4}{a} = \dfrac{2}{2} = 1.$

Using radian measure, $u_4 = \widehat{AB} = \pi/2.$ We can approximate the other values u_1, u_2, u_3 by using Theorem (8c-1). Recall also that we have agreed on the value $u_0 = 0$ for $\widehat{AA}.$ Using these results, we have approximately,

for $(\widehat{AA})$, $(\widehat{AP}_1)$, $(\widehat{AP}_2)$, $(\widehat{AP}_3)$, and $(\widehat{AB})$,

$$u_0 = 0,$$
$$u_1 \approx 0.61,$$
$$u_2 \approx 1.06,$$
$$u_3 \approx 1.32,$$
$$u_4 = \frac{\pi}{2} \approx 1.57, \text{ respectively.}$$

Using these and other values that could be obtained by similar methods, a graph of sine (u) for values of u is obtained. (See Fig. 8.38.)

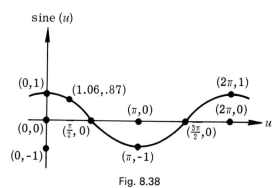

Fig. 8.38

Note that *no vertical line will ever intersect the locus* $\{[u, \text{sine } (u)]\}$ *more than once.* By Theorem (5f-1), then, this locus is a function. Similarly, $\{[u, \text{cosine } (u)]\}$ and the other ratios of Definition (7-n) are functions. (This fact could be precisely established in a more rigorous treatment than seems suitable here.) Because of this result, the abbreviation $cf(u) = cf(\widehat{AP})$ is suitable to represent any of this set of six functions.

The fact that $cf(u)$ is a function allows us to establish a useful fact. Suppose $\overset{\frown}{A'B'} \cong \overset{\frown}{AB}$ for arcs in the same or congruent circles. Then $(\overset{\frown}{A'B'}) = (\overset{\frown}{AB})$ by Theorem (8c-1), and because a function is single valued, $cf(\overset{\frown}{A'B'}) = cf(\overset{\frown}{AB})$.

Theorem (8i-1): Circular functions determined by congruent arcs in the same or congruent circles are equal.

This principle means that the circular functions are *independent of position* in the plane in spite of the fact that we defined them for a circle with center at the origin. It turns out that they are even less restricted than Theorem (8i-1) would indicate.

We know that each arc in a circle determines a central angle. It should be possible to relate the circular functions to angles in some way. Now consider Fig. 8.39. α determines both $\overset{\frown}{AB}$ and $\overset{\frown}{A'B'}$. Does it seem possible that $cf(\overset{\frown}{A'B'}) = cf(\overset{\frown}{AB})$?

Let us consider this problem by looking at the case illustrated in Fig. 8.40. Consider the two circles:

$$\mathscr{K}_1: \quad x^2 + y^2 = a_1{}^2$$
$$\mathscr{K}_2: \quad x^2 + y^2 = a_2{}^2.$$

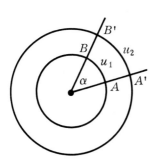

Fig. 8.39

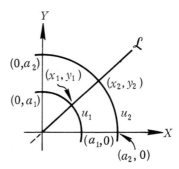

Fig. 8.40

In addition, we need points (x_1, y_1) and (x_2, y_2) such that

$$(x_1, y_1) \in \mathscr{K}_1$$
$$(x_2, y_2) \in \mathscr{K}_2.$$

For these two circles and these two points we may write

(1)
$$x_1{}^2 + y_1{}^2 = a_1{}^2$$
$$x_2{}^2 + y_2{}^2 = a_2{}^2.$$

By Corollary (6b-1a), $\mathscr{L}$ has equation $y = mx$ and intersects $\mathscr{K}_1$ at (x_1, y_1) and $\mathscr{K}_2$ at (x_2, y_2).   Also,

(2)
$$y_1 = mx_1$$
$$y_2 = mx_2$$

are true by Theorem (4e-3).   Solving each equation of (2) for m, we obtain

$$m = \frac{x_1}{y_1} \qquad m = \frac{x_2}{y_2}.$$

Hence we have that the tangent (u_1) = tangent (u_2).   That is,

(3)
$$\frac{y_1}{x_1} = \frac{y_2}{x_2}, \qquad x_1 \neq 0, \quad x_2 \neq 0.$$

We now show that the ratios for the sine and cosine of arcs u_1 and u_2 are equal.

Substituting (2) into (1), we obtain

$$x_1^2 + m^2 x_1^2 = a_1^2$$
$$x_2^2 + m^2 x_2 = a_2^2.$$

Dividing by x_1^2 and x_2^2, respectively, yields

$$\frac{a_1^2}{x_1^2} = 1 + m^2$$

$$\frac{a_2^2}{x_2^2} = 1 + m^2.$$

Setting these equal to each other gives us the fact that cosine (u_1) = cosine (u_2). That is,

$$\frac{x_1^2}{a_1^2} = \frac{x_2^2}{a_2^2},$$

or taking the square root of both members,

$$\left| \frac{x_1}{a_1} \right| = \left| \frac{x_2}{a_2} \right|.$$

Making a similar argument [this time we solve (2) for x_1 and x_2 and substitute into (1)], we obtain

$$\left| \frac{y_1}{a_1} \right| = \left| \frac{y_2}{a_2} \right|.$$

This establishes that sine (u_1) = sine (u_2).   From Theorem (7h-2) it is easy to obtain the result that the secant, cosecant, and cotangent are similarly related.   Theorem (8i-1) establishes for us the fact that the circles need not be concentric.   Thus the following proposition has been established.

Theorem (8i-2):   Circular functions of arcs determined by the same central angle or by congruent central angles are equal.

The results of Theorems (8i-1) and (8i-2) indicate that circular functions of angle measure might be just as reasonable as circular functions of arc measure.

From Definition (8-d) we learned that for an angle α the measure of a was given by

(4)
$$(\alpha) = ks_\alpha,$$

where s_α is the length of the arc determined by the central angle α. Letting $u = s_\alpha$ we obtain for u, from (4),

(5)
$$u = \frac{1}{k}(\alpha).$$

Now we write the circular functions in terms of (5). That is,

(6)
$$cf(u) = cf\left[\frac{1}{k}(\alpha)\right].$$

If $k = 1$, then (6) becomes

(7)
$$cf(u) = cf[(\alpha)].$$

That is, when the measure of the arc equals the measure of the central angle that determines it, then the circular functions of the arc are each equal to the corresponding circular functions of the angle. Now, if we choose a central angle α or any central angle congruent to α, then by Theorem (8c-2) all the arcs of circles determined by these central angles have their ratios of Definition (7-a) correspondingly equal. This means that these ratios are all respectively equal to the ratios determined by an arc u where $(\alpha) = (u)$ or, put another way, where $k = 1$. But this means that equation (7) is true. Thus we can always use our ratios in terms of the measure of the angles in place of the measures of their arcs. The following theorem summarizes this discussion.

Theorem (8i-3): $cf(\widehat{AP}) = cf(\alpha)$, where $\widehat{AP}$ is any arc determined by central angle α.

Combining this result with preceding ones, we have the following corollary.

Corollary (8i-3a): Circular functions determined by congruent angles are equal and conversely.

Example 1: What are the values of sine (α) and cosine (α) in Fig. 8.41 if $(\alpha) = 30°$ and tangent $(\alpha) = \sqrt{3}/3$?

Solution: By the preceding theorems, the circular functions have values independent of the length of radius (OA). Let us choose $(OA) = 1$. By Definition (7-n), we have tangent $(\alpha) = \sqrt{3}/3 = y/x$ and $x^2 + y^2 = 1$. We write $y = \sqrt{3}x/3$. Then $x^2 + 3x^2/9 = 1$, whence $12x^2 = 9$. We may use $x > 0$, since $(\alpha) = 30°$ determines an angle in the first quadrant. Hence $x = \sqrt{3}/2$ and $y = \frac{1}{2}$. Therefore cosine $(\alpha) = (\sqrt{3}/2)/1 = \sqrt{3}/2$ and sine $(\alpha) = \frac{1}{2}$.

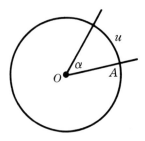

Fig. 8.41

Exercise Set

1. Determine values of sine (α) and cosine (α) if tangent (α) = 1 for $x > 0$ and $y > 0$.

2. Determine values of sine (α) and tangent (α) if cosine (α) = $-\frac{1}{2}$ and $y > 0$.

*3. Make the argument for the case when $x_1 = x_2$ in the proof of Theorem (8i-2).

In Exercises 9 through 14 of Section 7h, the results have been expressed in terms of arcs. Rework each problem with the arc being replaced by the appropriate angle in the manner of Example 1.

4. (AP_1) by $(\alpha_1) = 53°$.   5. (AP_2) by $(\alpha_2) = 45°$.

6. (AP_3) by $(\alpha_3) = 0°$.   7. (AP_4) by $(\alpha_4) = 30°$.

8. (AP_5) by $(\alpha_5) = 90°$.   9. (AP_6) by $(\alpha_6) = 15°30'$.

*10. Read through the proof of Theorem (8i-2). Does it seem that tangent (u) = m for the line $y = mx$ and α determined by that line and $\overrightarrow{OX}$?

*11. Using part (a) of Theorem (7h-3), show that A and B are acute angles of a triangle iff sine² (A) + sine² (B) = 1.

chapter 9

Properties of Triangles

9a   Special Triangles

We recall that a triangle is the geometric figure formed by the union of three line segments whose endpoints contain three noncollinear points. These triangles are now divided into various subsets depending on their angles or sides.

A triangle having no two sides congruent is called a **scalene triangle**. A triangle having an obtuse angle is called an **obtuse triangle**. A triangle including only acute angles is called an **acute triangle**. Some specialized triangles are so important that we state their properties as formal definitions.

Definition (9-a):   A triangle having two sides congruent is called an **isosceles triangle**.

Definition (9-b):   A triangle having all three sides congruent is called an **equilateral triangle**.

Definition (9-c):   A triangle having all three interior angles congruent is called an **equiangular triangle**.

When two sides of a triangle are congruent, the third side is called the **base**. Hence any side of an equilateral triangle is a base. The angles that include the base as one of their sides are called the **base angles**. The angle opposite the base in an isosceles triangle is called the **apex** of the triangle. (See Fig. 9.1.)

Definition (9-d):   A side of a triangle containing points interior to an angle is called the **side opposite** that angle.

Theorem (9a-1):   The base angles of an isosceles triangle are congruent.

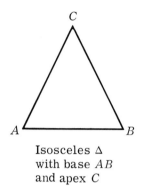

Isosceles △
with base AB
and apex C

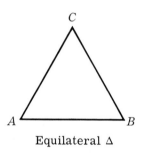

Equilateral △

Fig. 9.1

PROOF

Given: Isosceles triangle ABC
with $AB \cong BC$.
To Prove: $\angle A \cong \angle C$.

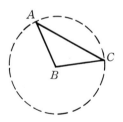

1. There is an isosceles △ABC such that $AB \cong BC$.	1. Hypothesis
2. There is a circle on A with center at B.	2. Why?
3. $(AB) = (BC)$.	3. Why?
4. BC is a radius of (B,BA).	4. Why?

5. Points *A* and *C* determine a chord.	5. Why?
6. $\angle A \cong \angle C$. Q.E.D.	6. Why?

Corollary (9a-1a): An equilateral triangle is equiangular.

Theorem (9a-2): If two angles of a triangle are congruent, then the sides opposite these angles are congruent.

PROOF

Given: $\triangle ABC$ where $\angle A \cong \angle B$.
To Prove: $AC \cong BC$.

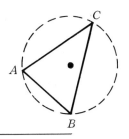

1. $\triangle ABC$ has $\angle A \cong \angle B$.	1. Hypothesis
2. There is a circle on *A,B,C*.	2. Theorem (5d-3)
3. $\angle A$ and $\angle B$ are inscribed angles.	3. Definition (7-g)
4. $AC \cong BC$. Q.E.D.	4. Theorem (8g-6)

Corollary (9a-2a): An equiangular triangle is equilateral.

Definition (9-e): A **right triangle** is a triangle that determines a right angle.

Definition (9-f): The **hypotenuse** of a right triangle is the side interior to the right angle.

Note that since the sum of the measures of the interior angles is $2(\gamma)$ for some right angle γ, a measure of (γ) is all that is left for the sum of the measures of the two nonright angles. It then becomes clear that these two remaining angles must be acute angles.

In Fig. 9.2, *BC* is the hypotenuse where $\angle CAB$ is the right angle. Sides *AB* and *AC* are referred to as the **legs** of the right triangle. If we discuss

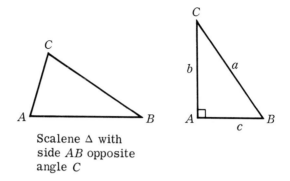

Scalene △ with
side *AB* opposite
angle *C*

Fig. 9.2

acute angle *B*, for example, we call side *AB* its included side.   Thus *AC* is
the included side of angle *ACB*.
   The following is one of the most famous theorems in all of mathematics.

   Theorem (9a-3) (*Theorem of Πυθαγορας*):   The square of the length of the
hypotenuse of any right triangle equals the sum of the squares of the lengths
of the legs.

PROOF

Given: Right △*ABC* with *C* the
right angle.
To Prove: $(AC)^2 + (BC)^2 =$
$(AB)^2$.

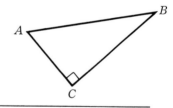

1. There is a right △*ABC* with *C* the right angle.	1. Hypothesis
2. $AC \perp BC$.	2. Definition (8-b)
3. $(AB)^2 + (BC)^2 = (AB)^2$.	3. Theorems (4h-1) and (6c-9)

   We shall make a convention that for any triangle *ABC*, the $(BC) = a$,
where *a* is opposite vertex *A*, $(AB) = c$, where *c* is opposite vertex *C*, and
$(CA) = b$, where *b* is opposite vertex *B*.   (See Fig. 9.2.)

   Theorem (9a-4):   If the sides of a triangle are so related that $a^2 = b^2 + c^2$
for sides of length *a*, *b*, and *c*, then the triangle is a right triangle with right
angle opposite the side of length *a*.

PROOF

Given: $\triangle AOB$ where $A(h,k)$, $B(a,0)$, and $O(0,0)$ such that $(AO) = b$, $(AB) = c$, $(OB) = a$, and $a^2 = b^2 + c^2$.

To Prove: AOB is a right triangle with angle A the right angle.

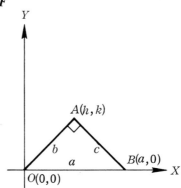

1. There is a $\triangle AOB$ where $A(h,k)$, $B(a,0)$, and $O(0,0)$ such that $(AO) = b$, $(AB) = c$, $(OB) = a$, and $a^2 = b^2 + c^2$.	1. Hypothesis
2. $m_c = \dfrac{k - 0}{h - a}, h \neq a;$ $m_b = \dfrac{k}{h}, h \neq 0.$	2. Definition (6-a)
3. $m_c \cdot m_b = \dfrac{k^2}{h^2 - ah}.$	3. Why?
4. $b = \sqrt{h^2 + k^2};$ $c = \sqrt{(h - a)^2 + k^2}.$	4. Definition (6-k)
5. $b^2 = h^2 + k^2;$ $c^2 = (h - a)^2 + k^2.$	5. Why?
6. $a^2 = h^2 + k^2 + (h - a)^2 + k^2.$	6. Why?
7. $h^2 - ha = -k^2$ or $-1 = \dfrac{k^2}{h^2 - ah}.$	7. Why?
8. $m_c \cdot m_b = -1.$	8. Why?
9. $\measuredangle A$ is a right angle.	9. Definition (8-b)
10. $\triangle AOB$ is a right triangle.	10. Definition (9-e)
11. Cases where $h = a$ or $h = 0$ are left to the exercises.	

Example 1: In right triangle ABC with hypotenuse AC, $(AC) = 5$, $(BC) = 3$. Find (AB).

Solution: Using Theorem (9a-3), we have

$$(AB)^2 + (BC)^2 = (AC)^2$$
$$(AB)^2 + 3^2 = 5^2$$
$$(AB)^2 = 16$$
$$(AB) = 4.$$

Example 2: If the vertices of a triangle are $A = (2,2)$, $B = (2,8)$, and $C = (10,2)$, is the triangle a right triangle?

Solution: First we should locate the points on the plane. This will facilitate the order in which we find the lengths of the sides of the triangle. (See Fig. 9.3.) We find the lengths

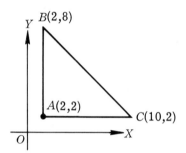

Fig. 9.3

$$(AC)^2 = |10 - 2|^2$$
$$(AB)^2 = |8 - 2|^2$$
$$(BC)^2 = (8 - 2)^2 + (2 - 10)^2.$$

Thus we have

$$64 + 36 = 36 + 64.$$

Hence $\triangle ABC$ is a right triangle.

If we consider any scalene triangle ABC and draw the line $\mathscr{L}$ through C and perpendicular to AB, from vertex C we have the model illustrated in Fig. 9.4. The line $\mathscr{L}$ intersects AB at D. We now have right triangles

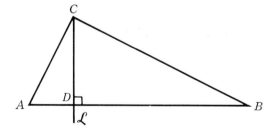

Fig. 9.4

ADC and *DBC* in addition to the given scalene triangle. The segment *CD* included in $\mathscr{L}$ is of special importance.

Definition (9-g): An **altitude** of a triangle is a perpendicular segment from a vertex of the triangle to the line which includes the side opposite that vertex.

The triangles of Fig. 9.4 are called overlapping triangles. Figure 9.5

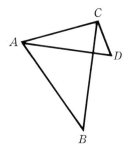

Fig. 9.5

illustrates overlapping triangles *ABC* and *ADC*. An altitude of a triangle may or may not be interior to the angle whose vertex it contains. Figure 9.6 illustrates some examples of altitudes.

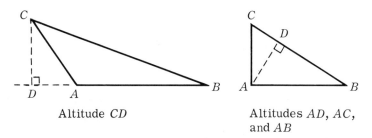

Altitude *CD*   Altitudes *AD*, *AC*,
                                  and *AB*

Fig. 9.6

Exercise Set

1. *Prove:* An equilateral triangle is isosceles. Is the converse true? Explain.

2. Finish the proof of Theorem (9a-1).

3. Prove Corollary (9a-1a).

4. Prove Corollary (9a-2a).

5. Restate Theorems (9a-1) and (9a-2) as a single proposition.

6. Prove Theorem (9a-2) using radii on the center of the inscribed circle and Theorem (8g-2).

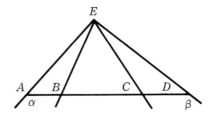

Fig. 9.7

For Exercises 7 through 12, use Fig. 9.7 and the given information.

7. If $AE \cong DE$, prove $\alpha \cong \beta$.

8. If $\triangle BCE$ and $\triangle ADE$ are isosceles, prove that $\angle AEB \cong \angle CED$.

9. If $AB \cong CD$, $\angle AEC \cong \angle BED$, and $\angle EBD \cong \angle ECA$, prove that $\triangle AED$ is isosceles.

10. If $AE \cong AD$ and $\angle ADE \cong \angle DAE$, prove that $\triangle ADE$ is equilateral.

11. If $AE \cong EC$, $BE \cong DE$, and $\angle AEC \cong \angle BED$, prove $\angle EBC \cong \angle ECA$.

12. If $\alpha \cong \beta$, prove that $\triangle AED$ is isosceles.

13. Complete the missing reasons in the proof of Theorem (9a-4).

*14. Prove Theorem (9a-3) without using Theorems (4h-1) or (6c-9).

*15. Prove Theorem (9a-3) using Theorem (9c-1).

*16. Prove Theorem (9a-4) for cases where $h = 0$ or $h = a$.

9b   Positional Equivalence of Triangles

The three sides and the three angles determined by the three noncollinear points of Definition (6-p) are often called the **six parts of a triangle**. To make efficient use of our coordinate system when working with triangles, we need to establish the positional equivalence of triangles.

This principle was discussed previously in Section 6e with respect to line segments, in Section 7d with respect to circles, and in Section 8b with respect to angles. We use these previous theorems to complete the proof for triangle positional equivalence. We have omitted the proof here, but it can be found in the Appendix.

Theorem (9b-1):   For any triangle and any point in a line, there is a triangle having all its parts congruent to the corresponding parts of the given triangle in such a way that one of its vertices is the given point and one of its sides is included in the given line.

Figure 9.8 illustrates the principle of this theorem.   That is, if OAB is any triangle in the plane and if O' is the origin on the x axis, then Theorem

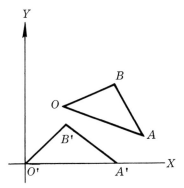

Fig. 9.8

(9b-1) guarantees that there is a triangle $O'A'B'$ such that the following is true. $O'A' \cong OA$, $A'B' \cong AB$, $B'O' \cong BO$, $\sphericalangle B'O'A' \cong \sphericalangle BOA$, $\sphericalangle O'A'B' \cong \sphericalangle OAB$, and $\sphericalangle A'B'O' \cong \sphericalangle ABO$.

9c Trigonometric Ratios

In Section 8i it was shown that the circular functions of Section 7h are determined by measures of central angles as well as by arc lengths. Although these functions derive their fundamental properties from relationships in a circle, some useful applications can be made to triangles as a special case.

Consider a right triangle ABC. Either of the acute angles A and C determines circular functions by Theorem (8i-3). Let us first examine the case where acute angle A is at the origin. (See Fig. 9.9.) Theorem (7b-3) guarantees the existence of a circle (A,AC). By Theorem (7a-4) this circle intersects $\overrightarrow{OX}$ at a point D. Hence $\sphericalangle CAD$ is a central angle. Since

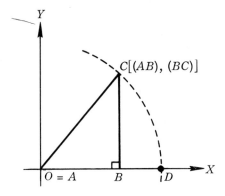

Fig. 9.9

$AB \perp BC$, these legs are grid loci, and $C = [(AB), (BC)]$. By Definition (7-n) and Theorem (8i-3), sine $(\angle CAB) = (BC)/(AC)$, cosine $(\angle CAB) = (AB)/(AC)$, and tangent $(\angle CAB) = (BC)/(AB)$. The remainder of the circular functions can be expressed in a similar fashion.

Thus we have the following theorem.

Theorem (9c-1): For any right triangle and either acute angle of the triangle, the ratio of the length of the opposite side to the length of the hypotenuse is the sine of that acute angle and the ratio of the length of the included side to the length of the hypotenuse is the cosine of that acute angle.

When circular functions are related to right triangles in this manner, they are traditionally called trigonometric ratios. (Note the use of the term *trigon* for "triangle" in this context. See Exercise 1, Section 11a.) The following theorem provides a way of using these ratios with more general triangles.

Theorem (9c-2) (*Law of Sines*): For any triangle ABC,

$$\frac{\text{sine } (\angle A)}{a} = \frac{\text{sine } (\angle B)}{b} = \frac{\text{sine } (\angle C)}{c}.$$

PROOF

Given: $\triangle ABC$ with lengths of the sides a,b,c.

To Prove:

$$\frac{\text{sine } (\angle A)}{a} = \frac{\text{sine } (\angle B)}{b}$$
$$= \frac{\text{sine } (\angle C)}{c}.$$

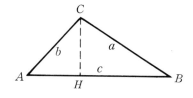

1. There is a $\triangle ABC$ with length of sides a,b,c.	1. Hypothesis
2. There is an altitude on C that is $\perp$ to AB at H.	2. Why?
3. $\angle AHC$ and $\angle BHC$ are right angles.	3. Why?
4. sine $(\angle A) = \dfrac{(CH)}{b}$ and sine $(\angle B) = \dfrac{(CH)}{a}$.	4. Theorem (9c-1)
5. $b \cdot$ sine $(\angle A) = (CH)$ and $a \cdot$ sine $(\angle B) = (CH)$.	5. Why?

6. $\dfrac{\text{sine }(\sphericalangle A)}{a} = \dfrac{\text{sine }(\sphericalangle B)}{b}$.

6. Why?

7. With the altitude on AC, we have $\dfrac{\text{sine }(\sphericalangle A)}{a} = \dfrac{\text{sine }(\sphericalangle C)}{c}$.

7. Steps 2 through 6

8. $\dfrac{\text{sine }(\sphericalangle A)}{a} = \dfrac{\text{sine }(\sphericalangle B)}{b} = \dfrac{\text{sine }(\sphericalangle C)}{c}$.

8. Why?

Q.E.D.

Exercise Set

1. In a scalene triangle, if the sine $(30°) = \frac{1}{2}$ and sine $(45°) = \sqrt{2}/2$, find the length of the side opposite the angle of $30°$ if the side opposite the angle of $45°$ has length $5\sqrt{2}$. (*Hint:* Use Law of Sines.)

2. Prove the Theorem of Pythagoras using Theorem (9c-1).

3. Complete the proof of Theorem (9c-2).

For Exercises 4 through 8, find the sine (A), cosine (B), and the tangent (A), where A and B are the acute angles of the given right triangles.

4. $(AC) = 3, (CB) = 4, (AB) = 5$.

5. $(AC) = 5, (CB) = 12, (AB) = 13$.

6. $(AC) = 7, (CB) = 24, (AB) = 25$.

7. $(AC) = 51, (CB) = 140, (AB) = 149$.

8. $(AC) = 4, (CB) = 4, (AB) = 4\sqrt{2}$.

For Exercises 9 through 12, find the specified number for the given conditions on $\triangle ABC$. (*Hint:* Use Law of Sines.)

9. $(AC) = 4$, sine $(B) = \frac{1}{2}$, $(CB) = 2$; find sine (A).

10. $(AB) = 9$, sine $(A) = \frac{1}{3}$, $(AC) = 5$; find sine (C).

11. $(CB) = 16$, sine $(A) = \frac{1}{8}$, sine $(B) = \frac{1}{3}$; find b.

12. sine $(A) = $ sine $(B) = \frac{1}{2}$, $(AC) = \frac{1}{2}$; find a.

13. Find the cosine (B) of the right triangle having vertices $A(1,2)$, $B(1,9)$, $C(2,8)$.

14. Find the secant (C) of the right triangle having vertices $A(-4,-3)$, $B(1,2)$, $C(3,-1)$.

*15. Would it be possible for sine $(A) = 0$ in right triangle ABC? Explain.

*16. Would it be possible for cosine $(B) = 0$ in right triangle ABC? Explain.

**17. *Prove:* For any right triangle, the sine of the measure of one acute angle equals the cosine of the measure of the other acute angle.

9d   Similarity of Right Triangles

We now establish a relationship between triangles that is based only on the real number lengths associated with the sides of triangles.

Definition (9-h):   Two triangles are **similar** ($\sim$) if and only if there is a positive $k \in \mathcal{R}$ such that the length of each side of one triangle is k times the length of the corresponding side of the other triangle.

The constant k in this definition is often called the **ratio of similitude** of the triangles.

Example 1:   Consider triangles ABC and DEF of Fig. 9.10.   If $(AC) = 4$, $(AB) = 6$, $(BC) = 8$, C and $(DE) = 2$, $(FD) = 3$, $(FE) = 4$, are the triangles similar?

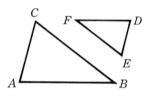

Fig. 9.10

Solution: We see that

$$(AC) = 2(DE)$$
$$(AB) = 2(FD)$$
$$(BC) = 2(FE).$$

Thus the triangles are similar and the ratio of similitude is 2.

Example 2:   If two triangles ABC and DEF are similar and if $(AB) = 24$, find the length of the corresponding side (DE) if the ratio of similitude is 3.

Solution: Since the triangles are similar, we have

$$(AB) = 3(DE)$$
$$24 = 3(DE)$$
$$8 = (DE).$$

However, we could have

$$3(AB) = (DE)$$
$$3(24) = (DE)$$
$$72 = (DE).$$

Thus we see that we have two possibilities for the side (DE).   Which one is correct?   We cannot tell unless we are given additional information.

The transitive property of similarity holds, for similarity depends directly on the real numbers.

Theorem (9d-1): If each of two triangles is similar to a third triangle, then they are similar to each other.

The following example illustrates this theorem. The formal proof is left to the exercises.

Example 3: If $\triangle ABC \sim \triangle DEF$ and the ratio of similitude is k, and if $\triangle GHI \sim \triangle ABC$ and the ratio of similitude is k_2, what is the ratio of similitude between triangles DEF and GHI?

Solution: Since $\triangle ABC \sim \triangle DEF$, we have

$$(AB) = k_1(DE)$$
$$(BC) = k_1(EF)$$
$$(CA) = k_1(FD).$$

Also, since $\triangle ABC \sim \triangle GHI$, we have

$$(AB) = k_2(GH)$$
$$(BC) = k_2(HI)$$
$$(CA) = k_2(IG).$$

Substituting these values into the previous set, we have

$$k_2(GH) = k_1(DE)$$
$$k_2(HI) = k_1(EF)$$
$$k_2(IG) = k_1(FD).$$

Dividing by k_2, we obtain

$$(GH) = \frac{k_1}{k_2}(DE)$$

$$(HI) = \frac{k_1}{k_2}(EF)$$

$$(IG) = \frac{k_1}{k_2}(FD).$$

Thus we have, by Definition (9-h), $\triangle DEF \sim \triangle GHI$, where the ratio of similitude is k_1/k_2.

For right triangles, we can use our definition of similar triangles and our knowledge of the special relationships of the length of its sides that were established by Theorem (9a-3). The use of the word *proportional* in all that follows means that two pairs of numbers are related by the same ratio of similitude.

Theorem (9d-2):   If two sides of one right triangle are correspondingly proportional to two sides of another right triangle, then the triangles are similar.   [There are two cases: (i) a leg and the hypotenuse are given as correspondingly proportional; (ii) the legs are correspondingly proportional. Only case (i) is proved here.   Case (ii) is left to the exercises.]

PROOF

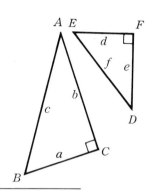

Given: Right triangles ABC and DEF with right angles C and F, respectively, such that $c = rf$ and $a = re$ for $r \in \mathscr{R}$.
To Prove: $\triangle ABC \sim \triangle DEF$.

1. There are right triangles ABC and DEF with right angles C and F, respectively, such that $c = rf$, $a = re$.	1. Hypothesis
2. $c^2 = r^2f^2$ and $a^2 = r^2e^2$.	2. Properties of $\mathscr{R}$
3. $c^2 - a^2 = r^2(f^2 - e^2)$.	3. Why?
4. $c^2 - a^2 = b^2$ and $f^2 - e^2 = d^2$.	4. Why?
5. $b^2 = r^2d^2$.	5. Why?
6. $b = rd$.	6. Why?
7. $\triangle ABC \sim \triangle DEF$.	7. Definition (9-h)

Example 4:   If two right triangles have hypotenuses of lengths 8 and 16 and legs of lengths 2 and 4, respectively, are the triangles similar?

Solution: The ratio of the two hypotenuses is 1 to 2.   The ratio of the two legs is 1 to 2.   Thus by Theorem (9d-2) the right triangles are similar.

Using this theorem and the trigonometric ratios of Section 9c, the following theorem can be proved.

Theorem (9d-3):   If one acute angle of one right triangle is congruent to the corresponding acute angle of a second right triangle, then the triangles are similar.

PROOF

Given: Right triangles *ABC* and *DEF* with right angles *A* and *E* and acute angles $B \cong F$.
To Prove: $\triangle ABC \sim \triangle EFD$.

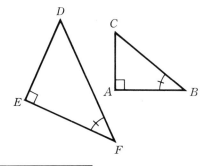

1. There are right triangles *ABC* and *EFD* with right angles *A* and *E* and acute angles $B \cong F$.	1. Hypothesis
2. Let $(AC) = k(ED)$ for some *k*.	2. Why?
3. $\text{sine}(\angle F) = \dfrac{(ED)}{(DF)}$, $\text{sine}(\angle B) = \dfrac{(AC)}{(CB)}$.	3. Why?
4. $\text{sine}(\angle B) = \text{sine}(\angle F)$.	4. Why?
5. $\dfrac{(DE)}{(DF)} = \dfrac{(AC)}{(CB)}$.	5. Why?
6. $\dfrac{(DE)}{(DF)} = \dfrac{k(DE)}{(CB)}$.	6. Why?
7. $(BC) = k(DF)$.	7. Why?
8. $\triangle ABC \sim \triangle EFD$.	8. Theorem (9d-2)
Q.E.D.	

Example 5: In Fig. 9.11, $DE \parallel AB$ and $\angle ABC$ is a right angle. Is $\triangle ABC \sim \triangle DEC$?

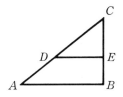

Fig. 9.11

Solution: Since $\sphericalangle ABC$ is a right angle, $\triangle ABC$ is a right triangle. Also, since $AB \parallel DE$, corresponding angles ABC and DEC are congruent. Thus $\sphericalangle DEC$ is a right angle and $\triangle DEC$ is a right triangle. $\sphericalangle ACB$ is an acute angle of *both* triangles. Therefore $\sphericalangle DCE \cong \sphericalangle ACB$. We have satisfied the hypothesis of Theorem (9d-3), and thus we may conclude that $\triangle ABC \sim \triangle DEC$.

Theorem (9d-4): The altitude on the hypotenuse of a right triangle determines two similar triangles, each similar to the given triangle.

PROOF

Given: Right triangle ABC with $\sphericalangle ACB$ the right angle and altitude $CD \perp$ to hypotenuse AB.
To Prove: $\triangle ADC \sim \triangle BDC \sim \triangle ACB$.

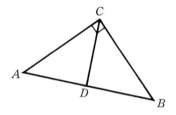

1. There is a right triangle ABC with $\sphericalangle ACB$ the right angle and altitude $CD \perp$ to hypotenuse AB.	1. Hypothesis
2. $\sphericalangle ADC$ and $\sphericalangle BDC$ are right angles.	2. Why?
3. $\triangle ADC$ and $\triangle BDC$ are right triangles.	3. Why?
4. $\sphericalangle B \cong \sphericalangle B$ and $\sphericalangle A \cong \sphericalangle A$.	4. Why?
5. $\triangle ABC \sim \triangle ADC$ and $\triangle DBC \sim \triangle ABC$.	5. Theorem (9d-3)
6. $\triangle ADC \sim \triangle BDC \sim \triangle ACB$.	6. Theorem (9d-1)
Q.E.D.	

Corollary (9d-4a): The altitude on the hypotenuse of a right triangle is the mean proportional between the segments determined on the hypotenuse.

The proof of this corollary is left to the exercises. The term mean proportional is used when two ordered pairs of real numbers are related by the same ratio of similitude and the second element of one pair is the same as the first element of the other pair. The common element is then called the **mean proportional**.

Example 6: Find the number p such that 7 is the mean proportional for the ordered pairs $(2,7)$ and $(7,p)$.

Solution: For 7 to be the mean proportional, we must have $2 = k7$ and $7 = kp$ for some $k \in \mathcal{R}$. From the first equations $k = \frac{2}{7}$. Then $7 = (\frac{2}{7})(p)$ or $p = \frac{49}{2}$. Thus 7 is the mean proportional between $(2,7)$ and $(7,\frac{49}{2})$.

Example 7: Consider the right triangle ABC such that $A = (-2,0)$, $B = (8,0)$, $C = (0,4)$. If CO is the altitude, where $O = (0,0)$, show that $\triangle AOC \sim \triangle OBC \sim \triangle ABC$. (See Fig. 9.12.)

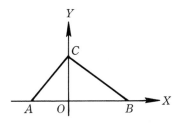

Fig. 9.12

Solution: To show similarity, we need to find a ratio of similitude. Finding the measures of the sides, we have

$\triangle ABC$: $(AB) = 10$ $\triangle AOC$: $(AC) = 2\sqrt{5}$ $\triangle OBC$: $(BC) = 4\sqrt{5}$

$(AC) = 2\sqrt{5}$ $(AO) = 2$ $(OB) = 8$

$(BC) = 4\sqrt{5}$, $(OC) = 4$, $(OC) = 4$.

If we multiply each length of the sides of $\triangle AOC$ by $\sqrt{5}$, we find that $(AB) = (AC)$, $(AC) = (AO)$, and $(BC) = (OC)$ for triangles ABC and AOC. Thus they have a ratio of similitude of $\sqrt{5}$ and they are similar. If we multiply each length of the sides of $\triangle OBC$ by $\frac{1}{2}$ and compare with the sides of $\triangle AOC$, we see they will be equal. Hence the ratio of similitude is $\frac{1}{2}$ and the triangles are similar. Following a similar argument, we see that the ratio of similitude between triangles OBC and ABC is $\sqrt{5}/2$. (Note that in each case, if we consider the ratio of similitude in the other direction, the number will be different. See Exercise 5.)

Theorem (9d-5): If two right triangles are similar, then their corresponding angles are congruent.

PROFF

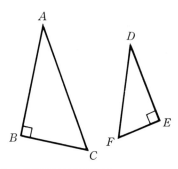

Given: $\triangle ABC \sim \triangle DEF$ where angles B and E are right angles.
To Prove: $\angle A \cong \angle D$, $\angle B \cong \angle E$, $\angle C \cong \angle F$.

1. There are triangles $ABC \sim DEF$ where angles B and E are right angles.	1. Hypothesis
2. $(AC) = k(DF)$ and $(BC) = k(EF)$ for some $k \in \mathscr{R}$.	2. Definition (9-h)
3. sine $(\angle A) = \dfrac{(BC)}{(AC)}$; sine $(\angle D) = \dfrac{(EF)}{(DF)}$.	3. Theorem (9c-1)
4. $\dfrac{(BC)}{(AC)} = \dfrac{k(EF)}{k(DF)} = \dfrac{(EF)}{(DF)}$.	4. Properties of $\mathscr{R}$
5. sine $(\angle A) = $ sine $(\angle D)$.	5. Axioms of equality
6. $\angle A \cong \angle D$.	6. Corollary (8i-3a)
7. $\angle B \cong \angle E$.	7. Theorem (8a-4)
8. $\angle C \cong \angle F$.	8. Theorem (8f-3)

Exercise Set

1. Complete the proof of Theorem (9d-2).
2. Complete the proof of Theorem (9d-3).
3. Complete the proof of Theorem (9d-4).
4. Prove that $\triangle ABC$ is a right triangle in Example 7.
5. In Example 7 find the other ratios of similitude that would establish the similarity of the triangles.
6. If (u,v) and (x,y) are proportional, show that $(u + v)/v = (x + y)/y$. (*Hint:* First write each equality in fraction form equal to the ratio of similitude. Then add 1 to each side of the resulting equality.)
7. If v is the mean proportional between u and w [i.e., if (u,v) and (v,w) are proportional], show that $v = \sqrt{uw}$ for positive u,v,w. Writen in this form, a mean proportional v is called the *geometric mean* between u and w.

8. Find the mean proportional x for $(2,x)$ and $(x,5)$.

9. Explain how we know that the division by k_2 in Example 3 is justified.

10. Prove case (ii) of Theorem (9d-2).

11. If $DB \perp AC$ as in Fig. 9.13, where AC is a semicircle, prove that (DB) is the mean proportional between (AB) and (BC).

12. Prove that any two equilateral triangles are similar.

13. Prove that any two equiangular triangles are similar.

14. State a definition for similarity of line segments using the basic principle of Definition (9-h). Then prove that any two line segments are similar to each other.

15. Repeat Exercise 14 for any two circles.

In Fig. 9.14, $AB \parallel ED$ and $FG \perp AB$. Prove that the following are true statements.

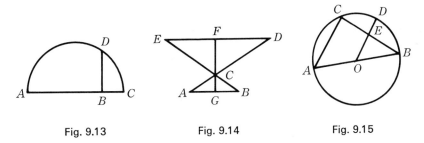

Fig. 9.13   Fig. 9.14   Fig. 9.15

16. $\triangle AGC \sim \triangle CDF$.

17. $\triangle GBC \sim \triangle EFC$.

18. If $\triangle ABC$ is isosceles, then $\triangle GCA \sim \triangle GBC$.

19. If $AD \perp BE$, then $\triangle GBC \sim \triangle CDF$ and $\triangle AGC \sim \triangle CFE$.

20. Prove Theorem (9d-1).

*21. Prove Corollary (9d-4a). Give an example of the corollary.

*22. In Fig. 9.15, AB is a diameter of (O,OA) such that OD bisects CB at E. Prove that $\triangle ABC \sim \triangle ODE$.

23. Prove the Theorem of Pythagoras using Corollary (9d-4a).

9e   General Triangle Similarity

We now call on the similarity theorems for right triangles to help us establish theorems of similarity for triangles in general. We carefully prove the following theorem.

Theorem (9e-1): Altitudes on any pair of corresponding sides in similar triangles separate the triangles into right triangles that are correspondingly similar.

PROOF

Given: $\triangle ABC \sim \triangle PQR$ with corresponding altitudes CD and RS.
To Prove: $\triangle ADC$, $\triangle DBC$, $\triangle PSR$, and $\triangle SQR$ are right triangles such that $\triangle ADC \sim \triangle PSR$ and $\triangle DBC \sim \triangle SQR$.

1. Triangles ABC and PQR are similar and have corresponding altitudes CD and RS.	1. Hypothesis
2. $\exists k \in \mathscr{R}$ such that $b = kq$, $f + g = k(t + u)$, $a = kp$.	2. Why?
3. $CD \perp AB$ and $RS \perp PQ$.	3. Why?
4. $\sphericalangle ADC$, $\sphericalangle BDC$, $\sphericalangle PSR$, $\sphericalangle QSR$ are right angles.	4. Why?
5. $\triangle ADC$, $\triangle BDC$, $\triangle PSR$, $\triangle QSR$ are right triangles.	5. Why?
6. $b^2 = d^2 + f^2$, $a^2 = d^2 + g^2$, $q^2 = s^2 + t^2$, $p^2 = s^2 + u^2$.	6. Theorem (9a-3)
7. $a^2 - b^2 = g^2 - f^2$, $p^2 - q^2 = u^2 - t^2$.	7. Subtraction in Step 6
8. $a^2 - b^2 = (g - f)(g + f)$, $p^2 - q^2 = (u - t)(u + t)$.	8. Why?
9. $a^2 - b^2 = p^2 k^2 - q^2 k^2 = k^2(p^2 - q^2)$.	9. Subtraction (Step 2 into Step 8)
10. $(g - f)(g + f) = k^2(u - t)(u + t)$.	10. Properties of equality
11. $(g - f)k(t + u) = k^2(u - t)(u + t)$.	11. Substitution (Step 2 into Step 10)

12. $g - f = k(u - t)$.	12. Properties of $\mathscr{R}$
13. $g - f = ku - kt$, $\quad g + f = kt + ku$.	13. Axiom R-12 (Step 2 and Step 11)
14. $2g = 2ku, \ -2f = -2kt$.	14. Addition, then subtraction
15. $g = ku, f = kt$.	15. Why?
16. $\triangle ADC \sim \triangle PSR$, $\quad \triangle DBC \sim \triangle SQR$.	16. Theorem (9d-2)

Example 1: In Fig. 9.16, $\triangle ABC \sim \triangle DEF$ and $CG \perp AB$. Prove that $DF \parallel AC$ and $BC \parallel EF$.

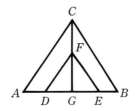

Fig. 9.16

Solution: CG is an altitude of both $\triangle ABC$ and $\triangle DEF$. Why? Therefore, by Theorem (9e-1), $\triangle AGC \sim \triangle DGF$ and $\triangle GBC \sim \triangle GEF$. By Theorem (9d-5), $\measuredangle CAG \cong \measuredangle FDG$ and $\measuredangle GBC \cong \measuredangle GEF$. Since the corresponding angles are congruent, Corollary (8e-3b) establishes that $DF \parallel AC$ and $BC \parallel EF$.

The following theorem states an important property of similar triangles. The proof is left to the exercises. It can be constructed by a straightforward application of the preceding theorem and Theorem (9d-5).

Theorem (9e-2): If two triangles are similar, then the corresponding angles are congruent.

The following theorem establishes the most useful test for determining similarity of general triangles.

Theorem (9e-3): If two triangles have two angles of one congruent respectively to two angles of the other, the triangles are similar.

PROOF

Given: $\triangle ABC$ and $\triangle DFG$ such that $\measuredangle A \cong \measuredangle D$ and $\measuredangle B \cong \measuredangle F$.
To Prove: $\triangle ABC \sim \triangle DGF$.

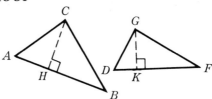

1. There are triangles ABC and DFG such that $\angle A \cong \angle D$ and $\angle B \cong \angle F$.	1. Hypothesis
2. There is a line on C such that $CH \perp AB$ and a line G such that $GK \perp DF$.	2. Why?
3. $\angle AHC$, $\angle BHC$, $\angle DKG$, $\angle FKG$ are right angles.	3. Why?
4. $\triangle AHC$, $\triangle BHC$, $\triangle DKG$, $\triangle FKG$ are right triangles.	4. Why?
5. $\triangle AHC \sim \triangle DKG$; $\triangle BHC \sim \triangle FKG$.	5. Theorem (9d-3)
6. There is a $k \in \mathscr{R}$ such that $(AC) = k(DG), (AH) = k(DK)$, and $(CH) = k(GK)$.	6. Why?
7. $(BC) = k(FG)$ and $(BH) = k(FK)$.	7. Why?
8. $(AB) = k(DK) + k(FK) = k(DF)$.	8. Why?
9. $\triangle ABC \sim \triangle DFG$.	9. Why?
Q.E.D.	

Example 2:   In Fig. 9.17, $AB \parallel CD$.   Is $\triangle ABE \sim \triangle ECD$?

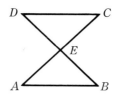

Fig. 9.17

Solution: The vertical angles AEB and DEC are congruent. $\angle BAC \cong \angle ACD$, for they are alternate interior angles determined by parallel lines. Thus Theorem (9e-3) ensures their similarity.

Theorem (9e-4) can be established by the use of the previous theorems and some algebraic manipulation.   The proof is left to the exercises.

Theorem (9e-4):   If two pairs of corresponding sides of two triangles are proportional and if the angles determined by these sides are congruent, then the triangles are similar.

This proposition is often referred to as the *side-angle-side* similarity theorem.   We could also state an *angle-side-angle* theorem, but this would be merely a different way of stating Theorem (9e-3).

Theorem (9e-5):   A line segment whose endpoints are in two sides of a triangle and that is parallel to a third side determines a triangle that is similar to the given triangle.

In Fig. 9.18 we see this theorem illustrated.   We are given that $D \in AC$

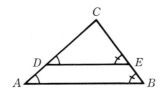

Fig. 9.18

and $E \in CB$ and that $DE \,/\!/\, AB$.   Angles CAB and CDE are congruent corresponding angles.   Angles ABC and DEC are similarily congruent. Thus Theorem (9e-3) established the similarity of triangles ABC and DEC.

Exercise Set

Use Fig. 9.19 for Exercises 1 through 10.   Give a formal proof for each question.

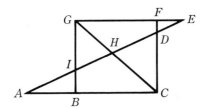

Fig. 9.19

1. If $GE \,/\!/\, AC$, prove that $\triangle ACH \sim \triangle EGH$.
2. If $GC \perp AE$ and $FC \perp GE$, prove that $\triangle HCD \sim \triangle FED$.
3. If $BG \,/\!/\, FC$, prove that $\triangle GHI \sim \triangle CHD$ by two different methods.
4. If AE and GC bisect each other, prove that $\triangle ACH \sim \triangle EHG$.
5. If $GB \perp AC$, $FC \perp GE$, and $GB \,/\!/\, FC$, prove that $\triangle ABI \sim \triangle EFD$.
6. If $AC \,/\!/\, GE$ and $GB \,/\!/\, FC$, prove that $\triangle ACD \sim \triangle EGI$.
7. If $AC \,/\!/\, GE$ and $GB \,/\!/\, FC$, prove that $\triangle GBC \sim \triangle FCG$.
8. If $(FD) = k(BI)$, $(DE) = k(IA)$, and $GB \,/\!/\, FC$, prove that $\triangle ABI \sim \triangle EFD$.

9. If $\triangle GHI \sim \triangle CHD$ and $(HI) = k(HD)$, prove that $FC \parallel GB$.

10. If $FC \perp AC$, $GC \perp AD$, and $(AD) = k(GC)$, prove that $\triangle ACD \sim \triangle CHD$.

11. Complete the missing reasons in the proof of Theorem (9c-1).

12. Complete the missing reasons in the proof of Theorem (9c-3).

13. Is Theorem (9e-3) a true converse of Theorem (9e-2)? If not, why not? What needs to be done to make it a true converse?

14. Prove Theorem (9e-2).

15. Prove Theorem (9e-3) under the assumption that $\sphericalangle A$ and $\sphericalangle D$ are obtuse, still using altitudes on vertices C and G.

*16. Using Fig. 9.20, prove that if $(\overset{\frown}{AB}) = (\overset{\frown}{BC})$, then $\triangle DAB \sim \triangle CBD$, where E is the center of the circle.

*17. Using Fig. 9.21, prove that $ABC \sim \triangle BCD$.

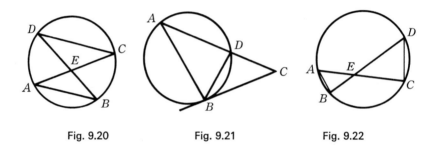

Fig. 9.20   Fig. 9.21   Fig. 9.22

*18. Using Fig. 9.22, prove that $\triangle ABE \sim \triangle CDE$.
*19. Prove Theorem (9e-4).   (*Hint:* Use an altitude.)

9f   Congruence of Triangles

Definition (9-i):   Two **triangles** are **congruent** iff they are similar triangles for which the ratio of similitude is $k = 1$.

Theorem (9f-1):   Corresponding parts of congruent triangles are congruent.

PROOF

Given: $\triangle ABC \cong \triangle DEF$.
To Prove: $AB \cong DE$, $AC \cong DF$,
$BC \cong EF$, $\sphericalangle A \cong \sphericalangle D$,
$\sphericalangle B \cong \sphericalangle E$, $\sphericalangle C \cong \sphericalangle F$.

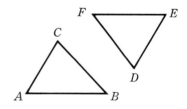

1. There are congruent triangles ABC and DEF.	1. Hypothesis
2. $(AB) = 1 \cdot (DE)$, $(AC) = 1 \cdot (DF)$, $(BC) = 1 \cdot (EF)$.	2. Definition (9-i)
3. $(AB) = (DE)$, $(AC) = (DF)$, $(BC) = (EF)$.	3. Properties of $\mathscr{R}$
4. $AB \cong DE$, $AC \cong DF$, $BC \cong EF$.	4. Definition (6-l)
5. $\angle A \cong \angle D$, $\angle B \cong \angle E$, $\angle C \cong \angle F$.	5. Theorem (9e-2)
Q.E.D.	

Theorem (9f-2):   If each side of one triangle is congruent to the corresponding side of another triangle, then the triangles are congruent.

PROOF

Given: $\triangle ABC$ and $\triangle DEF$ having $AB \cong DE$, $BC \cong EF$, $AC \cong DF$.
To Prove: $\triangle ABC \cong \triangle DEF$.

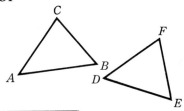

1. There are triangles ABC and DEF such that $AB \cong DE$, $BC \cong EF$, $AC \cong DF$.	1. Hypothesis
2. $(AB) = (DE)$, $(BC) = (EF)$, $(AC) = (DF)$.	2. Why?
3. $(AB) = 1 \cdot (DE)$, $(BC) = 1 \cdot (EF)$, $(AC) = 1 \cdot (DF)$.	3. Why?
4. $\triangle ABC \sim \triangle DEF$.	4. Why?
5. $\triangle ABC \cong \triangle DEF$.	5. Why?
Q.E.D.	

This theorem is often referred to as the *side-side-side* congruence theorem for triangles.   The following corollary is quickly established by the use of the Pythagorean Theorem.   Theorem (9f-3) is often called the *side-angle-side* congruence theorem for triangles.

Corollary (9f-2a):   If any two sides of one right triangle are congruent to the corresponding sides of another right triangle, then the two triangles are congruent.

Theorem (9f-3):   If two triangles have two sides and the included angle of one congruent to the corresponding two sides and included angle of the other, then the triangles are congruent.

PROOF

Given: $\triangle ABC$ and $\triangle DEF$ such that $AB \cong DE$ and $AC \cong DF$ and $\measuredangle A \cong \measuredangle D$.
To Prove: $\triangle ABC \cong \triangle DEF$.

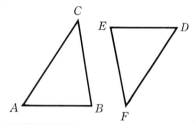

1. There are triangles ABC and DEF such that $AB \cong DE$, $AC \cong DF$, $\measuredangle A \cong \measuredangle D$.	1. Hypothesis
2. $(AB) = (DE)$ and $(AC) = (DF)$.	2. Why?
3. $(AB) = 1 \cdot (DE)$ and $(AC) = 1 \cdot (DF)$.	3. Why?
4. $\triangle ABC \sim \triangle DEF$.	4. Why?
5. $\triangle ABC \cong \triangle DEF$.	5. Why?
Q.E.D.	

The following theorem is called the *angle-side-angle* congruence theorem for triangles.   The proof of the theorem comes almost directly from Theorem (9e-3).   This corollary is often referred to as the *hypotenuse and acute angle* congruence theorem for right triangles.

Theorem (9f-4):   If two angles and the included side of one triangle are congruent to the corresponding angles and the included side of another triangle, then the two triangles are congruent.

Corollary (9f-4a):   If any side and an acute angle of one right triangle are congruent to the corresponding side and acute angle of another right triangle, then the two triangles are congruent.

The following set of exercises can be done almost entirely by synthetic methods.   The reader will have realized that our methods of proof have become more and more independent of the coordinate system.   The *analytic* method, as we have been using it, makes direct use of numbers such as the coordinates of points, slope, and distance.   The *synthetic* method, on the other hand, makes almost no use of algebraic operations but depends on the congruence theorems to establish important points in a proof.   We are now at the point where either technique can be chosen for many problems. Whichever method leads us most simply and quickly to the desired conclusion should be the one we employ.

Exercise Set

For Exercises 1 through 9, use Fig. 9.23. Write each proof in formal style.

1. If $\angle DAE \cong \angle FCE$, prove that $\triangle ADE \sim \triangle CFE$.
2. If $\angle DAE \cong \angle FCE$, $FC \perp AE$, and $AD \perp EC$, prove that $\triangle DAE \sim \triangle FCE$.
3. Using the same hypothesis as in Exercise 2, prove that $\triangle AFB \sim \triangle CDB$.
4. If AD and CF bisect each other, prove that $\triangle BFA \cong \triangle BCD$.
5. If $FB \cong DB$ and $\angle AFB \cong \angle CDB$, prove that $AB \cong CB$.
6. If $FE \cong DE$, $AE \cong CE$, prove that $\triangle ADE \cong \triangle CFE$.
7. If $\angle EFB \cong \angle EDB$, prove that $\triangle ADE \sim \triangle CFE$.
8. If $FC \perp AD$, $FB \cong DB$, and $\angle FAB \cong \angle DCB$, prove that $\triangle FBA \cong \triangle DCB$.
9. If $FE \cong DE$, $AE \cong CE$, $AB \cong CB$, and $FB \cong DB$, prove that $\triangle ABF \cong \triangle CDB$.

For Exercises 10 through 13, use Fig. 9.24. Write each proof in discussion style.

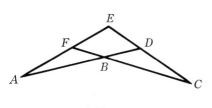

Fig. 9.23

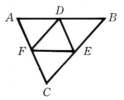

Fig. 9.24

10. If $\triangle ABC$ is isosceles with base AB, $CF \cong CE$, and D is the midpoint of AB, prove that $\angle AFD \cong \angle BED$.
11. If $AC \parallel DE$, $\triangle FDE$ is isosceles with base DE, and F is the midpoint of AC, prove that $\triangle ADF \cong \triangle CEF$.
12. If $\triangle FDE$ is equilateral, prove that $\triangle ABC$ is equilateral.
13. If $FE \parallel AB$, $AC \cong BC$, and $FD \cong ED$, prove that $AD \cong DB$ and $FC \cong CE$.

For Exercises 14 through 20, use Fig. 9.25. Write each proof in formal style.

14. If $EC \parallel AB$, $\triangle AFB$ is isosceles with base AB, and F is the midpoint of EC, prove that $\angle EAF \cong \angle CBF$.
15. If $\triangle EAF \sim \triangle CBF$, $AE \cong BC$, and F is the midpoint of EC, prove that $\triangle DEC$ is isosceles.
16. If $\triangle DEC \sim \triangle DAB$ and $(EC) = k(AB)$, prove that $EC \parallel AB$.
17. If $\triangle ABD$ is equiangular, and E, F, and C are the midpoints respectively of sides AD, EC, and BD, prove that $\angle EAF \cong \angle FBC$.

18. If $\triangle DEC$ and $\triangle DAB$ are isosceles with respective bases EC and AB, prove that $\triangle DEC \sim \triangle DAB$.

19. If $AD \cong BD$ and $EC \parallel AB$, prove that $AE \cong BC$.

20. If AF bisects $\sphericalangle BAE$, BF bisects $\sphericalangle ABC$, and $EC \parallel AB$, prove that $\triangle BCF$ and $\triangle AEF$ are isosceles.

For Exercises 21 through 24, use Fig. 9.26.   Write each proof in formal style.

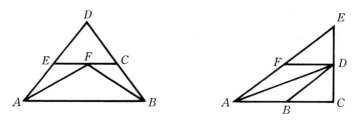

Fig. 9.25   Fig. 9.26

21. If AD bisects $\sphericalangle EAC$, $FD \parallel AC$, and $BD \parallel AE$, prove that $FD \cong BD$.

22. If $FD \parallel AC$ and $\sphericalangle EFD \cong \sphericalangle DBC$, prove that $AE \parallel BD$.

23. If AD bisects $\sphericalangle FDB$, $\triangle BCD$ is isosceles with base BD, and $FA \parallel DB$, prove that $\triangle FAD$ is isosceles.

24. If $FD \parallel AC$ and $FD \perp CE$, prove that $\triangle FDE \sim \triangle ACE$.

25. Prove that if the perpendicular bisector of the base of an isosceles triangle passes through the vertex, it bisects the angle at that vertex.

26. Prove that if the perpendicular bisector of a side of a triangle bisects the angle opposite that side, then the triangle is isosceles.

27. Prove that the bisector of a chord determines congruent triangles with the radii on the endpoints of the chord.

In Exercises 28 through 30, use Fig. 9.27. AP and BP are tangents, and O is the center.

28. *Prove:* $\triangle BPC \cong \triangle APC$.

29. *Prove:* $\sphericalangle BPC \cong \sphericalangle APC$.

30. *Prove:* $OA \cong BP$.

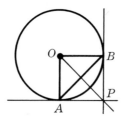

Fig. 9.27

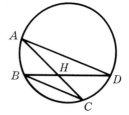

Fig. 9.28

In Fig. 9.28, $AB \cong DC$. Use this figure for Exercises 31 through 33.

31. *Prove:* $\triangle ADB \cong \triangle DAC$.

32. *Prove:* $\triangle AHD \sim \triangle BHC$.

33. *Prove:* $\triangle AHB \sim \triangle DHC$.

34. Complete the proof of Theorem (9f-2).

35. Complete the proof of Theorem (9f-3).

*36. In Fig. 9.28, prove that $BH \cong CH$ if $\overset{\frown}{AB} \cong \overset{\frown}{DC}$.

*37. In Fig. 9.29, prove that diameter $AB \perp$ chord CD if $BC \cong BD$.

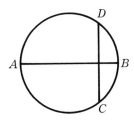

Fig. 9.29

*38. Prove that the midpoint of the hypotenuse of a right triangle is equidistant from the three vertices. Provide a synthetic proof involving isosceles triangles and a second proof using the coordinate system.

*39. Prove that if through any point in the bisector of an angle a line is drawn parallel to either side of the angle, the triangle formed is isosceles.

Prove by both analytic and synthetic methods the following propositions.

*40. The line segments joining the midpoints of a triangle divide the triangle into four congruent triangles.

*41. If the measure of one acute angle in a right triangle is twice the measure of the second acute angle, then the length of the hypotenuse is twice the length of the shorter leg.

*42. If one of the congruent sides of an isosceles triangle is extended through the vertex by its own length, the line segment whose endpoints contain the endpoint of the side extended and the endpoint of the nearer end of the base is perpendicular to the base. (*Hint:* Use the Law of Sines.)

*43. Prove Corollary (9f-2a).

*44. Prove Theorem (9f-4).

*45. Prove Corollary (9f-4a).

9g Triangles and Lines

The following two theorems provide for the existence of intersection points when a line enters a triangle. (See Fig. 9.30.) The proofs are left to the exercises.

Theorem (9g-1):   Any line that intersects a triangle on a vertex and contains a point interior to that angle also intersects the third side on one point.

Corollary (9g-1a):   Any line that intersects one side of a triangle on a single point that is not a vertex intersects a second side on a single point.

The following corollary is obtained by direct use of Corollary (9g-1a) and Theorem (9e-5).   The proof is left to the exercises.

Corollary (9g-1b):   A line that is parallel to one side of a triangle and contains the midpoint of a second side also contains the midpoint of the third side.

Example 1:   If $EC \parallel AB$ and E is the midpoint of side AD, prove that $CB \cong DC$.   (See Fig. 9.31.)

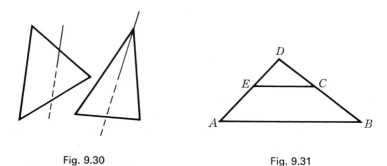

Fig. 9.30   Fig. 9.31

Solution: By Corollary (9g-1b) C is the midpoint of side DB.   Therefore $DC \cong CB$ by the definition of a midpoint.

Example 2:   If $EC \parallel AB$ and $(DA) = 14$, $(EA) = 6$, and $(DB) = 35$, what is the measure of (CB)?

Solution: By Theorem (9e-5) the sides are divided proportionally by the parallel line EC.   Thus we have

$$\frac{(DA)}{(EA)} = \frac{(DB)}{(CB)}$$

or

(1)
$$\frac{14}{6} = \frac{35}{(CB)}.$$

Solving (1) we obtain $(CB) = 15$.

Theorem (9g-2):   The line segment containing the midpoints of two sides of a triangle is parallel to the third side and has length equal to one half its length.

PROOF

Given: $\triangle ABC$ with DE on points $D(f,e/2)$, $E(b,e/2)$.
To Prove: $DE \parallel AB$ and $(DE) = \frac{1}{2}(AB)$.

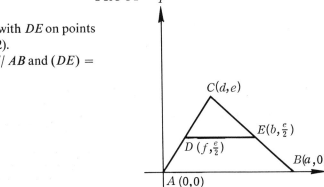

1. There is a $\triangle ABC$ with DE on points $D\left(f,\frac{e}{2}\right)$, $E\left(b,\frac{e}{2}\right)$, where $D \in AC$ and $E \in CB$.	1. Hypothesis
2. Slope of $DE = \dfrac{e/2 - e/2}{b - f} = 0$, slope of $AB = \dfrac{0}{a - 0} = 0$.	2. Why?
3. $DE \parallel AB$.	3. Why?
4. $(DE) = \sqrt{(f - b)^2 + (e/2 - e/2)^2}$.	4. Why?
5. $(DE) = \lvert f - b \rvert$.	5. Why?
6. $f = \dfrac{d}{2}$ and $b = \dfrac{d + a}{2}$.	6. Why?
7. $a = 2b - 2f = 2(b - f)$.	7. Properties of $\mathscr{R}$
8. $a = (AB) = 2(b - f)$.	8. Why?
9. $(DE) = \frac{1}{2}(AB)$.	9. Why?

Example 3: If $(AB) = 10$ and D and E are the midpoints of sides AC and BC of $\triangle ABC$, what is the length of DE? (See Fig. 9.32.)

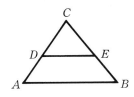

Fig. 9.32

Solution: By Theorem (9g-2), $DE \parallel AB$ and $(DE) = \frac{1}{2}(AB)$.   Thus we have $(DE) = \frac{1}{2} \cdot (10) = 5$.

Theorem (9g-3): If parallel lines intercept congruent segments on one transversal, they intercept congruent segments on any other transversal.

PROOF

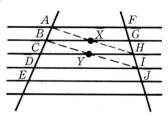

Given: $AF \parallel BG \parallel CH \parallel DI \parallel EF \parallel \ldots J$; $AB \cong BC \cong CD \cong DE \cong \ldots$
To Prove: $FG \cong GH \cong HI \cong IJ \cong \ldots$

1. There are parallel lines AE, BG, CH, DI, EJ, ... and congruent segments AB, BC, CD, DE, ...	1. Hypothesis
2. There are lines AH and BI.	2. Theorem (5c-3)
3. $AH \cap BG = X$; $BI \cap CH = Y$.	3. Theorem (6c-5)
4. $AX \cong XH$ in $\triangle ACH$, $BY \cong YI$ in $\triangle BDI$, ...	4. Corollary (9g-1b)
5. $FG \cong GH$ in $\triangle AFH$, $GH \cong HI$ in $\triangle BGI$, ...	5. Corollary (9g-1b)
6. $\therefore FG \cong GH \cong HI \cong \ldots$	6. Transitive property of $\cong$

We now state four theorems dealing with "concurrent lines."

Definition (9-j): Two or more lines are said to be **concurrent** if they intersect in one and only one point.   (See Fig. 9.33.)

Fig. 9.33

Theorem (9g-4): The lines including the altitudes of a triangle are concurrent.

PROOF

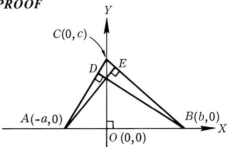

Given: $\triangle ABC$ where $A(-a,0)$, $B(b,0)$, and $C(0,c)$ and altitudes AE, BD, CO.

To Prove: AE, BD, CO intersect at a point P.

1. There is a $\triangle ABC$ such that $A = (-a,0)$, $B = (b,0)$, and $C = (0,c)$ having altitudes AE, BD, CO.	1. Hypothesis
2. Slope of AB: $m_{AB} = 0$ $\quad CO$: no slope $\quad BC$: $m_{CB} = \dfrac{-c}{b}$ $\quad AE$: $m_{AE} = \dfrac{b}{c}$ $\quad CA$: $m_{CA} = \dfrac{c}{a}$ $\quad BD$: $m_{BD} = \dfrac{a}{c}$.	2. Definitions (6-a) and (6-c)
3. Equation of $\quad CO$: $x = 0$ $\quad AE$: $y = \dfrac{b}{c}x + a$ $\quad BD$: $y = \dfrac{-a}{c}x - b$.	3. Corollary (6b-1c)
4. AE intercepts CO at $\left(0, \dfrac{ab}{c}\right)$. $\quad BD$ intercepts CO at $\left(0, \dfrac{ab}{c}\right)$.	4. Properties of $\mathscr{R}$
5. AE, BD, CO have exactly one common point.	5. Definition (4-a)
6. AE, BD, CO are concurrent.	6. Definition (9-j)

The point of intersection of the altitudes of a triangle is called the **orthocenter**.

Definition (9-k): A **median** of a triangle is a line segment whose endpoints are a vertex of the triangle and the midpoint of the side opposite that vertex.

Theorem (9g-5):   The medians of a triangle are concurrent.

The proof of this theorem can be easily constructed using the positional equivalence of triangles and the coordinate system.   (See Exercise 22.)   The point of intersection of the medians is called the **centroid**.   This is the "balance point" of the triangle.

Theorem (9g-6):   The lines including the perpendicular bisectors of the sides of a triangle are concurrent.

This theorem also has an easy analytic proof.   (See Exercise 23.)   The point of intersection of the perpendicular bisectors of the sides of a triangle is called the **circumcenter**.   It is the center of a circle determined by the three vertices of the triangle.

Theorem (9g-7):   The angle bisectors of a triangle are concurrent.

By repeated use of the definition of a bisector of an angle, this theorem can be quickly established by synthetic techniques.   The point of intersection of the angle bisectors of a triangle is called the **incenter**.   It is the center of a circle that is tangent to the three sides of a triangle.

Figure 9.34 illustrates these four theorems.

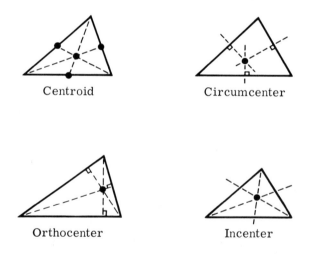

Centroid   Circumcenter

Orthocenter   Incenter

Fig. 9.34

Example 4:   Prove that the bisector of the apex angle of an isosceles triangle is the perpendicular bisector of the base.

Solution: In Fig. 9.35, $\triangle ABC$ is isosceles with base AB.   Line $\mathscr{L}$ is the bisector of angle C.   By Theorem (9g-1) we are guaranteed that $\mathscr{L}$ intersects

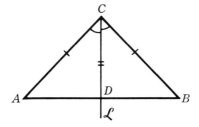

Fig. 9.35

AB in *D*. Since *AC* ≅ *BC* by Definition (9-a), ∢*ACD* ≅ ∢*BCD* by the definition of an angle bisector, and *CD* is a common side to triangles *ADC* and *BDC*, we have that △*ADC* ≅ △*BDC* by the *side-angle-side* congruence theorem. Thus *AD* ≅ *BD* by Theorem (9f-1). By the same theorem, ∢*ADC* ≅ ∢*BDC*. ∢*ADC* and ∢*BDC* are adjacent angles by Definition (5-n). Corollary (8c-4c) establishes that *ℒ* ⊥ *AB*. Thus *CD* is the *perpendicular bisector* of *AB*. We also note that *CD* is a *median* of △*ABC*.

Another illustration of the methods of this chapter as applied to circles is the following example.

Example 5:   Prove that the angles determined by two intersecting tangents to a circle and the line containing both the point of intersection of the tangents and the center of the circle are congruent.

Solution: Figure 9.36 illustrates the problem.   There are congruent radii

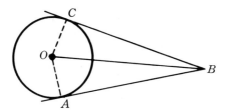

Fig. 9.36

OA and *OC*.   Moreover, we know that *OA* ⊥ *AB* and *OC* ⊥ *CB* by Theorem (7f-2).   Thus triangles *OAB* and *OCB* are right triangles with a common hypotenuse *OB*.   Corollary (9f-2a) establishes △*AOB* ≅ △*COB*.   Therefore, by Theorem (9f-1), ∢*CBO* ≅ ∢*ABO*.   We also note that the same corollary tells us that *AB* ≅ *CB*.   We call *AB* and *BC* tangent segments.

Exercise Set

1. Prove Corollary (9g-1b).
2. Complete the proof of Theorem (9g-2).

3. *A* is any point in the base *DF* of isoceles triangle *DEF* in Fig. 9.37.   The side *DE* is extended from *D* to *B* so that *DA* ≅ *DB*.   A line ℒ is drawn through *BA*.   Prove that ℒ intersects *FE* at a point *C* and that (∢*ECB*) = 3(∢*CBE*).

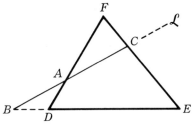

Fig. 9.37

4. If *BC* and *FD* bisect each other at *A* in Fig. 9.37, prove that △*BDA* ≅ △*ACF*.
5. Prove that in an isosceles triangle the perpendicular bisector of the base bisects the vertex angle.
6. Prove that the centroid is always interior to the angles.
7. Prove that the incenter is always interior to the triangle.
8. In what triangle would the circumcenter be contained in a side of the triangle?

For Exercises 9 through 14, use Fig. 9.38.   Write out each proof in formal style. Use either synthetic or analytic methods.

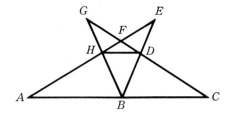

Fig. 9.38

9. If *H* is the midpoint of *AE*, *HD* || *AC*, *HB* ≅ *BD*, prove that *HB* ≅ *DE*.
10. If △*HBD* is equilateral, *B* is the midpoint of *AC*, *HD* || *AC*, prove that △*BHA* ≅ △*BDC*.
11. If △*ACF* is isosceles, *B* is the midpoint of *AC*, *HDB* is equilateral, and *HD* || *AC*, prove that △*ABE* ≅ △*CBG*.
12. Using the hypothesis of Exercise 11, prove that △*ABH* ≅ △*CBD*.
13. Using the hypothesis of Exercise 11 and the conclusion of Exercise 12, prove that △*HFD* is isosceles.
14. Using the hypothesis of Exercise 11 and the conclusions of Exercises 12 and 13, prove that △*GHF* ≅ △*EDF*.
15. If two transversals intersect a set of parallel lines and the segments cut off on one transversal have lengths 2, 4, 6, and 8, what are the lengths of the

segments on the second transversal if its segment of greatest length has measure 24?

16. Two tangents to a circle determine an angle of 60°. If the length of a radius is 12 inches, find the length of the tangent segments.

17. If $EC \parallel FB$ in Fig. 9.39, and if $BF \perp AD$ and $AB \cong CD$, show that $BF \cong CE$.

18. Prove that if AB and BC are tangents to circle (O,OD) in Fig. 9.40, then D is equidistant from AB and BC.

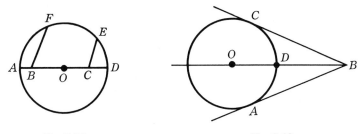

Fig. 9.39   Fig. 9.40

19. Prove that in a circle or in congruent circles, congruent chords are equidistant from the center. See Fig. 9.41.

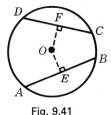

Fig. 9.41

*20. Prove the converse of the theorem in Exercise 19.

*21. Prove that the bisector of an angle of a triangle divides the opposite side in segments whose lengths are proportional to the lengths of the adjacent sides.

*22. Prove that the bisector of an exterior angle of a triangle intersects the opposite side extended on a point whose distance from the extremities of that side are proportional to the lengths of the other two sides.

*23. Using Exercise 21, if the triangle has sides of length 9, 18, and 21, find the length of the segments of the side of length 21 made by the bisector of the opposite angle.

*24. Develop a numerical example of the proposition of Exercise 17.

*25. Prove Theorem (9g-1). [*Hint:* Use positional equivalence of triangles, the coordinate system, and Theorems (6c-4), (9c-5), (9e-5), and (3d-4).]

*26. Prove Corollary (9g-1a).

*27. Prove Theorem (9g-5).

*28. Prove Theorem (9g-6).

*29. Prove Theorem (9g-7).

chapter 10

Constructions

10a A Construction and Its Proof

In Section 6e the positional equivalence of line segments was established. What we propose to do now is actually to "construct" such a line segment.

The terms *construct* and *construction* imply the use of tools rather than the use of logical arguments. The tools that we shall use are as simple as they were in Euclid's time. The first tool is a *straightedge*; that is, a ruler along which we draw a pencil to produce a mark called a straight line. The second tool is called a *compass*. This consists of two straightedges fixed at one end. Certainly our modern-day compasses are more efficient than those of the Greeks, but essentially it is the same instrument. Figure 10.1 illustrates a typical compass. We shall refer to the leg that has the steel point as the "fixed end" of the compass. The other leg holds the pencil and does all

Fig. 10.1

the marking. The compass, of course, makes circles. These two tools will be the *only* ones we shall allow ourselves to use.

The actual process of construction adds no new material to geometry. In fact, it does almost the opposite. By performing various constructions, we illustrate that the theorems do indeed establish concurrent lines, parallel lines, congruent angles, concentric circles, and all the other properties of figures that we have established. This very use of construction in its relation to the theorems makes it a worthwhile subject to study.

In all constructions, we prove that the results of our steps are valid. These proofs are an integral part of constructions. As an example, we shall carefully prove the problem that we originally proposed. In the remainder of the chapter, the proofs of the constructions are left to the exercises.

Figure 10.2 illustrates the problem. We want to copy line segment AB

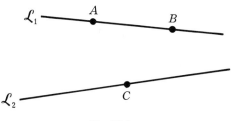

Fig. 10.2

of line $\mathscr{L}_1$ onto line $\mathscr{L}_2$ in such a way that one of the endpoints of copied segment AB is at point C and the other endpoint of AB lies in $\mathscr{L}_2$. We want the new line segment to be congruent to AB.

First fix the compass on AB so that the points of the compass lie on both A and B. Next, move the compass, without changing its extension, and place the fixed end at point C. Then draw a circle and label the points D and D' where $\mathscr{L}_2$ intersects the circle. We now claim that CD and CD' are each congruent to AB. That is, we have copied AB onto $\mathscr{L}_2$. Figure 10.3 illustrates the construction.

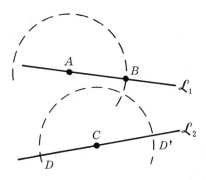

Fig. 10.3

We now proceed to prove that $AB \cong CD \cong CD'$. There are two important parts to the proof to be completed before one can absolutely state that $CD \cong AB$.

First we must prove that the points D and D' exist.

We agreed that the compass makes a circle and that the fixed end of the compass lies on the line. Thus we have a line containing the center of the circle. Theorem (7a-4) ensures us of the existence of the two points D and D'.

We must now make the easy argument that indeed $CD \cong AB$. Since we have circles (Fig. 10.3) on both lines with congruent radii (Remember, we did not change the compass!), Theorem (7b-4) and Definition (7-h) complete the proof. That is, since the two circles are congruent, their radii must also be congruent. And since AB, CD, and CD' are all radii, $AB \cong CD \cong CD'$. This is the general pattern for proofs of construction.

10b   Copying Angles and Triangles

Angles

See Fig. 10.4. Consider any angle ABC and any line segment $A'B'$.

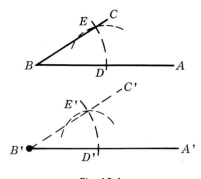

Fig. 10.4

Place the fixed end of the compass at B and draw any arc that intersects AB at D and BC at E. Draw a congruent arc with the fixed end of the compass at B'. Let this arc intersect $B'A'$ at D'. Now place the compass so that its points lie on D and E. Leaving the extension unchanged, place the fixed end at D' and draw an arc that intersects the arc containing D'. Call the point of intersection E'. Draw $B'E'$. This gives $\sphericalangle A'B'C' \cong \sphericalangle ABC$.

Triangles

See Fig. 10.5. Consider a triangle ABC and a ray $\overrightarrow{A'F}$. At A' copy angle BAC as done above. This is $\sphericalangle D'A'E'$, where D' is in the ray $\overrightarrow{A'F}$. Copy the line segment AB, as in Section 10a, so that $A'B' \cong AB$ and B'

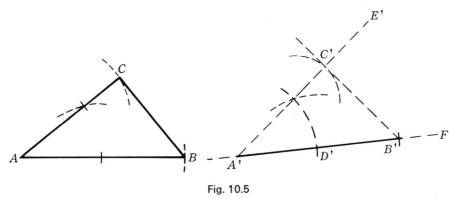

Fig. 10.5

is in ray $\overrightarrow{A'F}$.   At A' draw a circle with the compass having radius AC and intersecting $A'E'$ at C'.   Draw $C'B'$ with the straightedge.   Thus $\triangle ABC \cong \triangle A'B'C'$.

Exercise Set

1. Draw the following types of angles and then copy them.
   (a) obtuse   (b) acute   (c) right   (d) straight.
2. Draw the following types of triangles and then copy them.
   (a) obtuse   (b) scalene   (c) right.
3. Construct a triangle having sides of the following lengths:
   (a) 6, 8, and 10 inches.
   (b) 2, 12, and 15 inches.
   (c) 3, 3, and 6 inches.
4. Provide an alternate way to copy triangles.
5. Provide proofs for the copying of
   (a) angles   (b) triangles.
*6. Draw any angle and pick any point in one of its sides.   On that point construct a line parallel to the remaining side.

10c   Bisectors and Perpendiculars

In this section we introduce additional techniques of construction.   Each result should still be proven as in Sections 10a and 10b.   We shall leave these proofs to the exercises.

Bisectors

See Fig. 10.6.   Consider a line segment AB.   Using the compass with an extension clearly greater than half the length of AB yet less than that length, draw a circle with its center at *A*. Using the *same extension*, draw a second circle having its center at *B*. These two circles intersect at points *C* and *D*. Draw *CD*. *CD* intersects *AB* at *E*. *E* is the midpoint of *AB*. Line *CD* bisects *AB*.

Furthermore, we can say that *CD* is *perpendicular* to *AB*. Thus *CD* is the *perpendicular bisector* of *AB*. Why?

Consider any angle as in Fig. 10.7. Draw any circle whose center is at

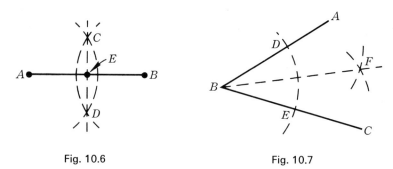

Fig. 10.6   Fig. 10.7

the vertex *B* of angle *ABC*. The circle will intersect ⊰*ABC* at *D* and *E*. Now, using an extension greater than half the length of *DE*, draw a circle with center at *D*. Using the same extension, draw a second circle having center *E*. These two circles will intersect at point *F*. Draw *BF*. *BF* is the bisector of ⊰*ABC*.

Perpendiculars

In finding the midpoint of a line segment we saw that the line which intersected the line segment was also perpendicular to it. Since this line meets the two qualifications required, it is a perpendicular bisector of the line segment. Note that *only* a line segment has a perpendicular bisector.

Consider a line 𝓛 containing point *A* as in Fig. 10.8. To construct a perpendicular at point *A*, we draw a circle of any radius with center at *A*. This circle will intersect line 𝓛 on points *B* and *C*. From this point our construction is similar to the one for the perpendicular bisector discussed previously. The problem is completed in Fig. 10.9.

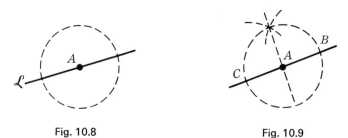

Fig. 10.8   Fig. 10.9

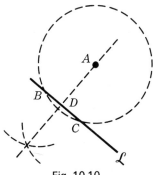

Fig. 10.10

Now consider a line $\mathscr{L}$ and a point A not in $\mathscr{L}$. See Fig. 10.10. To construct a line that contains A and is perpendicular to $\mathscr{L}$, we first draw a circle with center at A using a compass extension large enough to guarantee that $\mathscr{L}$ will be a secant to the circle. Points B and C are the points of intersection of the secant $\mathscr{L}$ with the circle. Using the previous construction, we find the midpoint of line segment BC. Call the midpoint D. Draw AD. Thus AD is perpendicular to $\mathscr{L}$. Note that we actually do not need to find the midpoint D. Why?

Exercise Set

Draw an example of the following and then bisect the line segment or angle.

1. Line segment 4 inches in length.
2. Line segment $2\frac{3}{4}$ inches in length.
3. Line segment $3\frac{1}{3}$ inches in length.
4. Obtuse angle.
5. Straight angle.
6. Acute angle.
7. Right angle.
8. Construct a circle with a given line segment as one of its chords. Does it pass through the center of the circle? What theorem is illustrated by this construction?
9. Construct any angle and then find its bisector. Pick any point in the bisector and find the perpendicular lines to the sides of the angles from the given point. What theorem is illustrated by this construction?
10. Construct the three median lines of a scalene triangle. What theorem is illustrated by this construction?
11. Construct a scalene triangle. From each vertex construct a line perpendicular to the side opposite that vertex. What theorem is illustrated by this construction?
12. Construct a triangle. For each angle of the triangle construct its bisector. What theorem is illustrated by this construction?

13. Construct a triangle. Construct the perpendicular bisectors of each side. What theorem is illustrated by this construction?

14. Construct a circle with any radius. Choose any point on the circle and construct the radius to that point. Construct a line perpendicular to this radius at the point on the circle. What theorem is illustrated by this construction?

15. Construct a line $\mathscr{L}$ and a point P not in $\mathscr{L}$. Construct a line $\mathscr{M}$ that contains P and is parallel to $\mathscr{L}$. What theorem is illustrated by this construction?

16. Construct a scalene triangle. Locate the midpoint of any side. Then construct a line through this midpoint parallel to a second side. Where does this parallel line intersect the third side of the triangle? What theorem is illustrated by this construction?

17. Repeat Exercise 12. Then construct a perpendicular from the point of intersection found by Exercise 6 to any side of the triangle. Using that new line segment as a radius and the point of intersection of the angle bisectors as the center, draw a circle. What appears to be true? The circle constructed is called the inscribed circle of the triangle. The point of intersection of the bisectors has a name. What is it?

18. Repeat Exercise 13. Using your compass, draw a circle with the fixed end on the point of intersection of the perpendicular bisectors and the other end on any vertex. This circle is called the circumscribed circle of the triangle. The center of this circle has a name. What is it?

Prove the following constructions as in Section 10a.

*19. Midpoint of line segment.

*20. Perpendicular bisector of a line segment.

*21. Angle bisector.

*22. Perpendiculars to a line at a point in a line.

*23. Perpendiculars to a line from a point not in a line.

10d   Division, Euler's Line, and Nine-Point Circle

Some topics in constructions by the very nature of their relation to each other can be extremely interesting. In this section we discuss a few of them.

Many times we are asked to divide a line segment into a given number of congruent segments. This problem, too, can be solved using only the compass and the straightedge.

In Fig. 10.11, we want to divide line segment AB into three congruent segments. We first construct any ray $\overrightarrow{AC}$. Setting our compass at any extension and using A as center, we mark off successively three points in $\overrightarrow{AC}$ so as to determine congruent segments. (These have been labeled D, E, and F.) We now draw FB. Then on D and E we construct lines parallel to FB. These parallels cut AB at G and H. Thus we have the three congruent segments AG, GH, and HB. The proof is left to the exercises.

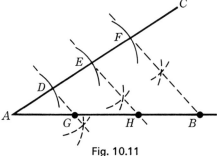

Fig. 10.11

Another example is the location of irrational numbers on the real number line. A construction process can establish the location of such numbers.

Suppose we ask, for example, for the location of $\sqrt{2}$ on the real number line. In Fig. 10.12, $\mathscr{L}_1$ is the real number line. We have fixed zero at A

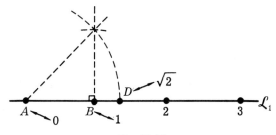

Fig. 10.12

and taken as our unit measure the length of the line segment AB. At B we construct a perpendicular line $\mathscr{L}_2$ and mark off on it (with our compass) a segment congruent to AB; that is, BC. We can now draw AC. From the Pythagorean Theorem of Chapter 9 we find that line segment AC has length $\sqrt{2}$. We now construct a circle having a radius AC and center A. The circle will intersect $\mathscr{L}_1$ at D. Why? Thus the point D will be the location of $\sqrt{2}$ on the real number line.

In a triangle we have discovered that the median lines intersect at a unique point, the perpendicular bisectors intersect at a unique point, and the altitudes intersect at a unique point. Recall that these points are called the *centroid*, the *circumcenter*, and the *orthocenter*, respectively. Figure 10.13 illustrates the three points.

The **Euler line** is the line segment whose endpoints are the orthocenter and the circumcenter of a triangle. The centroid must also be in the Euler line.

The **Nine-Point Circle** is a circle that is *uniquely* determined by nine special points. These nine points are located by various constructions performed

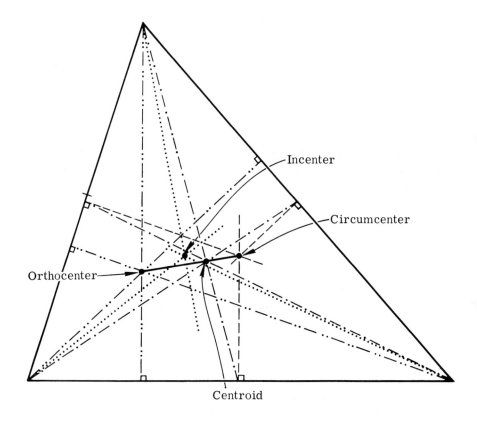

Fig. 10.13

on the perpendicular bisectors of the sides, the angle bisectors, and the medians of any given triangle.

We shall now list these nine points and illustrate them in Fig. 10.14. Locating these points involves most of the construction techniques that have been discussed so far.

The *center* of the nine-point circle is the *midpoint of the Euler line.* (Remember, the Euler line is a line segment.)   The letters refer to Fig. 10.14.

(a) Feet of altitudes, that is, points *D*, *E*, and *F*.

(b) Midpoints of the sides, that is, points *G*, *H*, and *K*.

(c) Midpoints of the line segments *AO*, *BO*, and *CO*, that is, points *P*, *Q*, and *R*.

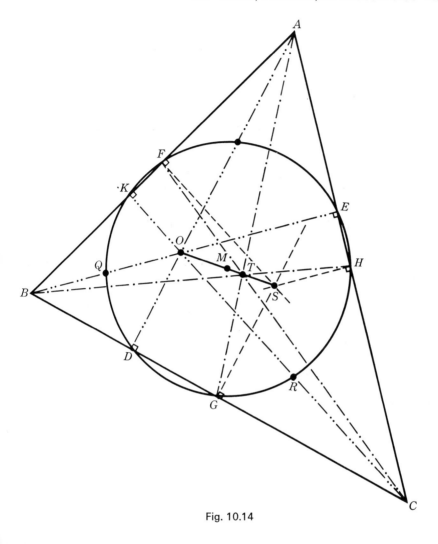

Fig. 10.14

Exercise Set

1. Construct a 6-inch line segment and divide it into five congruent segments by methods given in this section.

2. Locate the $\sqrt{5}$ on the real number line.

3. Construct a large scalene triangle and construct the orthocenter, the circumcenter, and the centroid.

4. Repeat Exercise 3, but this time construct only two median lines, two altitudes, and two perpendicular bisectors of the sides. Why is it unnecessary to construct the third line for each of these in order to locate the centroid,

circumcenter, and orthocenter? What theorem are you applying? Construct the nine-point circle.

5. In Fig. 10.14, using the points P, Q, and R as the vertices of a triangle, prove that $\triangle ABC \sim \triangle PQR$.

6. In Fig. 10.14, prove that $\angle FSH \cong \angle BOC$.

7. In Fig. 10.14, prove that $BO \parallel GR$.

8. In Fig. 10.14, prove that $\angle EQR \cong \angle OFE$.

9. Construct any angle. On one side, lay off with your compass n congruent segments, $n > 4$. Then construct parallel lines in such a way that the second side of the angle has been divided into $n > 4$ congruent segments. What theorem has been illustrated in this construction?

10. Construct an acute triangle. Divide one of the sides of the triangle into three congruent segments using the methods described in this section. Then construct two lines, one through each division point of the divided side and the vertex opposite the divided side. What appears to be true about the three new angles with the common vertex? Now repeat the instructions above except use an obtuse triangle and divide the side opposite the obtuse angle. What appears to be true this time about the three new angles with the common vertex? Based on these two previous conclusions, what might appear to be a general conclusion concerning the trisection of an angle?

chapter 11

Polygons

11a   Convex Polygons

In Section 6f we developed figures determined by intersecting line segments. We now formalize these concepts.

Definition (11-a):   A **polygon** is a set of n line segments, $n \geq 3$, having exactly n nonempty intersections, each of which contains exactly one endpoint of each of exactly two of the line segments.

Fig. 11.1

If we examine this definition carefully, we see that the geometric illustrations of Fig. 11.1 are polygons. We also find that many figures are excluded. Examples of nonpolygons can be found in Fig. 11.2.

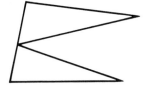

Fig. 11.2

The element of each intersection of Definition (11-a) is called a *vertex* of the polygon.   The line segments are called the *sides* of the polygon.   Two sides having a common endpoint are said to be *consecutive*.   Two vertices are said to be consecutive if they are endpoints of the same side.

A polygon is **convex** if the line including any side does not contain any other points in the polygon.   Figure 11.3 illustrates convex polygons.   Polygons

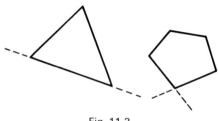

Fig. 11.3

that are not convex are called **concave**.   Figure 11.4 illustrates concave polygons.

In discussing only the convex polygons, the concave polygon is not being slighted.   It can be shown, although we shall not do it here, that all concave polygons can be divided into convex polygons.   Since this is true, and convex polygons are somewhat more adaptable to our purposes, we shall use the word polygon to mean convex polygon unless it is specially stated to the contrary.

A polygon is named by the number of sides it includes.   At this point we can redefine a triangle as a polygon of three sides.   (See Section 6f.)

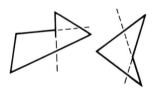

Fig. 11.4

Definition (11-b):   A polygon of four sides is called a **quadrilateral**.

Definition (11-c):   A polygon of five sides is called a **pentagon**.

In naming further polygons we continue the pattern of this definition.   A Greek number is prefixed to -*gon*.   For example, **hexagon, heptagon, octagon,** and **nonagon** are the names for polygons of six, seven, eight, and nine sides. (See Fig. 11.5 and page xi.)

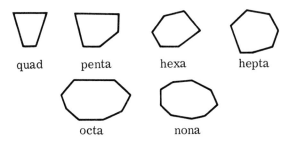

quad   penta   hexa   hepta

octa   nona

Fig. 11.5

Definition (11-d):   A line segment whose endpoints are two nonconsecutive vertices of a polygon is called a **diagonal**.

Figure 11.6 illustrates a polygon *ABCDEF* with diagonals *AC, DB, EC, DA,* and *EB*.   Are there any more diagonals?

In the preceding chapters we carefully established positional equivalence of each new geometric locus in order to use our coordinate system to its full advantage.   We now discuss the positional equivalence of polygons.

Since we are limiting ourselves to convex polygons, it can be shown that any *n*-sided polygon, $n \geq 3$, can be divided into $n - 2$ triangles by constructing all the diagonals from a given vertex.   (See Fig. 11.7.)   We have already

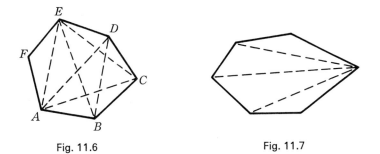

Fig. 11.6   Fig. 11.7

established positional equivalence of triangles.   Thus we have the positional equivalence of polygons directly.   It is useful to use the term *parts* in statements of properties of polygons.   This expression means the sides and the interior angles determined by the sides.

Theorem (11a-1):   For any *n*-sided polygon in the plane, $n \geq 3$, there is another polygon in some other position such that all the parts of the second polygon are congruent to all the parts of the first polygon.

Exercise Set

1. We note that, according to the system of naming polygons, a triangle should be called a trigon and a quadrilateral should be called a tetragon. Explore historically why these names are not used for polygons of three and four sides.

2. Explain why the geometric models of Fig. 11.2 are not polygons.

3. We call a polygon a **closed figure**. Can you name any other closed geometric figures that are not polygons?

4. Which polygons of Figs. 11.1 and 11.2 are convex?

*5. Prove Theorem (11a-1) for a polygon of six sides.

11b   Quadrilaterals

Using our definition of quadrilateral as a starting point, we now make definitions of particular types of quadrilaterals. (See Fig. 11.8.)

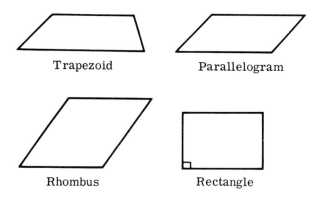

Trapezoid   Parallelogram

Rhombus   Rectangle

Fig. 11.8

Definition (11-e): A quadrilateral having exactly one pair of opposite sides parallel is called a **trapezoid**.

Definition (11-f): A quadrilateral having two pairs of opposite sides parallel is called a **parallelogram**.

Definition (11-g): A parallelogram having a pair of consecutive sides congruent is called a **rhombus**.

Definition (11-h): A parallelogram that determines one right angle is called a **rectangle**.

In a rectangle we give special names to nonparallel sides. The measure of the side of greater length is usually called the **length** and the measure of the second side is called the **width** of the rectangle. Both terms refer to *measures* of line segments. That is, a rectangle having length 5 and width 3 would be a rectangle whose sides have lengths of 3 and 5.

Definition (11-i): A rectangle having a pair of consecutive sides congruent is called a **square**.

We shall now state several theorems. Most are direct results of previous theorems and definitions. The proofs have been left to the exercises.

It should be reemphasized that we have two methods of proof at our disposal, the analytic and the synthetic. In the following material, the method that seems most appropriate to the exercise or theorem at hand is the one that is used.

Theorem (11b-1) is proven twice. The first proof involves the use of slope, which is a number (analytic) concept. The second method uses only the concepts of parallel lines and the transitive property of congruence. This second method is a synthetic proof of the theorem.

Theorem (11b-1): The opposite angles of a parallelogram are congruent.

PROOF

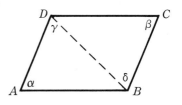

Given: Parallelogram $ABCD$.
To Prove: $\alpha \cong \beta$ and $\delta \cong \gamma$.

1. $ABCD$ is a parallelogram.	1. Hypothesis
2. $AB \parallel DC$ and $AD \parallel BC$.	2. Definition (11-f)
Analytic Method:	
3. Slope of AB = slope of DC; slope of AD = slope of CB.	3. Definition (6-b)
4. $\therefore$ $\alpha \cong \beta$ and $\delta \cong \gamma$.	4. Theorem (8d-1)
Synthetic Method:	
3a. There is a line on B and D.	3a. Theorem (5c-3)
4a. $\angle ABD \cong \angle BDC$; $\angle ADB \cong \angle DBC$.	4a. Theorem (8e-2)
5a. DB is common to both $\triangle ABD$ and $\triangle BDC$.	5a. Axiom E-1
6a. $\triangle ADB \cong \triangle DBC$.	6a. Theorem (9f-4)
7a. $\alpha \cong \beta$.	7a. Theorem (9f-1)

8a. $(\sphericalangle ABD) + (\sphericalangle DBC) =$ $(\sphericalangle ADB) + (\sphericalangle BDC).$	8a. Properties of $\mathscr{R}$
9a. $\therefore (\sphericalangle ABC) = (\sphericalangle ADC).$	9a. Corollary (8c-3a)
10a. $\therefore \delta \cong \gamma.$	10a. Theorem (8c-2)
Q.E.D.	

We should note that Step 2 of Theorem (11b-1) claims the existence of slope for the sides of the parallelogram. Theorem (11a-1) is what allows us to choose a parallelogram such that the sides *will* have slope.

We now list theorems concerning the parallelogram and the rhombus.

Theorem (11b-2):   A rectangle has four right angles.

Theorem (11b-3):   The opposite sides of a parallelogram are congruent.

Theorem (11b-4):   The diagonals of a parallelogram bisect each other.

Theorem (11b-5):   The diagonals of a rhombus are perpendicular.

There is another special quadrilateral called a **kite**. The name implies its shape. A kite has two distinct pairs of congruent adjacent sides. Figure 11.9 illustrates a kite for which $AB \cong BC$ and $AD \cong DC$. We can easily

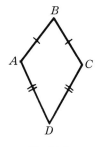

Fig. 11.9

see that a rhombus and a square must also be kites, for all their adjacent sides are congruent. This means, of course, that whatever we prove true about a kite will also be true for the rhombus and the square.

Theorem (11b-6):   The diagonals of a kite are perpendicular.

The proof of this theorem is a straightforward application of the side-side-side triangle congruence theorem, followed by showing that various angles become congruent. (See Exercise 17.) We also want to note that an analytic proof would be much more involved. That is, for this particular problem, the synthetic method is more practical than an analytic method.

If the nonparallel sides of a trapezoid are congruent, we call the polygon an **isosceles trapezoid**. Generally we call the included angles of the smaller parallel side the **summit angles** and the included angles of the larger parallel side the **base angles**. Angles ADC and BCD are summit angles and angles DAB and CBA are base angles in the trapezoid of Fig. 11.10. Furthermore,

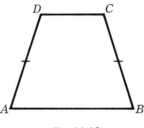

Fig. 11.10

in Fig. 11.10, if $AD \cong CB$, then trapezoid $ABCD$ is isosceles.

Theorem (11b-7): The base angles of an isosceles trapezoid are congruent.

PROOF

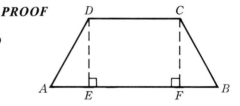

Given: Isosceles trapezoid $ABCD$ with $AB \parallel CD$ and $AD \cong BC$.
To Prove: $\sphericalangle DAB \cong \sphericalangle CBA$.

1. Isosceles trapezoid $ABCD$ has $AB \parallel CD$ and $AD \cong BC$.	1. Hypothesis
2. There are lines DE and $CF \perp AB$.	2. Why?
3. $DE \parallel CF$.	3. Why?
4. $DE \cong CF$.	4. Why?
5. $\triangle AED$ and $\triangle FBC$ are right triangles.	5. Why?
6. $\triangle AED \cong \triangle FBC$.	6. Why?
7. $\sphericalangle DAB \cong \sphericalangle CBA$.	7. Why?
Q.E.D.	

The following exercise set contains many problems that are, in fact, theorems. The reader should study these propositions carefully and relate them to the geometry that has been developed. A sketch or model of the relationships in each exercise would be an excellent way to help understand the concept under discussion. Moreover, it is hoped that the reader will provide the simple proof for each of the exercises.

Exercise Set

1. Prove that the adjacent angles of parallelogram $ABCD$ are supplementary. See Fig. 11.11.

2. Prove that the diagonal AC divides parallelogram $ABCD$ into two congruent triangles.   See Fig. 11.12.

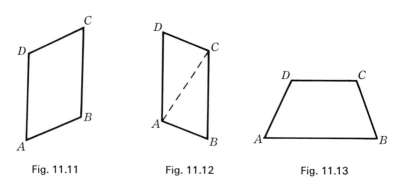

| Fig. 11.11 | Fig. 11.12 | Fig. 11.13 |

3. Prove that the diagonals of isosceles trapezoid $ABCD$ are congruent.   See Fig. 11.13.

4. Prove that if the quadrilateral $ABCD$ has one pair of parallel and congruent sides, then it is a parallelogram.   See Fig. 11.12.

5. Prove that the line joining the midpoints of the isosceles sides of trapezoid $ABCD$ is parallel to the two remaining sides.   See Fig. 11.13.

6. Prove that the summit angles of isosceles trapezoid $ABCD$ are congruent. See Fig. 11.13.

7. Prove that if two adjacent angles of a trapezoid are congruent, then it is isosceles.

8. Prove that a quadrilateral that has both pairs of opposite angles congruent is a parallelogram.

9. Prove that if the diagonals of a quadrilateral bisect each other, the quadrilateral is a parallelogram.

10. Prove that if the midpoints of any quadrilateral are joined together successively by line segments, the quadrilateral formed is a parallelogram.

11. Prove that if two sets of parallel lines intersect each other, the opposite angles are congruent.

12. Prove that if the diagonals of a quadrilateral are perpendicular and bisect each other, the quadrilateral is a rhombus.

13. Prove Theorem (11b-2).

14. Prove Theorem (11b-3).

15. Prove Theorem (11b-4).

16. Prove Theorem (11b-5).

17. Prove Theorem (11b-6).

18. Prove that exactly one diagonal of a kite is the perpendicular bisector of the other diagonal.

19. Prove that the diagonals of a rhombus bisect the angles of the rhombus.

20. Prove that the diagonals of a square are congruent.

21. List all the properties that you now know to be true about a parallelogram, kite, trapezoid, rectangle, rhombus, and square.

22. Show that the sum of the measures of the interior angles of any quadrilateral is equal to the measure of four right angles.

*23. Given two triangles ABC and ABD with the same base AB, and on the same side of AB, the vertices D and C of the triangle are each outside the other triangle. Prove that if AC is congruent to AD, then BC cannot be congruent to BD. See Fig. 11.14. (*Hint:* Prove by contradiction.)

*24. In a parallelogram $ABCD$ the line BQ bisects AD and DP bisects BC. Prove that BQ and DP trisect AC. See Fig. 11.15.

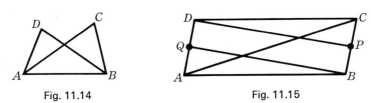

Fig. 11.14   Fig. 11.15

*25. Prove that the bisectors of two consecutive angles of a parallelogram are perpendicular to each other.

*26. Prove that the opposite angles of the quadrilateral formed by the bisectors of the interior angles of any quadrilateral are supplementary.

*27. Prove that the line joining the midpoints of the parallel sides of a trapezoid passes through the midpoints of the two diagonals.

*28. If the opposite sides of a hexagon are congruent and parallel, prove that the diagonals whose endpoints are opposite vertices meet at a point.

*29. Prove the proposition of Exercise 5 for a general trapezoid. (*Hint:* Try an analytic approach.)

**30. Prove that in an inscribed quadrilateral the product of the lengths of the diagonals is equal to the sum of the products of the lengths of the opposite sides. (*Hint:* Construct DE, where E is the center of the circle. Then look for similar triangles.) See Fig. 11.16.

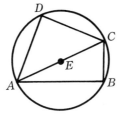

Fig. 11.16

**31. From M, the midpoint of a line CD, ME is constructed oblique to CD. Prove that DE is not congruent to CE.

11c   Regular Polygons

We now consider a special set of polygons that have certain characteristics lacking in general polygons.

Definition (11-j):   A **regular polygon** is a convex polygon, all of whose angles and sides are congruent.

Theorem (11c-1):   The exterior angles of a regular polygon are congruent.

The proof is left to the exercises.   Figure 11.17 illustrates a regular hexagon and its exterior angles.

We now choose a vertex of any regular polygon and proceed to construct diagonals to all the remaining nonadjacent vertices.   Using this procedure, we obtain two less triangles than the number of sides of the polygon.   (See Fig. 11.18.)

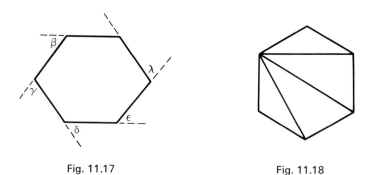

Fig. 11.17   Fig. 11.18

We know that the sum of the measure of the interior angles of a triangle is equal to the measure of two right angles.   Therefore the sum of the measures of the interior angles of an n-sided regular polygon must be $(n - 2)$ times twice the measure of a right angle.   This can be established by the principle of mathematical induction.   Such a proof, however, is beyond the scope of this book.

The measure of the exterior angles of an n-sided polygon can be found as easily as the measure of the interior angles.   There are as many interior angles as sides.   Since the measure of an exterior angle plus the measure of an interior angle equals the measure of two right angles, we arrive at the following formula.   Let the measure of a right angle be equal to m and let e be the measure of an exterior angle.   Thus

$$e + \frac{(n - 2)2m}{n} = 2m$$

(1)
$$e = \frac{1}{n}(-2nm + 4m + 2nm)$$

$$e = \frac{4m}{n}.$$

Hence we have the measure of an exterior angle equal to four times the measure of a right angle divided by the number of sides of the regular polygon.

Example 1:   What is the sum of the measures of the interior angles of a regular pentagon if the measure of a right angle is $\pi/2$ radians?   What is the sum if the measure of a right angle is $90°$?

Solution: The sum of the measures would be

$$s_1 = 2(n - 2)\left(\frac{\pi}{2}\right),$$

where n is the number of sides.   Since a pentagon has five sides, our formula becomes

$$s_1 = 2(5 - 2)\left(\frac{\pi}{2}\right)$$

$$= 3\pi \text{ radians.}$$

Using $90°$ as the measure of a right angle, we have

$$s_2 = 2(n - 2)90°$$

$$= 2(5 - 2)90°$$

$$= 540°.$$

Example 2:   What is the measure of an interior angle of a regular octagon if the measure of a right angle is $\pi/2$ radians?   An exterior angle?

Solution: Our formula of Example 1 is divided by the number of angles that are equal to the number of sides—that is, eight—for an octagon has eight sides.   Thus we have

$$i = \frac{2(n - 2)(\pi/2)}{n}$$

$$= \frac{2(8 - 2)(\pi/2)}{8}$$

$$= \frac{12(\pi/2)}{8}$$

$$= \frac{3}{4}\pi \text{ radians.}$$

The exterior angle has measure

$$e = \pi - \frac{3}{4}\pi$$

$$= \frac{\pi}{4},$$

since the angles are supplementary. If we apply formula (1) directly, we obtain

$$e = \frac{4(\pi/2)}{8}$$

$$= \frac{\pi}{4}.$$

Example 3:   What is the measure of the interior and exterior angles of a regular nonagon if the measure of a right angle is 90°?

Solution: Using formula (1) for the measure of the exterior angle, we have

$$e = \frac{4(90°)}{9}$$

$$= 40°.$$

Since the exterior and interior angles are supplementary, for the measure of an interior angle we have

$$i = 180° - 40°$$

$$= 140°.$$

Based on these examples and on Fig. 11.17, we can conclude that as n becomes very large, the measure of an interior angle approaches the measure of two right angles.   Why?   (See Exercises 1 through 6.)

Example 4:   What is the measure of an interior angle of a regular polygon of 1000 sides where the measure of a right angle is 90°?

Solution: Using the formula of Example 1, we have

$$i = \frac{2(n - 2)(90°)}{n}$$

$$= \frac{2(1000 - 2)(90°)}{1000}$$

$$= 179.65°.$$

We are very close to a straight angle!

Exercise Set

If the measure of a right angle is m, find the measures of the interior and exterior angles of the following regular polygons.

1. Pentagon, $m = 90°$.   2. Hexagon, $m = \pi/2$.
3. Decagon, $m = \pi/2$.   4. 16 sides, $m = 90°$.
5. 24 sides, $m = \pi/2$.   6. 32 sides, $m = 90°, \pi/2$.
7. What is the sum of the measures of the interior and exterior angles of the regular polygons of Exercises 1 through 6?

Which of the following are regular polygons? Find the sum of the measures of the interior angles.

8. Rhombus.   9. Rectangle.
10. Square.   11. Isosceles trapezoid.
12. Parallelogram.   13. Equiangular triangle.
14. Using your compass, construct a circle of some given radius. Then, without changing the extension, lay off equal arcs on the circle. What happens? Are there any conclusions that might be made?

For Exercises 15 through 20, determine the number of sides of the regular polygons.

15. Exterior angle has measure 72°.
16. Exterior angle has measure $\pi/5$.
17. Exterior angle has measure $\pi/10$.
18. Interior angle has measure 140°.
19. Interior angle has measure $249\pi/250$.
20. Interior angle has measure 179.91°.
21. What conclusion can be drawn from Example 4 and Exercise 20 in terms of inscribing a regular polygon in a circle?
**22. Construct a regular polygon with only a compass and a straightedge.

11d   Similar Polygons

We would like now to recall our definition of similar triangles.

Definition (9-h): Two triangles are **similar** ($\sim$) if and only if there is a positive $k \in \mathscr{R}$ such that the length of each side of one triangle is k times the length of the corresponding side of the other triangle.

By choosing any vertex of a convex n-sided polygon we can, as seen in Section 11c, divide the polygon into $n - 2$ triangles. Using these triangles as our basis, we make the following definition.

Definition (11-k): Two convex n-sided polygons, $n \geq 3$, are **similar** iff the $n - 2$ triangles of one polygon are similar respectively to the corresponding $n - 2$ triangles of the other polygon.

Theorem (11d-1): The corresponding interior angles of two similar polygons are congruent.

We leave the formal proof of this theorem for a heptagon to the exercises. The proof for the general case is omitted.   Example 1 illustrates the argument of the proof.

Example 1:   Consider two similar convex polygons as in Fig. 11.19.

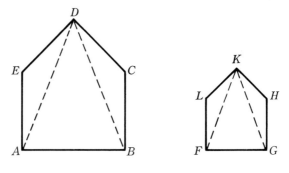

Fig. 11.19

From vertices D and K we have drawn the diagonals of the polygons.   Since the polygons are similar, the triangles are correspondingly similar.   Theorem (9e-2) establishes the congruence of the angles of the corresponding triangles. Thus we quickly see the validity of Theorem (11d-1).   A numerical technique can also be used to illustrate this theorem for a regular polygon.

Example 2:   Consider the two regular hexagons of Fig. 11.20.   Show that

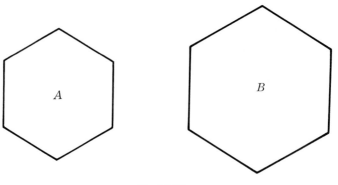

Fig. 11.20

the interior angles have equal measure.

Solution: By the formula of Section 11d, we have for hexagon A,

$$i_1 = \frac{2(6 - 2)m}{6}.$$

The formula for hexagon B is

$$i_2 = \frac{2(6 - 2)m}{6}.$$

But $i_1 = i_2$; therefore we conclude that corresponding angles are congruent.

At this point we could formulate a theorem about the similarity of regular polygons. For example, all regular pentagons are similar. Why? Furthermore, all regular octagons are similar. The proof of this case would be identical to the previous case. We now give a general theorem that includes all n-gons.

Theorem (11d-2): All regular polygons of n sides for a particular n, $n \geq 3$, are similar. (n is a natural number.)

The proof is easily derived by considering a series of triangles, starting with a triangle that includes two sides of the polygon. Exercise 2 asks for the proof of the similarity of two regular pentagons. The proof for the general case is omitted.

Exercise Set

1. Prove Theorem (11d-1) for the case of a heptagon.
2. Prove Theorem (11d-2) for the case of a pentagon.
3. If the diagonals of two polygons from particular vertices are all respectively congruent, are the polygons similar? Give an illustration verifying your answer.
4. Is it possible for a regular polygon to be similar to a polygon that is not regular? Why or why not?
5. Can a rectangle be similar to a square? A rhombus? A parallelogram?
*6. Given some line segment, construct a regular pentagon.
*7. Given any circle, construct a regular octagon that is inscribed in the circle.

chapter 12

Area and Perimeter

12a Polygons

When we use the term *area*, our intuition seems to tell us the meaning of the word. Certainly, we think, no one is ever confused by the concept of area! However, we must develop the concept of area in a sound mathematical manner. What we need is a definition. In order to arrive at a definition, let us examine some of the relationships involved.

We first consider a square of unit length; that is, each side of the square has length one. If we call the "area" of the square 1, we have associated a real number with a geometric model in the same manner that we associated "length" with a line segment. We now consider a rectangle of length 3 and width 2. What real number do we associate with the geometric model this time? If we divide the rectangle in the manner of Fig. 12.1, where each

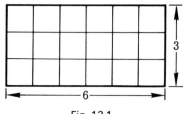

Fig. 12.1

segment has length 1, we obtain 6 squares of unit length. It would seem reasonable to call the "area" of this rectangle 6. The rectangle in the figure itself might have "area" 18.

Figure 12.2 illustrates a rectangle of length $6\frac{1}{2}$ and width $3\frac{1}{4}$. Using our intuitive idea of area, we obtain 21 unit squares plus $\frac{1}{8}$ of a unit square. The rectangle in Fig. 12.3 is divided into such unit squares. We should be able

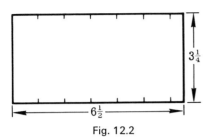

Fig. 12.2

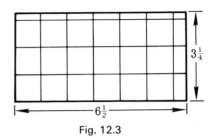

Fig. 12.3

to count 21 unit squares plus $\frac{1}{8}$ of an additional unit square. These arguments are summed up in the following definition.

Definition (12-a): The real number product of the length and width of a rectangle is called the **area of the rectangle**.

Theorem (12a-1): If a rectangle has length l and width w, then the rectangle has area $A = l \cdot w$.

This is an existence theorem for areas and can be proved by a direct application of Axiom R-7. (See Exercise 2.) The next question of importance is whether we can add areas together in a manner similar to arcs and lengths of line segments. The proof comes from the definition. (See Exercise 3.) In the next few theorems, we use the word "combined." This is a nontechnical word meaning the union of the interiors of the two rectangles where the interiors themselves are disjoint (they have no points in common).

Theorem (12a-2): If rectangle $ABCD$ has area r and rectangle $A'B'C'D'$ has area s, then the area of the combined rectangles is $t = r + s$.

In Chapter 11 we proved that the diagonals of a parallelogram divide the parallelogram into two congruent triangles. (See Exercise 2, Section 10b.) This information leads us to the area of a triangle.

Certainly half the area of a rectangle will be $lw/2$. Figure 12.4 shows that $lw/2$ would be a likely candidate for the area of a triangle except that both triangles ABD and DBC are right triangles. This would make the definition too restrictive. In Fig. 12.5 we consider any triangle ABC and any one

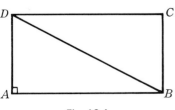

Fig. 12.4

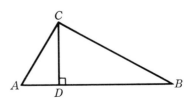

Fig. 12.5

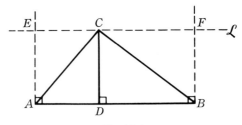

Fig. 12.6

altitude *CD*.   In Fig. 12.6 we have constructed perpendiculars to *AB* at *A* and *B* on the same side of *AB*.   We then constructed line $\mathscr{L}$ through *C* and parallel to *AB* intersecting the perpendiculars at *E* and *F*.   We can prove that *ABFE*, *ADCE*, and *DBFC* are rectangles.   (See Exercise 1.) We see that the △*ABC* has become, intuitively, half of the rectangle *ABFE*. Why?   Note that $CD \cong EA \cong FB$.   We have thus created a more general case of the argument that the "area" of a triangle appears to be half the area of a rectangle.   We make the following definition for the area of the special polygon called a triangle.

Definition (12-b):   The **area of a triangle** is that real number $lw/2$ for which *l* is the length of any side of the triangle and *w* is the length of the altitude to that side.

Lengths of line segments are real numbers, and the existence axiom R-7 states that for $(l,w) \in \mathscr{R}$, $l \cdot w = x, \exists x \in \mathscr{R}$.   Thus we are assured that the area of a triangle exists.

Theorem (12a-3):   If a triangle *ABC* has a side of length *b* and an altitude on that same side of length *h*, then the triangle has area $bh/2$.

Theorem (12a-4):   If a triangle *ABC* has area *r* and a triangle *A'B'C'* has area *s*, then the area of the combined triangles is $t = r + s$.

The proofs of these theorems are left to the exercises.

Using the fact that the ratio of similitude of congruent triangles is 1, and that congruent triangles have corresponding altitudes congruent, we can prove the following theorem.   The proof is left to the exercises.

Theorem (12a-5):   Congruent triangles have equal areas.

Thus far area has been defined for two special polygons.   We now give a definition for convex polygons of four or more sides.

Definition (12-c):   The **area of a convex polygon of four or more sides** is equal to the sum of the areas of its $n - 2$ triangles.

Example 1:   Find the area of the parallelogram having a side of length 8 and an altitude of length 4.

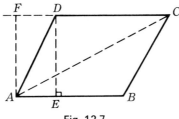

Fig. 12.7

Solution: Figure 12.7 illustrates the problem. $(AB) = 8$ and $(DE) = 4$. First construct AC. Then construct altitude AF and note that $DE \cong AF$. Therefore $(DE) = (AF) = 4$. Area of triangle $ACD = \frac{1}{2}(8)(4) = 16$. Using the fact that a diagonal divides a parallelogram into two congruent triangles, plus Theorem (12a-1) and Definition (12-c), we find that $ABCD$ has area $2(16) = 32$. [We adopt the notation $(ABCD)$ as meaning the area of the polygon in question. For example, $(\triangle ACD) = 16$ and $(ABCD) = 32$.]

Example 2: Find the area of an isosceles trapezoid whose sides have length 5 and whose bases are 16 and 8.

Solution: Figure 12.8 illustrates the problem. We construct diagonal

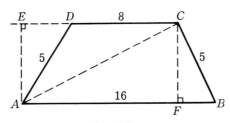

Fig. 12.8

AC. Constructing the perpendiculars AE and CF, we note that they are congruent and are the respective altitudes of the triangles ACD and ABC. Clearly $(ED) = 4$ and $(EA) = 3$. Therefore $(\triangle ADC) = \frac{1}{2}(3)(8) = 12$. $(\triangle ABC) = \frac{1}{2}(3)(16) = 24$. Hence $(ABCD) = 36$.

Exercise Set

1. Explain carefully the use of Axiom R-7 in the definitions of area for a triangle, a rectangle, and a polygon.
2. Develop the formula $A = \frac{1}{2}h(b + b')$ for the area A of a trapezoid whose altitude has length h and whose bases have lengths b and b'.

Consider a triangle ABC with altitude having a length h to side AB at D. Find its area if the following conditions are met.

3. $h = 3, (AB) = 4$.

4. $h = 4, (AC) = 5, (DB) = 6$.

5. $h = 1, (AD) = 1, (\triangle DBC) = \frac{1}{2}$.

6. $h = 4, (AC) = 5, (BC) = 6$.

7. Prove Theorem (12a-2).

8. Prove Theorem (12a-4).

9. Prove Theorem (12a-5).

10. If the length of a rectangle is $\sqrt{6}$ and the width is $\sqrt{3}$, find its area.

11. A triangle has a base of measure 40 and an area of 100.   Find the length of its altitude.

12. Find the area of an isosceles right triangle if one leg has length 6.

13. An equilateral triangle has side of length 5.   Find its area.

14. Prove the theorem that the area of a parallelogram can be expressed as the product of the lengths of its base and altitude.

15. In Example 2, develop a second method of finding the area of the trapezoid. Is this an acceptable way of using the given definitions of area?   Why?

16. An equilateral triangle has side of length 13.   Find its area.

17. An isosceles right triangle has area 8.   What is the length of its hypotenuse?

Find the altitudes of the triangles whose areas and bases respectively are given as follows.

18. 176, 32.   19. 30, 3.

20. $3\sqrt{14}, \sqrt{6}$.   21. 27, 6.

Find the altitudes of the trapezoids whose areas and bases respectively are given as follows.

22. 33, 5, 6.   23. 15, 4, 6.

24. 70, 9, 11.   25. 13, 9, 5.

*26. If the ratio of similitude of two similar triangles is 3, how do their areas compare?

*27. Two equilateral triangles have as the ratio of their areas 4 to 9.   What will be their ratio of similitude?

*28. Develop the concept that the product of the lengths of the diagonals of a kite equals twice the area of the kite.

*29. Prove that if two triangles have an angle of one congruent to an angle of the other, the areas have the same ratio as do the products of the lengths of the sides that determine the congruent angles.

*30. Prove that the areas of two similar polygons are in the same ratio as are the squares of the lengths of any two corresponding sides.   [*Hint:* Use Definition (12-c) and Exercise 11.]

*31. From one end of a rectangular sheet of paper of length 20 a square piece is cut off, leaving an area of 100 square inches in the rest of the sheet.   How wide is the sheet?

*32. Find the area of a triangle having vertices
   (a) (2,2), (7,2), (2,14);
   (b) (3,1), (6,1), (9,6).
**33. Find the area of the triangle having vertices (3,1), $(-3,4)$, and (5,6).

12b   Circles

In Section 7g we introduced the real irrational number π as a factor of the unscaled arc length of a circle.   We now use this number again in the definition of area for a circle.

Definition (12-d):   The **area of a circle** is the product of the square of the length of the radius and π; that is, $a = \pi r^2$.

Theorem (12b-1):   If the length of radius of a circle is r, then the number πr^2 for the area of the circle exists.

Theorem (12b-2):   If a circle P has area u and a circle P' has area w, then the area of the combined circles is $u = v + w$.

Theorem (12b-1) establishes the existence of area for all circles.   This is clearly an application of Axiom R-7.   Theorem (12b-2) guarantees that we can add areas together.   The proofs are left to the exercises.

The actual derivation of the constant π is an interesting one, but one that involves the concept of a limit.   In this book we have not explored *limits*, except indirectly.   The derivation of π will be left to another course.   Whenever π is used in the exercises that follow, its decimal approximation has been avoided.   We suggest the reader do the same.

Example 1:   Find the area of a circle with diameter 14.

Solution: Since the diameter is 14, the radius is $\frac{14}{2}$ or 7.   Thus the area, according to Definition (12-d), is $a = \pi r^2 = \pi \cdot 7^2 = 49\pi$.

Example 2:   If the area of a circle is 32π, what is its diameter?

Solution: Since $a = \pi r^2$, we must have $32\pi = \pi r^2$, or $r^2 = 32$.   Hence we get $r = \sqrt{32}$.   This simplifies to $r = 4\sqrt{2}$.   But $d = 2r$, and therefore $d = 8\sqrt{2}$.

Exercise Set

Find the area of the circles given the radius of length r, or diameter of length d, or its locus of points.

1. $r = 3$.   2. $r = \sqrt{5}$.   3. $d = 2\sqrt{3}$.
4. $r = \pi$.   5. $d = 12.3$.   6. $d = 2$.
7. $x^2 + y^2 = 4$.   8. $(x - 1)^2 + (y + 1)^2 = 24$.   9. $x^2 + y^2 + 2y = 3$.

Find the length of both (a) the radius and (b) the diameter of the circles having the following areas.

10. 2π.

11. 24.

12. $16\pi^2$.

13. $\dfrac{\pi}{3}$.

14. $(x + 2)^2\pi$

15. 128π.

16. Prove that congruent circles have equal areas.

*17. Consider the circle $x^2 + y^2 = 8$ and the triangle with vertices $(-2,-2)$, $(2,-2)$, and $(0,2,\sqrt{2})$.   Find
  (a) the area of the circle;
  (b) the area of the triangle;
  (c) the area inside the circle but outside the triangle.

*18. Consider the points $(0,0)$, $(4,0)$, and $(2,2)$.   Find
  (a) the area of the triangle;
  (b) the area of its circumscribed circle;
  (c) the equation for the locus of the circumscribed circle.

*19. Prove Theorem (12b-1).

*20. Prove Theorem (12b-2).

12c   Perimeters

Definition (12-e):   The **perimeter** of a polygon is the sum of the lengths of its sides.

Definition (12-f):   The **circumference** of a circle is the real number $2\pi r$, where r is the length of the radius.

Note, particularly, that we are using the words *perimeter* and *circumference* to mean *real number lengths*.   When we say circle, we mean the continuous locus illustrated in Fig. 12.9, but not that which is interior to the circle (illustrated by the shaded region).   Similarly, the words square, rhombus,

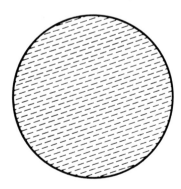

Fig. 12.9

and so on, mean only the loci themselves. They do not include what is interior to the locus.

Example 1: What is the circumference of the circle

$$(x + 2)^2 + (y - 1)^2 = 4?$$

Solution: Since $(x - h)^2 + (y - k)^2 = r^2$ is the general equation for the locus of the circle having center (h,k) and length of radius r, we have $r = 2$. Thus the circumference $c = 2\pi r = 2\pi(2) = 4\pi$.

Example 2: Find the perimeter of a rectangle with area of 40 and length 10.

Solution: The area of a rectangle is $a = lw$. Thus $40 = lw$, and since $1 = 10$ we have $40 = 10w$, or $w = 4$. The perimeter of a rectangle would be $2l + 2w$. Why? Hence we have the perimeter $p = 2(10) + 2(4)$, or $p = 28$.

Exercise Set

Find the perimeters or circumferences of the following loci. If not possible, explain why.

1. $x^2 + y^2 = 16$.
2. Square with side of length 3.
3. Isosceles triangle with congruent sides of length 5 and altitude of length 4.
4. Triangle with sides of length $\sqrt{8}$, $\sqrt{12}$, $\sqrt{24}$.
5. Square with area 64.
6. Rectangle with area 45 and width 3.
7. $x^2 + (y - 1)^2 = 3^2$.
8. Circle with diameter of length 14.
9. Isosceles trapezoid with bases of lengths 6 and 8 and side of length 4.
10. Kite having lengths of diagonals 4 and 8.
11. Parallelogram with sides of lengths 6 and 8.
12. Regular hexagon with side of length 4.
13. Isosceles trapezoid with bases of lengths 8 and 16 and altitude of length 3.
14. Equilateral triangle with area $64/\sqrt{3}$ and altitude of length 8.

What is the perimeter of a triangle having the following vertices?

15. $(2, -1)$, $(3,4)$, $(-4,2)$.
16. $(0,0)$, $(2,\frac{1}{3})$, $(-4,1)$.
17. $(2,2)$, $(-2,-2)$, $(2,-2)$.
18. Find the perimeters of the triangles of Exercise 32 of Section 12a.
19. A rectangle with width 20 and length 40 has a square with side 4 removed from each corner. What is the original perimeter of the rectangle and its perimeter after the squares have been removed?

20. Which has a greater length—the perimeter of a square with side 4 or a circle with radius 4? What would have to be the radius of the circle so that its circumference is equal to the perimeter of the square?

*21. Consider a circle with a radius of 10 and a regular polygon whose side has some undetermined length. Form an argument that would show that the perimeter of a regular polygon can approximate the circumference of the given circle. Give illustrations. (*Hint:* Try regular polygons that have sides of various lengths.)

*22. Assume that the radius of the earth has a length of 4000 miles. Suppose that the earth were smooth and that a rope were stretched taut along the equator. If the rope were made a yard longer and again stretched taut above the equator so as to be everywhere equidistant from the surface, could a mouse crawl under?

chapter 13

3-Space Concepts

13a Coordinates for 3-Space

In Chapter 4 we developed the Cartesian coordinate plane. If we changed the axioms stated there, we could develop other grid systems, including the one described below. For our purpose, however, we shall leave the actual axiomatic adjustments to more advanced work. In fact, one of the axioms is violated immediately in the opening statement of the following development of a new coordinate system.

Let us now consider three Cartesian planes. Since we can intuitively think of a plane as a "flat expanse" with no thickness (sheets of paper, blackboard, table top), we *could* arrange these planes in a manner similar to Fig. 13.1. That is, the planes *could* all intersect in some prescribed manner.

Fig. 13.1

If we take, for example, a Cartesian plane A and any line $\mathscr{L}_1 \in A$ and then take a second plane B and any line $\mathscr{L}_2 \in B$ such that $\mathscr{L}_1 \in B$ and $\mathscr{L}_2 \in A$, we would have the model illustrated in Fig. 13.2. Now, taking a third plane C with a line $\mathscr{L}_3 \in C$ and making the plane C intersect both planes A and B, we would have the model illustrated in Fig. 13.3. There is a point that is common to all three planes; that is, $A \cap B \cap C = \{P\}$. Would there be more than one? It turns out that there is *at most one point common to*

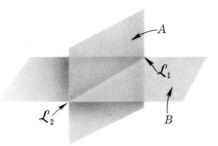

Fig. 13.2

three distinct planes. Using this procedure, we imagine a fourth plane that does not intersect *A*, a fifth plane that does not intersect *B*, and a sixth plane that does not intersect *C*. Thus a model, as illustrated in Fig. 13.4, begins to appear.

Examining the possibilities for locating loci in this model, we immediately

Fig. 13.3

note that there are five directions in which we can move from any one point of intersection of three planes. Assuming that all the lines in one plane are nonintersecting to the lines in a second plane or that they intersect at right angles to the lines in a second plane, we can move left-to-right, right-to-left, up-or-down, front-to-back, or back-to-front. Figure 13.5 illustrates this

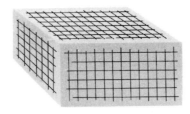

Fig. 13.4

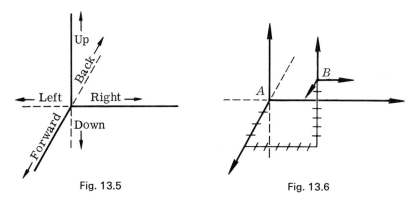

Fig. 13.5   Fig. 13.6

with only the line of intersection. If we start at point A in Fig. 13.6 and count the steps to reach point B along the lines of intersection of the three planes intersecting at A and B, we have 4 forward from A, then 6 to the right, and finally 7 up. Thus we can associate an ordered triple of numbers [in this case, (4,6,7)] with the intersection point of three planes. This we shall do.

To review our position, we have three Cartesian planes all mutually perpendicular as in Fig. 13.7. Now the real numbers are associated in

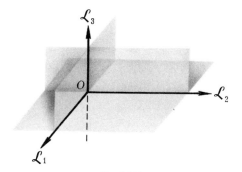

Fig. 13.7

one-to-one correspondence with points in lines $\mathscr{L}_1$, $\mathscr{L}_2$, and $\mathscr{L}_3$.

The number zero is associated with the point O in each of the three number lines; that is, $O = (0,0,0)$. With every point in the line $\mathscr{L}_1$, a real number $(a,0,0)$ is associated. Similarly, for points in $\mathscr{L}_2$ and $\mathscr{L}_3$, we have $(0,b,0)$ and $(0,0,c)$. Figure 13.8 illustrates the model.

The planes containing the intersecting lines $\mathscr{L}_1$ and $\mathscr{L}_2$, $\mathscr{L}_2$ and $\mathscr{L}_3$, $\mathscr{L}_1$ and $\mathscr{L}_3$ are called the **coordinate planes**. Lines $\mathscr{L}_1$, $\mathscr{L}_2$, and $\mathscr{L}_3$, which all intersect at $O = (0,0,0)$, we call the **coordinate axes** and label them $\overleftrightarrow{OX}$, $\overleftrightarrow{OY}$, and $\overleftrightarrow{OZ}$.

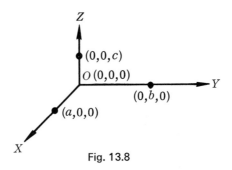

Fig. 13.8

For a point not in one of these axes, we make two agreements for our purpose here. First, forward, to the right, or up is always positive. Second, the first element of any ordered triple is associated with $\overleftrightarrow{OX}$, the second with $\overleftrightarrow{OY}$, and the third with $\overleftrightarrow{OZ}$. This means that the point $(2, -3, 4)$ would be 2 forward, -3 to the left, and 4 up, from the starting point $(0,0,0)$. Figure 13.9 illustrates the procedure. Since the grid loci in this new system are all

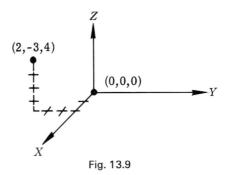

Fig. 13.9

mutually perpendicular, we call it a **rectangular coordinate system for 3-space**. The axes $\overleftrightarrow{OX}$, $\overleftrightarrow{OY}$, and $\overleftrightarrow{OZ}$ are called the **x axis**, the **y axis**, and the **z axis**, respectively. The **origin** is the point $(0,0,0)$.

Many of the theorems and definitions developed for 2-space in the previous chapters must be restated to make them hold true for 3-space. The most important one, the one that truly makes our coordinate system rectangular, is the definition of distance. The word *proposition* is used in the following material to indicate that we are making only an *informal development* and hence no formal distinction between a definition and a theorem.

Proposition (13a-1): The distance between any two points (x_1, y_1, z_1) and (x_2, y_2, z_2) in 3-space is the real number

$$d = \sqrt{(x_1 - x_2)^2 + (y_1 - y_2)^2 + (z_1 - z_2)^2}.$$

This definition is easily developed from the one in 2-space. (See Exercise *11.)

Example 1: Find the distance between the points $(2,3,-1)$ and $(2,0,-2)$.

Solution: By Proposition (13a-1) we have

$$d = \sqrt{(2-2)^2 + (3-0)^2 + [-1-(-2)]^2}$$
$$= \sqrt{3^2 + 1}$$
$$= \sqrt{10}.$$

Exercise Set

For each of the following exercises, draw the coordinate axes for 3-space and locate the following points.

1. $(2,-1,3)$, $(4,1,1)$, $(0,1,1)$.
2. $(2,1,0)$, $(0,2,3)$, $(-2,-1,0)$.
3. $(1,0,1)$, $(2,0,3)$, $(5,6,1)$.
4. $(-2,4,0)$, $(4,2,-4)$, $(-3,5,-1)$.

Find the distances between the following sets of points.

5. $(2,-1,3)$, $(2,-1,0)$.
6. $(8,9,-1)$, $(-2,-1,1)$.
7. $(-3,-4,1)$, $(5,-2,0)$.
8. $(-3,0,-2)$, $(9,-2,1)$.
9. $(0,-1,0)$, $(1,0,1)$.
10. $(-1,-1,-1)$, $(1,1,1)$.

*11. Develop the definition of distance [Proposition (13a-1)] by considering the problem of finding the distance from one corner of a room and floor to the opposite corner of a room and ceiling. Use the Pythagorean Theorem twice.

*12. Give examples of other three-dimensional coordinate systems and explain their uses.

*13. Which axioms of Chapter 4 have we violated?   How could they be reworded?

14. Find the perimeter of the triangle having vertices $(-1,2,3)$, $(10,-2,11)$, and $(2,16,0)$.

*15. Show by distances that points $(1,-2,5)$, $(3,1,11)$, and $(-1,-5,-1)$ lie in a straight line.

13b Lines and Planes

If we attempt to make our definition of a straight line for 2-space work in 3-space, we have an immediate problem. A third variable has been introduced. Suppose we take

$$px + qy + rz + s = 0$$

as our definition of a straight line.

Choosing any such locus, say

(1) $$3x + 4y - 4z + 1 = 0,$$

we have the points

(2) $$(1,1,2), (1,0,1), (0,0,\tfrac{1}{4}),$$

which satisfy (1).   Locating the points (2) in the coordinate system, we see (Fig. 13.10) that these three points certainly do not lie in a straight line. Nevertheless, these three distinct points may well determine some other geometric locus.   As shown in Fig. 13.11, we could place a "flat board" or

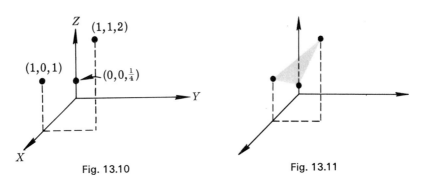

Fig. 13.10   Fig. 13.11

plane on these three points.   This fact illustrates the concept that *three noncollinear points determine a plane*.

We now note that if the point $(0,0,0)$ were included with the set (2), the four points *would not* determine a unique plane.   Is any plane determined by three points the same as the plane that was established by the axioms of Chapter 4?   It can be shown that each such plane *has* the same properties as the plane of 2-space.

Proposition (13b-1):   The locus of ordered-number triples $\{(x,y,z) \mid px + qy + rz + s = 0\}$ is called a **plane**.

We say that a set of points is **coplanar** if there is a plane that contains all the points of the set. For example, the points of (2) are coplanar.

Proposition (13b-2):   Two **planes are parallel** iff they have no common points.

Since each plane established here has the same properties as the plane obtained from the axioms, we can conclude that two points in a plane determine a straight line and all the points contained in the line are also contained in the plane.   That is, the locus of a line is always coplanar with itself.

Proposition (13b-3):   There is exactly one plane containing a line and a point not in the line.

Figure 13.12 illustrates this proposition and the next one.

Proposition (13b-4):   There is exactly one plane containing two intersecting lines.

The method of determining parallel lines in 3-space requires an added condition from the case in 2-space.   In 3-space, the concept of slope is not used because a line can be oriented many other ways besides simply vertical, horizontal, or oblique.   For example, the lines of Fig. 13.13 are not parallel

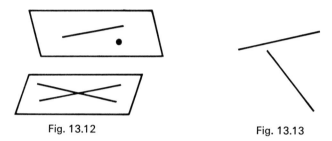

Fig. 13.12   Fig. 13.13

but they also may not even intersect.   To ensure parallelism, the lines must be in the same plane.

Proposition (13b-5):   Two coplanar lines having no common points are called **parallel lines**.

Proposition (13b-6):   Two noncoplanar lines having no points in common are said to be **skew lines**.

The lines of Fig. 13.13 may be skew lines.   Note that the lines of Fig. 13.14 are parallel if plane A is parallel to plane B.

Figure 13.14 also illustrates how we determine straight lines in 3-space. That is, *the intersection of two planes determines a straight line.*   As was done for a plane, we could write down a defining equation for a straight line in 3-space.   According to the principle just stated, it would be determined by the simultaneous solution of the equation of two planes.   However, such solutions will not be undertaken in this course.

Consider a line $\mathscr{L}$ in plane P (Fig. 13.15) intersecting $AB \in \mathscr{L}$.   The line

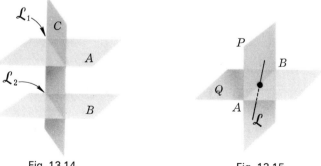

Fig. 13.14   Fig. 13.15

$\mathscr{L}$ intersects the plane in one and only one point.   This illustrates the general principle that *if two points of a line are such that one point is contained in a plane and a second point is not contained in the plane, then the line intersects the plane in one and only one point.*   Figure 13.16 illustrates this concept.

The following is only a representative list of the principles dealing with planes, lines, and points in 3-space.   Some differ considerably from the corresponding 2-space concept.   Others are merely an immediate extension of the properties of 2-space.

Proposition (13b-7):   A line is **perpendicular** to a plane if it is perpendicular to each of two intersecting coplanar lines at their point of intersection.

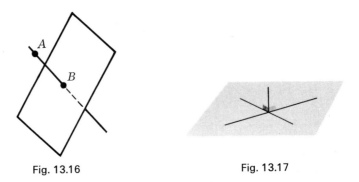

Fig. 13.16   Fig. 13.17

Proposition (13b-8):   A line perpendicular to a plane is called a **normal** to the plane.

Proposition (13b-9):   The **angle** between two planes is the angle between two intersecting normals.

Figures 13.17 and 13.18 illustrate these three definitions.   The angle α determined by the two planes of Fig. 13.18 is called a **dihedral angle.**

Proposition (13-10):   The **distance** of a point from a plane is the length of the normal line segment whose endpoints are the given point and a point in the plane.

As with the corresponding case for 2-space, this proposition makes use of the concept of distance along the perpendicular from the point to the plane. Figure 13.19 illustrates this principle.

Proposition (13b-11):   The distance between two planes is the length of the common perpendicular segment.

Proposition (13b-12):   The locus of points equidistant from two fixed points is a plane such that a normal of the plane contains the two given points. (See Fig. 13.20.)

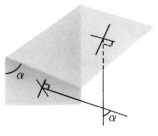

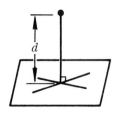

Fig. 13.18   Fig. 13.19

Proposition (13b-13): Two normals to the same plane are coplanar.

Proposition (13b-14): There is one and only one plane that contains a given point and is perpendicular to a given line.

This proposition requires that a normal of the plane at the given point must either be parallel to or coincident with the given line. Figure 13.21

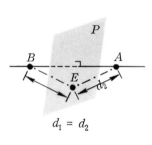

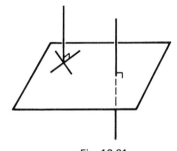

Fig. 13.20   Fig. 13.21

illustrates this proposition.

Proposition (13b-15): On a given point there is one and only one line perpendicular to a given plane.

Proposition (13b-16): Two planes are perpendicular if a pair of intersecting normal lines are respectively perpendicular.

Additional propositions could also be stated here. However, for our purpose of taking an intuitive look at 3-space, this list is adequate.

Exercise Set

In the following exercises, locate the points on the 3-space grid system and estimate whether the points are coplanar.
1. $(3,3,-5)$, $(1,1,-1)$, $(0,0,1)$, $(6,-3,-2)$.
2. $(1,1,6)$, $(0,-1,-1)$, $(2,2,9)$, $(5,-3,10)$.

3. $(2,4,-1)$, $(3,7,1)$, $(2,9,-6)$, $(4,-2,3)$.

4. $(2,1,3)$, $(0,0,3)$, $(1,0,1)$, $(9,5,5)$.

5. $(6,-1,3)$, $(-3,-2,-1)$, $(4,3,-1)$, $(6,-8,9)$.

In each of Exercises 6 through 11, find three ordered triples that are in the solution set of the given equation and locate them on the 3-space coordinate system. Then sketch the plane that corresponds to the given equation.

6. $3x - 2y + 5z = 0$.   7. $x - y + 2z + 1 = 0$.

8. $x + y + 3z - 4 = 0$.   9. $x + y + 1 = 0$.

10. $x = 5$.   11. $z = 3$.

For each proposition listed in Exercises 12 through 14, find a similar one for 2-space.

12. Proposition (13b-5).

13. Proposition (13b-6).

14. Proposition (13b-11).

15. Are two normals to the same plane parallel?

16. Are two planes perpendicular to the same line parallel?

17. Are all lines in 3-space mutually intersecting?   Can you name a coordinate system where they are?

*18. Find the equation of the plane determined by the points $(0,0,1)$, $(0,2,0)$, $(1,-1,1)$.

*19. Find the equation of the plane determined by the points $(1,-3,3)$, $(0,-2,2)$, $(-4,5,-4)$.

**20. Determine the equation of the line formed by the intersection of the planes $x + y - 7z + 1 = 0$ and $5x - y - 5z = 13$.

13c   Surfaces in 3-Space

For our purpose, *a surface in 3-space is a set of points in one-to-one correspondence with a particular set of ordered-number triples.*   Thus the locus of points determined by $\{(x,y,z) \mid px + qy + rz + s = 0\}$ is a **surface**.   We call this particular surface a **plane surface**.   Some surfaces may have *many* defining equations.   In addition, we sometimes specify a surface as a locus of points that is to satisfy some *geometric condition.*

A closed surface is one that we intuitively think of as having no "holes" in it.   That is, a point is in the locus, or "inside" the locus, or "outside" the locus.   In Fig. 13.22 point A is "inside" the closed surface, point B is contained in the locus, and point C is "outside" the locus.

Closed surfaces determined by planes (or faces) are called **polyhedra**. The surfaces have names similar to those of polygons.   For example, a tetrahedron has four faces, a pentahedron has five faces, and a hexahedron has six faces.   Figure 13.23 illustrates a representative of each of these polyhedra.

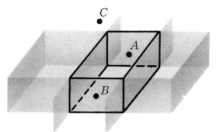

Fig. 13.22

Since we know that intersecting planes determine straight lines, the "edges" of the polyhedra are straight lines. A vertex of a polyhedron is the intersection of three or more of the determining planes.

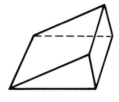
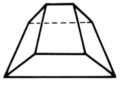

Fig. 13.23

A polyhedron having one vertex that is contained in all but one of its "determining" planes is called a **pyramid**. Figure 13.24 illustrates some pyramids. The geometric model of Fig. 13.25 would not be called a pyramid. It has eight bounding faces; thus it is an octahedron.

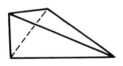

Fig. 13.24

Three sets of intersecting parallel planes determine what is called a **parallelepiped**. If the sets of planes are also mutually perpendicular, then we have a **rectangular box**. (See Fig. 13.26.)

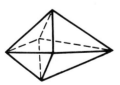
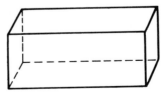

Fig. 13.25   Fig. 13.26

A **prism** is a closed surface such that two of its faces are polygons in parallel planes and the other faces are parallelograms. Thus the parallelepiped of Fig. 13.26 is also a prism.

In 2-space, the locus of points equidistant from a fixed point is a circle. In 3-space, the locus of points equidistant from a fixed point is called a **sphere**. Certainly this agrees with our intuitive concept of a sphere. As with the circle, we must remember that the points interior to the sphere are not in the locus. (See Fig. 13.27.)

In 3-space, the defining equation for a circle is

$$(x - h)^2 + (y - k)^2 + (z - j)^2 = r^2,$$

where (h,k,j) is the **center** of the sphere and r is the length of the **radius**.

Example 1: Locate the sphere $(x - 2)^2 + (y - 2)^2 + z^2 = 4$ on the 3-space coordinate system.

Solution: The center is $(2,2,0)$ and the radius is 2. The graph is illustrated in Fig. 13.28.

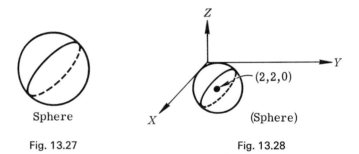

Sphere

Fig. 13.27

(Sphere)

Fig. 13.28

If there is a locus of a circle in some plane P and if some point B not in P is such that there is a set of lines on B containing all the points of the circle, then the surface that is determined is a **circular cone**. Figure 13.29 illustrates the formation of such a cone.

When the point B and the center of the circle are contained in the same normal of P, we call the surface a **right circular cone**. We could have cones of shapes determined by loci other than circles. If we consider a plane on the opposite side of B from P, we obtain a second portion of the circular cone. (See Fig. 13.30.)

If we again consider a plane P containing the locus of a circle O, and a second plane Q parallel to B, then the surface determined by the common normal lines to P and Q containing all the points of O is called a **right circular cylinder**. (See Fig. 13.31.)

Certainly if we slide the planes in opposite directions and no longer require them to be parallel, we can determine many different surfaces. Figure 13.32 illustrates several examples.

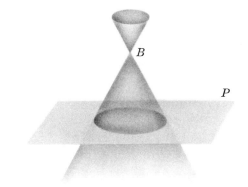

Fig. 13.29

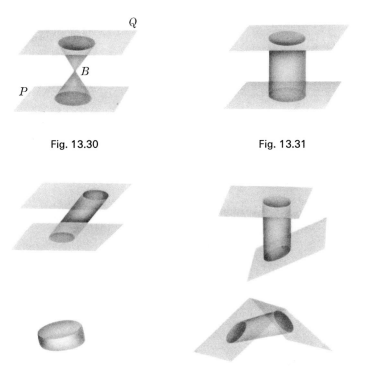

Fig. 13.30   Fig. 13.31

Fig. 13.32

Exercise Set

1. What do we call a hexahedron that has all six of its edges congruent?

2. Draw a heptahedron and a decahedron.

3. Draw a pyramid with four congruent equilateral triangles as the faces.

In Exercises 4 through 7, determine the center of the sphere and the radius and locate the model on the 3-space coordinate system.

4. $(x - 2)^2 + (y - 2)^2 + z^2 = 16$.

5. $(x + 3)^2 + (y - 1)^2 + (z - 2)^2 = 9$.

6. $(x + 1)^2 + y^2 + z^2 = 1$.

7. $(x + 3)^2 + (y + 3)^2 + (z + 3)^2 = 9$.

In the YX coordinate plane *only*, locate the following circles.   Then through the given point draw straight lines that contain points of the given circle.   State which are right circular cones.

8. $x^2 + y^2 = 9$, (4,4,4).

9. $(x - 4)^2 + y^2 = 16$, (0,0,4).

10. $(x - 3)^2 + (y - 3)^2 = 9$, (3,3,9).

11. $(x - 4)^2 + (y + 1)^2 = 9$, $(4, -1, -9)$.

In Exercises 12 through 15, graph the planes and determine what type of surface is formed.

12. $x = 4$, $y = 4$, $x = 0$, $y = 0$, $z = 0$, $z = 4$.

13. $x = y$, $x + y = 1$, $x = 0$, $z = 0$, $z = 4$.

14. $x + z = 4$, $z - x = 4$, $z = 0$, $y = 4$, $y = -4$.

15. $y = z$, $y = z + 10$, $x = 0$, $x = 5$, $z = 0$, $z = 8$.

*16. If we graph $x^2 + y^2 = 9$, $z = 0$, and $z = 9$, what type of surface is obtained?

*17. Is the following a sufficient definition for a regular polyhedron?   "A poly-hedron is regular if each of its faces is a regular polygon."   If not, what would be needed to make it a proper definition?

*18. If we intersect the cone $x^2 + y^2 - z^2 = 0$ by the planes $z = 1$, $y = 0$, $x = 0$, $z = x + 1$, and $y = 1$, what are the geometric models determined by each intersection?

13d   Surface Area and Volume

In Chapter 12 we discussed areas of polygons.   For polyhedra, the **surface area** would be the total area of the polygonal faces.

Example 1:   What is the surface area of a rectangular parallelepiped that has faces of area 6, 12, and 14?

Solution: Figure 13.33 illustrates the problem. Since a parallelepiped has opposite faces congruent, we have

$$\text{surface area} = 2(6) + 2(12) + 2(14)$$
$$= 12 + 24 + 28$$
$$= 64.$$

Polyhedra of more unusual shapes require much more computation to obtain their surface areas. The basic principle is the same, however.

As an example, let us consider the right circular cone. If the cone is cut in the manner of Fig. 13.34, it would be possible to find the area of the two separate surfaces. The area of the base is clearly the area of the circle; that is, $a_1 = \pi r^2$.

The second surface requires more attention. If we imagine it rolled out as in Fig. 13.35, can we find the area of that sector? Carefully imagine the

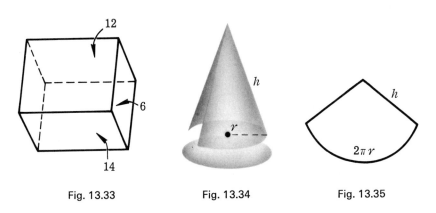

Fig. 13.33   Fig. 13.34   Fig. 13.35

process of "unrolling" the curved surface. Note that the slant height h of the cone actually becomes a radius of a circle and the arc has length $2\pi r$. Why? (To see the reason, try unfolding a conical-shaped drinking cup!) The area of a sector of a circle is given by the formula $s = \frac{1}{2}$ the length of the radius times the arc length of the sector. Thus we have $a_2 = \frac{1}{2}h(2\pi r) = \pi rh$. Therefore we have as the surface area of a right circular cone

(1) $$a = \pi r^2 + \pi rh,$$

where r is the length of the radius of the circle of the base and h is the slant height. The number πrh of (1) is often called the **lateral surface area** of a *right circular cone*.

The surface area of a right circular cylinder can be obtained in a manner similar to that for the cone. In Fig. 13.36, we have divided the locus into three separate surfaces. It is clear that the top and bottom surfaces of the cylinder have areas of πr^2.

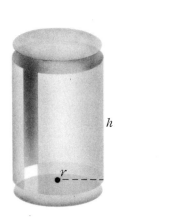

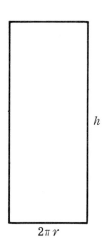

Fig. 13.36   Fig. 13.37

Uncurling the curved surface, we obtain the rectangle of Fig. 13.37.   The length of the rectangle is the circumference of its base (on top), and the width of the rectangle is the height of the cylinder.   Thus its area is $2\pi rh$.   Therefore the surface area of a right circular cylinder is

(2) $$a = 2\pi r^2 + 2\pi rh.$$

The number $2\pi rh$ in (2) is often called the **lateral surface area** of a *right circular cylinder*.

The surface area of a sphere is $4\pi r^2$, where r is the length of the radius of the sphere.   The surface area of the sphere with radius 3 in Fig. 13.38 is

$$a = 4\pi 3^2$$
$$= 36\pi.$$

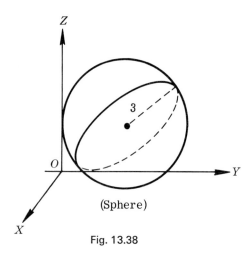

(Sphere)

Fig. 13.38

The volumes of surfaces are listed below. The unit of measure in 3-space is always taken to be cubic units when specific measuring units are used. Here, however, an unscaled measure is still being used.

Volume of a rectangular parallelepiped $= lwh$.
Volume of a right circular cone $= \frac{1}{3}\pi r^2 h$.
Volume of a right circular cylinder $= \pi r^2 h$.
Volume of a sphere $= \frac{4}{3}\pi r^3$.

Figure 13.39 illustrates the letters used in these formulas.

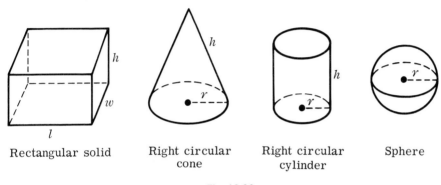

| Rectangular solid | Right circular cone | Right circular cylinder | Sphere |

Fig. 13.39

The volumes of irregular polyhedra require individual investigations. We shall not consider such polyhedra.

Exercise Set

A rectangular parallelepiped has the following measures. Find the required area, volume, or length.

1. Area of base is 20; height is 5; volume $=$?
2. Height is 10; length is 5; width is 4; volume $=$?
3. Height is 8; length is 4; volume is 64; width $=$?
4. Area of base is 20; volume is 40; height $=$?

Find the surface area and volume of the following spheres.

5. Radius 3.
6. Radius 2.
7. Radius $\frac{2}{3}$.
8. Radius π.
9. Radius $3/\pi$.
10. Radius 12.

For the following cones, find the (a) volume, (b) lateral area, and (c) total area.

11. Radius is 4; slant height is 6.
12. Radius is 12; slant height is 4.
13. Radius is 4; slant height is 12.

14. Radius is 1; slant height is 1.

For the following cylinders, find the required area, volume, or height.

15. Height is 10; volume is 100; area of bases = ?

16. Height is 5; radius is 4; lateral surface area = ?

17. Height is 5; radius is 5; volume = ?

18. Volume is 1000; radius is 20; height = ?

19. Find the radius of a sphere that has the same number of square units in its surface area as cubic units in its volume.

*20. A plane intersects a sphere such that the distance from the center of the sphere to the plane is 4.   If the radius of the sphere is 8, what is the radius of the intercepted circle?   (*Hint:* Make a sketch.)

*21. A sphere has a surface area of 50π.   Find its radius.

**22. A fustrum of a cone is that part of a cone between the base of the cone and a second base determined by a plane intersecting the cone parallel to the given base.   Develop

(a) a formula for the lateral surface area.

(b) a formula for its total surface area.

(c) a formula for its volume.

Appendix

4d Properties of the Grid System

Theorem (4d-3):   All grid loci are included in one system.

PROOF

There is at least one grid locus $\mathscr{L}_1$ by Axiom A-2.   Axiom A-4 requires that there be a grid locus on each point in $\mathscr{L}_1$.   In turn, these grid loci have an infinite number of other grid loci on their points, again by Axiom A-4. Thus we have all the grid loci in the two sets H and V.   Hence at least one grid system exists.

Now let us assume that a different grid system exists.   Consider a point P in this second system.   We know P exists by Theorem (4d-1).   Axiom A-7 requires that P either be in $\mathscr{L}_1$ or in some grid locus $\mathscr{L}_2$ that intersects $\mathscr{L}_1$. However, $\mathscr{L}_1$ is in the first grid system, and since $\mathscr{L}_2$ intersects $\mathscr{L}_1$ by Axiom A-7, it too is in the first grid system.   Thus P is in the first system.   Contradiction.   Therefore there is at most one grid system.   Thus the theorem is established.

6d Betweenness

Theorem (6d-1):   Given any two Cartesian points, there is at least one point between the given points.

PROOF

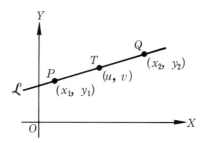

We let the given points be $P(x_1,y_1)$ and $Q(x_2,y_2)$ in a line $\mathcal{L}$. $P \neq Q$ by hypothesis. Therefore, if $x_1 \neq x_2$, we may assume $x_1 < x_2$ by Definition (4-j). There is a $u \in \mathcal{R}$ such that $x_1 < u < x_2$ by the properties of $\mathcal{R}$. Then

(1)
$$|u - x_1| + |x_2 - u| = |x_2 - x_1|,$$

and by the properties of $\mathcal{R}$ we have the same result for $x_2 < x_1$. The slope of $\mathcal{L}$ is $m = (y_2 - y_1)/(x_2 - x_1)$, for nonvertical $\mathcal{L}$. Thus

(2)
$$y_2 - y_1 = m(x_2 - x_1).$$

By definition, we have $x_1, y_1, m \in \mathcal{R}$. Therefore $(x_1 - u) \in \mathcal{R}$ and $m(x_1 - u) \in \mathcal{R}$. Why? There is a $v \in \mathcal{R}$ such that $y_1 = v + (mx_1 - mu)$ by the additive solvability property of $\mathcal{R}$. This yields

(3)
$$y_1 - v = mx_1 - mu.$$

Adding (2) and (3), we obtain

(4)
$$y_2 - v = mx_2 - mu.$$

Now $T(u,v)$ is a Cartesian point. Since $u \neq x_1$, $m = (y_1 - v)/(x_1 - u)$ from (3). That is, the slope of PQ equals the slope of PT. Therefore PQ and PT are coincident by Corollary (6b-2b). Now

$$(PT) + (TQ) = \sqrt{(u - x_1)^2 + (v - y_1)^2} + \sqrt{(x_2 - u)^2 + (y_2 - v)^2}$$

by Definition (4-1). From (2) and (3) we have

$$(PT) + (TQ) = \sqrt{(u - x_1)^2 + m^2(u - x_1)^2} + \sqrt{(x_2 - u)^2 + m^2(x_2 - u)^2}$$
$$= |u - x_1|\sqrt{1 + m^2} + |x_2 - u|\sqrt{1 + m^2}$$
$$= (|u - x_1| + |x_2 - u|) \cdot \sqrt{1 + m^2}.$$

From (1) we now have

$$(PT) + (TQ) = |x_2 - x_1|\sqrt{1 + m^2}$$
$$= \sqrt{(x_2 - x_1)^2 + m^2(x_2 - x_1)^2}.$$

Squaring (2) and substituting, we obtain

$$(PT) + (TQ) = \sqrt{(x_2 - x_1)^2 + (y_2 - y_1)^2}.$$

By Definition (4-1) we have for (PQ),

$$(PQ) = \sqrt{(x_2 - x_1)^2 + (y_2 - y_1)^2}.$$

Thus we have established that

$$(PT) + (TQ) = (PQ).$$

Hence the requirements for the existence of a T, such that PTQ provided $x_1 \neq x_2$, have been established. The vertical case $(x_1 = x_2)$ is left to the reader.

6e Line Segments

Theorem (6e-1): For any line segment and any point in any line, there is a line segment in the given line that has the given point as one of its endpoints and that is congruent to the given line segment.

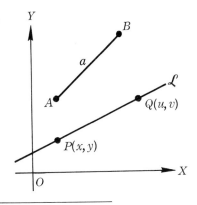

PROOF

Given: Line segment AB and a point $P(x_1, y)$ in a line $\mathscr{L}$.
To Prove: There is a point $Q \in \mathscr{L}$ such that $AB \cong PQ$.

1. There is a line segment AB and a point $P(x_1, y_1)$ in a line $\mathscr{L}$.	1. Hypothesis
2. Let $\mathscr{L}$ have equation $y = mx + b$ (vertical case left to the reader).	2. Corollary (6b-1a)
3. $\therefore\ y_1 = mx_1 + b$.	3. Theorem (4e-3)
4. Let $(AB) = a$.	4. Corollary (4h-2a)
5. $(a/\sqrt{1 + m^2}) \in \mathscr{R}$.	5. Properties of $\mathscr{R}$

6. $\exists u \in \mathcal{R}$ such that $x_1 = a/\sqrt{1 + m^2} + u.$ $\exists v \in \mathcal{R}$ such that $y_1 + mu = mx_1 + v.$	6. Axiom R-5
7. $mx_1 + b + mu = mx_1 + v.$	7. Substitution
8. $\therefore v = mu + b.$	8. Properties of $\mathcal{R}$
9. $\therefore (u,v) \in \mathcal{L}.$ Call the point $Q.$	9. Theorem (4e-3)
10. $x_1 - u = a/\sqrt{1 + m^2}$ $y_1 - v = mx_1 - mu.$	10. Properties of $\mathcal{R}$
11. $(PQ) = \sqrt{a^2/(1 + m^2) + m^2a^2/(1 + m^2)}$ $(PQ) = |a| = a.$	11. Definition (4-k)
12. $(AB) = (PQ).$	12. Axioms of Equality
13. $AB \cong PQ.$	13. Definition (6-l)

Axial Projections

Often in doing perspective drawings one has reason to project a line segment (or its length) onto a line. This would correspond to projecting the length of a geometric line segment in such a way that it would correspond to the length of some given segment in a line or plane.

Definition (6-m):   An **axial projection** of the length of a line segment is the absolute value of the difference of the abscissas (ordinates) of the endpoints of the line segments.

Example: Project the length of AB and PQ onto the x axis if $A(-4,3)$, $B(-1,5)$, $P(2,6)$, and $Q(5,4)$.

Solution: $|AB|_x = |-4 - (-1)| = 3, |PQ|_x = |2 - 5| = 3.$ (We have adopted the notation $|AB|_x$ to mean the projection of the line segment AB onto the x axis. We use the terms *absolute differences* and *absolute slopes* to mean the absolute values of the numbers involved.)

Since $(AB) = 13$ and $(PQ) = 13$, we have $AB \cong PQ$. Theorem (6e-1) shows, however, that there are an infinite number of line segments ending on any point which are congruent to a given line segment. For most of these, the absolute differences of abscissas will not be equal. Looking at line segments AB and PQ again, we have as their slopes, $m_{AB} = \frac{2}{3}$ and $m_{PQ} = -\frac{2}{3}$. Hence $|m_{AB}| = |m_{PQ}|$; that is, the slopes are *absolutely equal*.

Theorem (6e-2):   The axial length projections of congruent line segments having absolutely equal slopes are equal.

PROOF

Given: Line segments AB and CD with coordinates as indicated, $|m_{AB}| = |m_{CD}|$, and $AB \cong CD$.
To Prove: $|AB|_x = |CD|_x$ and $|AB|_y = |CD|_y$.

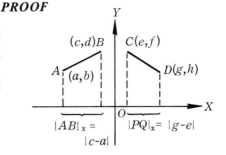

1. There are line segments AB and CD such that $AB \cong CD$ and $|m_{AB}| = |m_{CD}|$ and coordinates as indicated.	1. Hypothesis
2. $\left\|\dfrac{d-b}{c-a}\right\| = \left\|\dfrac{h-f}{g-e}\right\|.$	2. Definition (6-a)
3. $\|d-b\| = \dfrac{\|c-a\| \cdot \|h-f\|}{\|g-e\|}.$	3. Properties of $\mathscr{R}$
4. $(AB) = (CD).$	4. Definition (6-l)
5. $\sqrt{(d-b)^2 + (c-a)^2} = \sqrt{(h-f)^2 + (g-e)^2}.$	5. Definition (6-d)
6. $(d-b)^2 + (c-a)^2 = (h-f)^2 + (g-e)^2.$	6. Properties of $\mathscr{R}$
7. $\dfrac{(c-a)^2(h-f)^2}{(g-e)^2} + (c-a)^2 = (h-f)^2 + (g-e)^2.$	7. Substitution
8. $(c-a)^2 = (g-e)^2.$	8. Properties of $\mathscr{R}$
9. $|AB|_x = |CD|_x.$	9. Properties of $\mathscr{R}$
10. The proof that $|AB|_y = |CD|_y$ is left as an exercise.	

Corollary (6e-2a) is in the text.

Corollary (6e-2b): If AB and CD are line segments such that $(AB) = r \cdot (CD)$ for some $r \in \mathscr{R}$, and if $|m_{AB}| = |m_{CD}|$, then each projection of AB is r times the corresponding projection of CD and conversely.

The proof is omitted.

7f Circles and Tangents

Theorem (7f-1): A line tangent to a circle is perpendicular to the radius at the point of tangency.

PROOF

Using the positional equivalences of line segments and circles, we have the line $y = mx + b$ tangent to the circle $x^2 + y^2 = a^2$. Squaring the former, we have

(1) $y^2 = m^2x^2 + 2mxb + b^2.$

Using this value for y in the equation of the circle, we obtain

(2) $(1 + m^2)x^2 + 2mbx + b^2 - a^2 = 0.$

We see that (2) is a quadratic equation in x. Thus we have from the quadratic formula

(3) $x = \dfrac{-2mb}{2(1 + m^2)} \pm \sqrt{\dfrac{4m^2b^2 - 4(b^2 - a^2)(1 + m^2)}{2^2(1 + m^2)^2}}.$

But, since the line $y = mx + b$ is a tangent to the circle, their intersection must yield only one real root (Section 3c). Therefore the discriminant of (3) must equal zero. Thus we now have

$$x = \frac{-2mb}{2(1 + m^2)}.$$

The point of tangency $(x,y) = (x, mx + b)$ has become

(4) $\left[\dfrac{-mb}{1 + m^2},\ m\!\left(\dfrac{-mb}{1 + m^2}\right) + b \right].$

The slope of the radius to the point (4) is

$$m_1 = \left\{ \frac{[m(-mb)/1 + m^2] + b}{-mb/1 + m^2} \right\}$$

(5) $= \dfrac{-m^2b + b + m^2b}{-mb}$

$$= -\frac{1}{m}.$$

The slope of the tangent line is m. The product of these slopes is

$$-m\!\left(\frac{1}{m}\right) = -1.$$

By Definition (6-c) the lines must be perpendicular. The case for the vertical and horizontal tangent is left as an exercise.

8e   Angle Congruence and Straight Lines

Corollary (8e-2d): If two lines are cut by a transversal in such a way that the sum of the measures of the two interior angles on the same side of the transversal is less than the measure of two right angles, then the lines will intersect on the same side of the transversal as the two interior angles (*Euclid's fifth axiom*).

PROOF

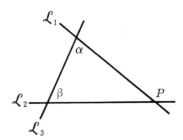

Given: Lines $\mathscr{L}_1$ and $\mathscr{L}_2$ with transversal $\mathscr{L}_3$ such that $(\alpha) + (\beta) < 2(\gamma)$ for γ a right angle.
To Prove: $\mathscr{L}_1$ and $\mathscr{L}_2$ intersect at P.

We have as hypothesis lines $\mathscr{L}_1$ and $\mathscr{L}_2$ with transversal $\mathscr{L}_3$ determining angles α and β interior to $\mathscr{L}_1$ and $\mathscr{L}_2$ on the same side of $\mathscr{L}_3$. Also, we know that $(\alpha) + (\beta) < 2(\gamma)$ for some right angle γ. *We shall construct our proof on the principle of contradiction.*

Let us assume that $\mathscr{L}_1$ *does not intersect* $\mathscr{L}_2$ on the same side of $\mathscr{L}_3$ as α and β. Therefore (i) $\mathscr{L}_1$ is either parallel to $\mathscr{L}_2$ (hence no intersection at all) or (ii) $\mathscr{L}_1$ intersects $\mathscr{L}_2$ in the opposite side of $\mathscr{L}_3$ from α and β.

If $\mathscr{L}_1$ is parallel to $\mathscr{L}_2$, then by Corollary (8e-2b) we have $(\alpha) + (\beta) = 2(\gamma)$, which contradicts our hypothesis.

Considering (ii), we have several things to conclude. First, we shall call the interior angles on the opposite side of $\mathscr{L}_3$ from α and β, δ and ϵ. (See Fig. 1.) By Corollary (8c-4b), we have

(1) $$(\alpha) + (\delta) = 2(\gamma).$$

Now through the point of intersection of $\mathscr{L}_1$ and $\mathscr{L}_3$ there is a line $\mathscr{L}_4$ such that $\mathscr{L}_4 \parallel \mathscr{L}_3$ by Theorem (6c-4). (See Fig. 2.) Since $\mathscr{L}_1$ intersects $\mathscr{L}_2$

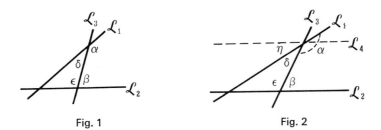

Fig. 1   Fig. 2

by our assumption (ii), then $\mathscr{L}_1$ and $\mathscr{L}_4$ intersect by Theorem (6c-5). Thus $\mathscr{L}_1$ and $\mathscr{L}_4$ determine an interior angle, call it η, on the same side of $\mathscr{L}_3$ as δ but on the opposite side $\mathscr{L}_1$ from δ. By Definition (8-d),

(2) $$(\eta) > 0.$$

Now using Theorems (8e-2) and (8c-3), we have

(3) $(\eta) + (\delta) = (\beta).$

However, by hypothesis,

(4) $(\alpha) + (\beta) < 2(\gamma).$

Substituting (3) into (4), we obtain

(5) $(\alpha) + (\eta) + (\delta) < 2(\gamma).$

Then subtracting (1) from (5) we have $(\eta) < 0$. This is a contradiction of (2). We have now shown that part (ii) under our assumption is false. Therefore our assumption must be false. Hence $\mathscr{L}_1$ must intersect $\mathscr{L}_2$ on the same side of $\mathscr{L}_1$ as α and β. The corollary is now established.

The foregoing has been an example of mathematical proof by contradiction and, indeed, one that involved a double conclusion and the use of De Morgan's Law.

9b Positional Equivalence of Triangles

Theorem (9b-1): For any triangle and any point in a line, there is a triangle having all its parts congruent to the corresponding parts of the given triangle in such a way that one of its vertices is the given point and one of its sides is included in the given line.

PROOF

Given: $\triangle ABC$ and a line $\mathscr{L}$ containing a point A'.
To Prove: There is a $\triangle A'B'C'$ whose parts are correspondingly congruent to those of $\triangle ABC$.

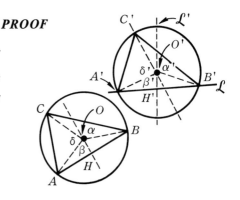

1. There is $\triangle ABC$ and a point A' in a line $\mathscr{L}$.	1. Hypothesis
2. On points A,B,C there is a circle Q with center O.	2. Theorem (5d-3)
3. On O there is a line perpendicular to AB at, say, H.	3. Theorem (6c-8)

4. OH bisects AB.

    4. Theorem (7b-5)

5. H is the midpoint of AB.

    5. Definition (6-o)

6. $AH \cong HB$.

    6. Definition (6-n)

7. In $\mathscr{L}$ there are $A'H'$ and $H'B'$ such that $A'H' \cong AH$, $H'B' \cong HB$.

    7. Theorem (6e-1)

8. $\overline{A'H'B'}$.

    8. Theorem (6d-1)

9. On H' there is a line $\mathscr{L}'$ such that $\mathscr{L}' \perp A'B'$.

    9. Theorem (6c-8)

10. In $\mathscr{L}'$ there is an $H'O' \cong HO$.

    10. Theorem (6e-1)

11. $AO \cong BO$.

    11. Theorem (7b-4)

12. $(AH) = (A'H')$, $(HB) = (H'B')$, $(OH) = (O'H')$, $(AO) = (BO)$.

    12. Definition (6-l)

13. $(OH)^2 + (AH)^2 = (AO)^2$, $(OH)^2 + (BH)^2 = (BO)^2 (O'H')^2 + (A'H')^2 = (A'O')^2$, $(O'H')^2 + (B'H')^2 = (B'O')^2$.

    13. Theorem (4h-1) or (6c-9)

14. $(A'O') = (AO) = (B'O') = (BO)$.

    14. Properties of $\mathscr{R}$

15. There is a circle with center at O' having lengths of radii $(A'O') = (B'O')$.

    15. Theorem (7b-3)

16. $(O',O'A') \cong (O,OA)$.

    16. Definition (7-h)

17. $(A'H') + (H'B') = (AH) + (HB)$.

    17. Properties of $\mathscr{R}$

18. $(A'B') = (AB)$.

    18. Properties of $\mathscr{R}$

19. $A'B' \cong AB$.

    19. Definition (6-l)

20. There are lines AO, BO, CO, $A'O'$, $B'O'$.

    20. Theorem (5c-3)

21. There is an $\angle B'O'D' \cong \angle BOC$ (i.e., $\alpha' \cong \alpha$).

    21. Theorem (8b-1)

22. $O'D'$ intersects $(O',O'A')$ at C'.

    22. Theorem (7a-4)

23. There are lines $A'C'$ and $B'C'$.

    23. Theorem (5c-3)

24. $\angle A'O'B' \cong \angle AOB$ (i.e., $\beta' \cong \beta$).

    24. Definition (8-a)

25. $(\alpha) + (\beta) + (\delta) = 4(\gamma)$, $(\alpha') + (\beta') + (\delta') = 4(\gamma)$, for some right angle γ.	25. Corollary (8c-4a)
26. $(\delta) = (\delta')$.	26. Properties of $\mathscr{R}$
27. $\delta \cong \delta'$.	27. Theorem (8c-2)
28. $A'C' \cong AC$ and $B'C' \cong BC$.	28. Definition (8-a)
29. $\sphericalangle B'A'C' \cong \sphericalangle BAC$, $\sphericalangle A'C'B' \cong \sphericalangle ACB$, $\sphericalangle C'B'A' \cong \sphericalangle CBA$.	29. Theorem (8g-5)

Q.E.D.

Answers to Selected Exercises

Section 1c.

1. Every y is a z. **3.** There are exactly three wires; there are exactly two wires on every bead. **5.** There are exactly five wires; every bead is on exactly two wires.

Section 2a.

1. Valid. **3.** Valid. **5.** Invalid. **7.** Valid.

Section 2b.

1. Proposition. **3.** Not a proposition. **5.** Proposition. **7.** Proposition.
9. Proposition. **11.** Not a proposition. **13.** ∀, an upside-down "A," stands for the "a" in "all." ∃, a backwards "E," stands for the "e" in "exists."

15.

p	p	$p \wedge p$
T	T	T
F	F	F

17.

p	$\sim p$	$p \vee \sim p$
T	F	T
F	T	T

19. The inverse of $p \Rightarrow q$ is $\sim p \Rightarrow \sim q$.

p	q	$\sim p$	$\sim q$	$\sim p \Rightarrow \sim q$
T	T	F	F	T
T	F	F	T	T
F	T	T	F	F
F	F	T	T	T

21. (a) Converse: If it is cold, then it snows. Inverse: If it does not snow, then it is not cold. Contrapositive: If it is not cold, then it does not snow. **(b)** Converse: If two line segments are congruent, then they are similar. Inverse: If two line segments are not similar, then they are not congruent. Contrapositive: If two line segments are not congruent, they are not similar.

23.

p	q	$(p \wedge q)$	$(p \wedge q) \Rightarrow p$
T	T	T	T
T	F	F	T
F	T	F	T
F	F	F	T

Section 2d.

1. (a) If it is not raining, then it is snowing. **(b)** If it is snowing, then it is not raining.　**3.** No.　Truth tables differ.　**5.** The lines are parallel and they do not intersect.　**7.** The lines are parallel or they intersect.　**9.** The lines do not intersect.

11.

p	$\sim p$	$p \wedge \sim p$	$\sim(p \wedge \sim p)$
T	F	F	T
F	T	F	T

13. $p \Rightarrow q$

p

―――― Valid

q

15. $p \Rightarrow q$

p

―――― Valid

q

Section 3a.

1. $S = \{1,2,3,\ldots\}$.　**3.** $S = \{-9,-8,-7,-6,\ldots,-1,0,1\}$.　**4.** $S = \{-1,1,-3, 3,-5,5,\ldots\}$.　**5.** $S = \{-2,2,-4,4,-6,6,\ldots\}$.　**7.** A,B,G; C,F; D,E.　**9.** $\emptyset,\{1\},\{2\}$, $\{1,2\}$.　**11.** $\emptyset,\{\alpha\}$, $\{\beta\}$, $\{\alpha,\beta\}$.　**13.** $\emptyset,\{0\},\{1\},\{2\},\{3\}$, $\{0,1\}$, $\{0,2\}$, $\{0,3\}$, $\{1,2\}$, $\{1,3\}$, $\{2,3\}$, $\{0,1,2\}$, $\{0,1,3\}$, $\{1,2,3\}$, $\{0,2,3\}$, $\{0,1,2,3\}$.　**15.** Infinite.　**17.** Finite.　**19.** Infinite.　**21.** (a) Not necessarily.　(b) Yes.

Section 3b.

1. $A \cap B = \emptyset$, $A \cup B = \{1,2\}$.　**3.** $A \cap B = \emptyset$, $A \cup B = \{-2,3,4,-1,5,6\}$.　**5.** $A \cap B = \emptyset$, $A \cup B = $ set of integers.　**7.** $A \cap B = \{-1\}$, $A \cup B = \{$negative integers$\}$.　**11.** $A \cup B = \{1,2,3,4,5,6\}$.　**13.** $A \cap B = \emptyset$.　**15.** $A \cap (A \cap C) = \{3\}$.　**17.** $A \cup (B \cap C) = \{1,2,3,4\}$.　**19.** Variable.　**21.** Variable.　**23.** Variable.　**25.** Variable.

Section 3c.

3. Trichotomy property.　**5.** Commutative property of multiplication.　**7.** Associative property of addition.　**9.** Uniqueness of product.　**11.** Solvability property of addition.　**13.** Solvability property of multiplication.　**15.** Closed.　**17.** (a) closed; (b) closed; (c) closed; (d) not closed.　**19.** (a) N,Z,Q; (b) Z,Q; (c) N,Z,Q; (d) Q.

Section 3d.

1. $\forall x,y$; if $y \neq x$, then $x \neq y$.　**3.** $x = 3$; $(x = 3) \vee (x^2 = y^2)$.　**5.** True.　**7.** $x = 3$.　**9.** No.

Section 4c.

1. The set of real numbers is in one-to-one correspondence with the points in each grid locus.　**3.** Given a point in one grid locus, A-4 states that this point "is also in exactly one other grid locus."

Section 4d.

1. Yes.　**5.** (a) yes; (b) yes; (c) yes.

Section 4e.

1. $2, 3, 6, 0, -2$; $-8, 0, 1, 4, -2$.   **3.** OX; horizontal OY; vertical.   **5.** Yes, no, no.

Section 4f.

1. 5.   **3.** 2.   **5.** $\sqrt{61}$.   **7.** 6.   **9.** 12 miles.   **11.** Unscaled distance 4.   **13.** $\frac{1}{3}$ centimeter per integral unit.   **15.** $a = 1, 7$.   **17.** $a = 4, 6$.   **19.** $y_2 = 0, 2$.

Section 4h.

5. 5.   **7.** $3\sqrt{2}$.   **9.** $(AB) < (AC) + (BC)$ **12.** Impossible.
$(AC) < (AB) + (BC)$
$(BC) < (AB) + (AC)$

Section 5a.

17. Function.   **19.** Function.   **21.** Function.   **23.** Not a function; yes; $y = \sqrt{16 - 4x^2}$, $y = -\sqrt{16 - 4x^2}$.   **25.** All real numbers except zero; has a "hole" at $x = 0$.   **27.** Yes; no; center is not "part" of a circle.

Section 5b.

1. Distinct.   **3.** Coincident.   **5.** Distinct.   **11.** Distinct.   **13.** Coincident.

Section 5c.

1. Oblique.   **3.** Vertical.   **5.** None.   **7.** None.   **13.** Definitions are always reversible.   **15.** $\{(x,y) \mid 4x + y - 8 = 0\}$.   **17.** $\{(x,y) \mid 7x + 4y - 2 = 0\}$.   **19.** $\{(x,y) \mid y = 4\}$.

Section 5d.

1. $(x - h)^2 + (y - k)^2 = 16$.   **3.** $(x + 2)^2 + (y - 0)^2 = 4$.   **5.** $(x - 2)^2 + (y - 3)^2 = 10$; $(x + 1)^2 + (y - 4)^2 = 10$.

Section 5e.

5. Yes, unless the intersecting straight line is parallel to the second side of the angle.   **7.** Yes.   **9.** Yes. $\overrightarrow{CB}$, $\overrightarrow{BA}$, $\overrightarrow{CA}$, $\overrightarrow{BC}$.

Section 5f.

1. $(7,0)$, $(0,7)$.   **3.** $(-4,0)$.   **5.** $(0,0)$.   **7.** $(2 - \sqrt{3}, 0)$, $(2 + \sqrt{3}, 0)$.   **9.** $(0,0)$.   **11.** $(0,0)$, $(0,0)$.   **13.** -3; -6.   **15.** Examples 1, 2, 3, 4, and 5.

Section 6a.

1. Division by zero is undefined.   **5.** No.   **7.** $\{(x,y) \mid px_1 + qy_1 + r = 0\}$.   **9.** $\frac{3}{4}$.   **11.** $\frac{-3}{11}$.   **13.** Does not exist.   **15.** $\{(x,y) \mid 3x - 7y + 41 = 0\}$.   **17.** $\frac{1}{2}$.

Section 6b (Exercise Set I).

1. $4x - y - 12 = 0$.   **3.** $6x - y - 22 = 0$.   **5.** $5x + 2y + 6 = 0$.   **7.** $11x - y = 0$.   **9.** $6x - 7y - 21 = 0$.   **11.** $y - 2 = 0$.   **13.** $y - b = 0$.   **15.** x-intercept does not exist; $m = 0$.

Section 6c (Exercise Set I).

1. Not parallel.   **3.** Not parallel.   **5.** Not parallel.   **7.** $5y - 3x - 18 = 0$.

Section 6c (Exercise Set II).

1. $-5x - 3y + 10 = 0$.   **3.** $y = -5$.   **5.** $x - 8y + 13 = 0$.   **7.** $3x - 2y - 1 = 0$; $3y + 2x - 18 = 0$.   **9.** $3y + 2x - 11 = 0$.   **17.** 104.   **23.** $L_1 \parallel L_2$.

Section 6d.

3. (a) $\overline{PQR}$.   **(b)** $m = \frac{4}{3}$.   **(c)** $3y - 4x - 5 = 0$.   **5. (a)** Not $\overline{PQR}$.   **(b)** $\overline{PQ}$, $m = \frac{3}{4}$; $\overline{QR}$, $m = \frac{3}{8}$; $\overline{PR}$, $m = \frac{1}{2}$.   **(c)** $4y - 3x - 8 = 0$; $8y - 3x - 18 = 0$; $2y - x - 2 = 0$.

Section 6e.

1. $(1, \frac{5}{2})$.   **3.** $(3, -1)$.   **5.** $(\frac{1}{4}, \frac{1}{4})$.   **7. (1)** $8x - 18y + 37 = 0$; **(2)** $4y + 5x - 25 = 0$; **(3)** $y - 3x + 10 = 0$; **(4)** $y - x + 6 = 0$; **(5)** $y + x - 1 = 0$; **(6)** $y - x = 0$; **(11)** $(\frac{29}{3}, -\frac{16}{5})$.

Section 6f.

3. $|AB|_x = 0$; $|AC|_x = 5$; $|BC|_x = 5$; $|AB|_y = 1$; $|AC|_y = 4$; $|BC|_y = 5$.
5. $(DE) = \sqrt{41}/2$; $(DF) = 5\sqrt{2}/2$; $(EF) = \frac{1}{2}$; $(AC) = \sqrt{41}$; $(BC) = 5\sqrt{2}$; $(AB) = 1$.   The lengths of the line segments joining the midpoints of a triangle equal $\frac{1}{2}$ the lengths of the respective sides of a triangle.

Section 7a.

1. No intersection.   **3.** Secant.   **5.** Tangent.   **7.** 1; (0,0).   **9.** 3; (2, -1).   **11.** 4; (0,0).   **17.** The slope of the radius and the slope of the tangent are negative reciprocals.   **21.** Secant.   **23.** Secant.

Section 7b.

1. True (7b-4).   **3.** False; AC is not necessarily congruent to DF.   **5.** True (7b-5).   **7.** True; CO is not a chord, but can be extended to become a chord. **9.** False; however, these angles have many of the same properties of inscribed angles.   **13.** $x + y - 2 = 0$.   **15.** $x + y = 0$.

Section 7c.

1. Not congruent.   **3.** Not congruent.   **5.** Not congruent.   **7.** $(x - 3)^2 + (y + 2)^2 = 4$.   **9.** Yes.

Section 7d.

1. No; no.   **3.** Yes; yes.   **5.** (1) No; no.   (2) Yes; yes.   (3) No; no.   (4) Yes; yes.   (5) No; no.   (6) Yes; yes.

Section 7e.

3. (a) Yes, (b) yes, (c) yes; $x = 4$.   **5.** (a) No, (b) no, (c) yes; $x - y = 0$.   **7.** (a) Yes, if $a^2 = 50$ or $b^2 = 50$; (b) yes, if (a) is true and $2a \geq b$ or $2b \geq a$; (c) yes; $x + y = 0$.

Section 7f.

1. Tangent.   **3.** $x = 0$ is a tangent; $y = 0$ is not a tangent.   **5.** $y = 1$ is a tangent; $x = 1$ is not a tangent.   **7.** $x + 3y + 1 = 0$.   **9.** $x + 4y = 0$.   **11.** $x = 0$.   **13.** $-\frac{4}{3}$.   **15.** 1.   **17.** $-\frac{1}{2}$.   **21.** $\sqrt{85}$.

Section 7g.

1. 4π.   **3.** $2\sqrt{2}\pi$.   **5.** $4\sqrt{2}\pi$.   **7.** $1000/13$.   **9.** 240 degrees.   **11.** True in the same or congruent circles.

Section 7h.

5. Sine $(AP) = \sqrt{3}/2$; cosine $(AP) = \frac{1}{2}$; tangent $(AP) = \sqrt{3}$; cosecant $(AP) = 2\sqrt{3}/3$; secant $(AP) = 2$; cotangent $(AP) = \sqrt{3}/3$.   **7.** Sine $(AP) = \sqrt{5}/5$; cosine $(AP) = 2\sqrt{5}/5$; tangent $(AP) = \frac{1}{2}$; cosecant $(AP) = \sqrt{5}$; secant $(AP) = \sqrt{5}/2$; cotangent $(AP) = 2$.   **9.** Sine $(AP_1) = \sqrt{5}/5$; cosine $(AP_1) = 2\sqrt{5}/5$; cosecant $(AP_1) = \sqrt{5}$; secant $(AP_1) = \sqrt{5}/2$; cotangent $(AP_1) = 2$.   **11.** Cosine $(AP_3) = \sqrt{3}/2$; tangent $(AP_3) = \sqrt{3}/6$; cosecant $(AP_3) = 4$; secant $(AP_3) = 2/\sqrt{3}$; cotangent $(AP_3) = 2\sqrt{3}$.   **13.** Sine $(AP_5) = \sqrt{3}/2$; tangent $(AP_5) = 2\sqrt{3}$; cosecant $(AP_5) = 2\sqrt{3}/3$; secant $(AP_5) = 4$; cotangent $(AP_5) = \sqrt{3}/6$.

Section 8a.

1. No.   **3.** Yes.   **5.** Yes.   **7.** No.

Section 8c.

3. $360°$.   **5.** $30°$.   **7.** $315°$.   **9.** $120°$.   **11.** $215°$.   **13.** $\pi/3$.   **15.** $2\pi/3$.   **17.** $\pi/12$.   **19.** $37\pi/180$.   **21.** When the arc is a semicircle.   **23.** Obtuse.   **25.** Acute.   **27.** Acute.   **29.** Supplementary.   **31.** $(\gamma) = 90$.   **33.** 90 is the measure of a right angle.

Section 8d.

5. 0.   **6.** (a) $m_3 = 7$, $m_4 = 1$.   (b) $m_3 = 2$, $m_4 = -2$.   (c) $m_4 = \frac{1}{2}$.

Section 8f.

1. $110°$.   **3.** 105.   **5.** $\pi/2$.   **7.** $a - b$.   **9.** $2a$.

Section 8g.

3. 90° or $\pi/2$ radians.   **18.** $\frac{1}{2}[(\widehat{AC}) + (\widehat{BC})]$.   **19.** One-half the difference of the measures of the intercepted arcs.

Section 8i.

1. Sine $(\alpha) = \sqrt{2}/2$ cosine $(\alpha) = \sqrt{2}/2$.   **2.** Sine $(\alpha) = \sqrt{3}/2$ tangent $(\alpha) = -\sqrt{3}$.

Section 9c.

1. 5.   **5.** Sine $(A) = 12/13$; cosine $(B) = 12/13$; tangent $(A) = 12/5$.   **7.** Sine (A) $= 140/149$; cosine $(B) = 140/149$; tangent $(A) = 140/51$.   **9.** 1.   **11.** 128/3.
13. $\sqrt{2}/8$.

Section 9d.

5. $\sqrt{5}/5$; 2.   **9.** $k_2 \neq 0$ since $k_2 > 0$; $(9 - h)$.

Section 9g.

8. Right triangle.   **15.** 6, 12, 18, 24.   **16.** $12\sqrt{3}$.   **23.** 7, 12.

Section 11a.

3. Circle, ellipse.   **4.** All but first and third figures of Figure 11.1.

Section 11c.

1. 108°; 72°.   **3.** $4\pi/5$; $\pi/5$.   **5.** $11\pi/12$; $\pi/12$.   **7.** (1) 540°; 360°.   (2) 4π; 2π.
(3) 8π; 2π.   (4) 14π; 2π.   (5) 2520°; 360°.   (6) 2700°; 360°; 30π; 2π.   **9.** Not a regular polygon; 360°.   **11.** Not a regular polygon; 360°.   **13.** Regular; 180°.
15. 5.   **17.** 20.   **19.** 500.

Section 12a.

3. 6.   **5.** 3/4.   **11.** 5.   **13.** $25/4\sqrt{3}$.   **17.** $2\sqrt{2}$.   **19.** 20.   **21.** 9.   **23.** 3.   **25.** 13/7.
27. 2 to 3.   **31.** 10.   **33.** 18.

Section 12b.

1. 9π.   **3.** 3π.   **5.** 37.82π.   **7.** 4π.   **9.** 3π.   **11.** $2\sqrt{6/\pi}$; $4\sqrt{6/\pi}$.   **13.** $\sqrt{3}/3$;
$2\sqrt{3}/3$.   **15.** $8\sqrt{2}$; $16\sqrt{2}$.   **17.** (a) 8π; (b) $4\sqrt{2} + 4$; (c) $8\pi - (4\sqrt{2} - 4)$.

Section 12c.

1. 8π.   **3.** 16.   **5.** 32.   **7.** 6π.   **9.** 22.   **11.** 28.   **13.** 34.   **15.** $\sqrt{26} + 3\sqrt{5} +$
$\sqrt{53}$.   **17.** $8 + 4\sqrt{2}$.   **19.** 120; 88.

Section 13a.

5. 3.   **7.** $\sqrt{69}$.   **9.** $\sqrt{3}$.

Section 13b.

1. Coplanar. **3.** Noncoplanar. **5.** Coplanar. **13.** Theorem (6c-2). **15.** Yes.
17. No, spherical. **19.** $x - 2y - 3z + 2 = 0$.

Section 13c.

1. Regular hexahedron. **5.** $(-3,1,2), r = 3$. **7.** $(-3,-3,-3), r = 3$. **9.** Right
circular cone. **11.** Right circular cone. **13.** Pentahedron. **15.** Parallelepiped.

Section 13d.

1. 100. **3.** 2. **5.** 36π; 36π. **7.** $16\pi/9$; $32\pi/81$. **9.** $36/\pi$; $36/\pi^2$. **11.** 32π;
24π; 40π. **13.** 64π; 192π; 208π. **15.** 20. **17.** 125π. **19.** $r = 3$. **21.** $5\sqrt{2}/2$.

Index

Boldface numbers indicate pages on which basic discussions or formal definitions of topics occur.